WITHDRAWN

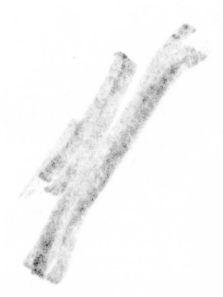

A Normal Country

A Normal Country

Russia after Communism

Andrei Shleifer

Harvard University Press
Cambridge, Massachusetts
London, England
2005

Library of Congress Cataloging-in-Publication Data
Shleifer, Andrei.
A normal country : Russia after communism / Andrei Shleifer.
p.   cm.
Includes bibliographical references and index.
ISBN 0-674-01582-7 (alk. paper)
1. Russia (Federation)—Economic conditions—1991–
2. Russia (Federation)—Politics and government—1991–
3. Post-communism—Russia (Federation).   I. Title.
HC340.12.S4937   2005
330.947—dc22   2004059915

Contents

Acknowledgments

I would first like to thank my collaborators on some of the chapters in this book: Nicholas Barberis, Olivier Blanchard, Maxim Boycko, Timothy Frye, Jonathan Hay, Simon Johnson, Daniel Kaufmann, Kevin M. Murphy, Daniel Treisman, Natalia Tsukanova, and Robert Vishny, both for working with me and for allowing me to include joint work in this volume.

Over the last fifteen years, many colleagues have offered me valuable comments on the various chapters of this book. I would particularly like to thank Anders Aslund, Gary Becker, Olivier Blanchard, Maxim Boycko, David Cutler, Cevdet Denizer, Padma Desai, Martin Feldstein, Stanley Fischer, Lev Freinkman, Alan Gelb, Edward Glaeser, Miriam Golden, Marshall Goldman, Roger Gordon, Sergei Guriev, Stephen Hanson, Arnold Harberger, Oleh Havrylishyn, James Hines, Jack Hirshleifer, Bengt Holmstrom, Simon Johnson, Lawrence Katz, David Laibson, Rafael La Porta, Ed Leamer, Normal Loayza, Florencio Lopez-de-Silanes, Kevin M. Murphy, Dwight Perkins, James Poterba, Sherwin Rosen, Jeffrey Sachs, Ratna Sahay, James Snyder, Lawrence Summers, Jakob Svensson, Timothy Taylor, Judith Thornton, Daniel Treisman, Robert Vishny, Michael Waldmann, Martin Weitzman, and Katia Zhuravskaya.

The research reported in this book was financed by a number of organizations, including the Bradley Foundation, the Brookings Institution, the Harvard Institute for International Development, and the National Science Foundation. I thank them for their support.

Finally, I would like to thank my editor at Harvard University Press, Michael Aronson, for improving the manuscript and Clare MacLean for all the help involved in putting the book together.

A Normal Country

— 1 —

Russia after Communism

1.1 Yeltsin's Challenge

On December 25, 1991, the last general secretary of the Communist Party of the Soviet Union, Mikhail Gorbachev, left the Kremlin, turning over leadership to the first popularly elected president of a now independent Russia, Boris Yeltsin. Gorbachev's fall was a pivotal moment in the demise of Soviet communism, the system of nearly complete control of economic, political, and social life of the country by the Communist Party. Over its 75-year life span, communism brought to Russia industrialization, high-quality education, a historic victory in the Second World War, nuclear capability, and a central role in world affairs. Yet it was also responsible for the destruction of tens of millions of innocent lives in Stalinist purges and famines; a mediocre record of economic performance, especially since the 1970s; and near-complete repression of political, cultural, and social expression.

Gorbachev's political demise dealt a tremendous setback to Soviet communism, but it did not destroy it. The state continued to control nearly the whole economy. Prices were still set by the State Planning Committee, rather than by market forces. The government retained ownership of factories, which were managed by the old communist elite and still subordinate to industrial planners. The state security system, the enforcement mechanism of the Communist order, remained intact. The press remained state-owned, although it grew increasingly critical of the government. If Yeltsin wanted to replace Soviet communism with a more normal society, his job had barely begun.

Yeltsin pursued normalization with alacrity. He introduced a new constitution, organized a series of parliamentary elections, and ran for re-election himself in 1996. The Communist Party stayed alive, but had to compete with other parties for the presidency and seats in parliament. Yeltsin's economic program included an immediate and nearly complete price liberalization, followed by mass privatization of state assets. In his foreign policy, Yeltsin reduced defense spending by an estimated 90 percent, pursued drastic nuclear arms reduction in cooperation with the United States, accepted the expansion of NATO, and participated in U.N.-led efforts to stop civil war in the former Yugoslavia. Yeltsin's Russia also saw perhaps the greatest era of personal freedom in its history, including the rise of a private and unencumbered press.

Yeltsin's clear intention in all his reforms was to destroy communism in Russia. Nowhere is this vision more clear than in his speech introducing the privatization program, given on August 19, 1992, on the first anniversary of the failed hard-line coup:

> The past year was the first without the absolute power of province and district Party committees. The boundless dictatorship of the CPSU [Communist Party of the Soviet Union], which has lasted for more than seven decades, came to an end. During that time, refined mechanisms for subjecting all of society to the will of the CPSU had been created ... There was a suffocating, poisonous atmosphere of the absence of freedom in society. But it was in this atmosphere that millions of people, several generations of them, were molded. We simply did not know a different life, we had never seen anything else. No one had taught or was able to teach us to live differently ... At this point, a very elementary thing has to be comprehended. We are taking just the very first steps toward a normal human life, and we are stumbling and falling ... Difficult as it may be, the majority of people understand that we cannot go back to the old ways. Under no circumstances, Russia simply cannot stand another Communist era. We must persistently continue the transformation and push ahead with the reforms.

As Yeltsin's speech made clear, the march toward normalcy did not come without pain. The fall of communism in Russia, already well underway in the 1980s, devastated the economic, political, and social order that the Communist Party had maintained. The disorder manifested itself in many ways. Even before Yeltsin's liberalization, Gorbachev's partial economic reforms created a bizarre mixture of plan and market that led to severe shortages. The inability of the law-and-order institutions to keep up with economic change allowed the mafia and other private enforcers of contracts to step into their place. The liberalization of economic life—alongside the weakness of nascent tax and regulatory institutions—led to an explosion of the unofficial economy. Last but not least, the regions and ethnic republics of the Russian Federation pursued their own economic and fiscal policies, aiming largely to increase transfers from the center. In the extreme case of Chechnya, separatism brought about a bloody and pointless civil war.

Herein lay Yeltsin's dilemma. To truly bury Soviet communism, he needed to destroy the mechanisms of state control, from the Communist Party as the institution of government itself, to Gosplan, to industrial ministries, to the omnipresent security apparatus. But a democracy and a market economy itself needed institutions, which could not be created either instantaneously or without the elimination of communist institutions that they were to replace. Although Yeltsin's reforms tried to balance these goals, the replacement was neither finely tuned nor as rapid as some had hoped. In retrospect, a significant institutional structure of a democracy and a market economy had been created in the 1990s. But the path was far from smooth.

From a political perspective, there were good reasons to speed up the destruction of communist institutions. Communism was not dead in Russia in 1992. The barely reformed Communist Party, with its solid support from the pensioners whose worldviews it molded for decades, consistently did well in parliamentary elections. Its leader, Gennady Zyuganov, was widely expected to win the presidency in 1996. But communists were not alone in wishing the return of massive state control in Russia: the former ministers, managers, security officials—not to mention a number of Western intellectuals—grieved the passing of the old order. To move toward normalcy, Yeltsin had to defeat these forces of the past, remove the mechanisms of their political and economic influence, and create new constituencies for change powerful enough to support the new institutions. One of Yeltsin's greatest legacies has been the creation of these new constituencies.

Yeltsin's policies are best understood as a balancing act between the twin goals of destroying old institutions and creating new ones. Without a doubt, this balancing act involved many missteps, compromises, and reversals. Politics delayed Russia's reforms and rendered them haphazard and incomplete, but it did not reverse their course. By the turn of the century, as Yeltsin yielded power to Vladimir Putin, it became clear that Yeltsin reached his goal. Russia became a normal country: a democratic market economy. It was a highly imperfect democracy and a highly imperfect market economy. But Soviet communism was dead in Russia.

1.2 Russia's Reforms

Boris Yeltsin did not initiate economic and political reform in Russia. Mikhail Gorbachev, the last general secretary of the Communist Party of the Soviet Union, who assumed power in 1985, pursued economic and political liberalization through programs known as "Perestroika" and "Glasnost," respectively. Gorbachev's economic policies allowed for a small amount of private business creation in the form of "cooperatives," as well as an increase in administrative discretion of managers of state enterprises. These reforms were slow and incremental: the economy, including most prices, remained centrally planned and entrepreneurship severely limited. Politically, Gorbachev allowed greater freedom of the press and improved Russia's relations with the West, but also pursued a new policy of nonintervention in Eastern Europe, accommodating a peaceful democratic revolution in that region. Still, Gorbachev always insisted that the Soviet Union must remain a communist state, and contemplated no reforms that would surrender either the Communist Party's monopoly on power or even the state's near monopoly on ownership. Nor would he accept the dissolution of the Soviet Union and independence of its republics.

Gorbachev's foreign policy was historic, and he deserves extraordinary recognition for his restraint. He also paid for it with his political life. When Gorbachev went on vacation to Crimea in August 1991, a group of hard-line members of the Politburo staged a coup, took over power, and declared a state of emergency. Although the coup failed, Gorbachev had to step down, and Yeltsin became the country's unquestioned leader. In December, Yeltsin agreed with the leaders of Ukraine and Belarus to dissolve the Soviet Union, leaving Russia independent.

Gorbachev's economic reforms failed, and Yeltsin came into office facing an economic crisis. The previous two years had seen declines in output, worsening shortages, and fears of a complete economic and political collapse. As of 1989, the average citizen spent 40–68 hours a month standing in line to purchase goods. In April 1991, "only 12 percent of respondents in a national survey claimed to have seen meat in state stores" and only 8 percent had seen butter (Aron, 2002). In the fall of 1991, CNN predicted imminent starvation that winter.

Yeltsin immediately appointed a reformist government headed by Yegor Gaidar. Over the following three years, the government pursued a radical economic transformation. In January 1992, most prices were freed. Queues disappeared and goods showed up in stores. During the year, the government developed a mass privatization program, which was then implemented between December 1992 and July 1994. Through this program, shares in most firms were transferred from the government to their managers, workers, and the public. By mid-1994, almost 70 percent of the Russian economy was in private hands. In 1995, with the help of the International Monetary Fund, Russia stabilized the ruble.

Less visibly, Yeltsin pursued an aggressive program of institutional reform. His government introduced a modern tax system, created a system of commercial courts, and steered through parliament a range of new commercial laws, including the civil code. Planning ministries were sharply curtailed or eliminated and replaced by regulatory agencies serving a market economy, including the antimonopoly commission in 1991 and a securities commission in 1993. The army, the police, and the security forces all went through major reforms.

All of these changes proved difficult. The parliament, the unreformed and well-organized Communist Party, and the entrenched industrial interests resisted almost every measure, and even the government itself could not establish an internal consensus. This is not surprising, since Yeltsin was replacing the institutions of the old order with those of the new one. To maintain political peace, Yeltsin dismissed one reformer after another, but popularity eluded him.[1]

In 1995, Yeltsin tried to broaden his support ahead of the 1996 presidential election, which the Communist Party leader Gennady Zyuganov was expected to win. As part of this political campaign, and in an attempt to balance the budget, Yeltsin agreed to a "loans-for-shares" program, whereby some valuable natural resource enterprises were turned over to existing industrial groups in exchange for loans to the government. The program accelerated the consolidation of a few large groups in the Russian economy, led by so-called oligarchs, who enjoyed great political and economic influence. In addition to financing his campaign, these businessmen helped Yeltsin with sympathetic coverage on television and in other media outlets they controlled.

Despite suffering a heart attack, which was concealed from the voters, Yeltsin came from behind to win a second presidential term. Although he successfully prevented the communists from regaining power in Russia, Yeltsin was in poor health, lacking political and popular support, and less attentive than before to economic policy. Much of his focus in subsequent years was on finding a successor. Russia's far-flung regions exploited the political weakness at the center to disrupt the central government's tax collections and to divert tax revenues to regional uses. The central government, in turn, resorted to massive debt finance of its deficits. As oil prices collapsed in 1997–98, so did the federal budget, and the financial turmoil that had started in East Asia spread to Russia. The crisis led to a debt default and a sharp depreciation of the ruble; yet, contrary to the expectations of some pundits, also to a rapid economic recovery.

Yeltsin ultimately found a successor, Vladimir Putin, whom he appointed Prime Minister in 1999. On January 1, 2000, Yeltsin resigned and Putin became acting president, subsequently winning the presidential election in March of that year. Over the next four years, Russia grew rapidly, helped by dramatic increases in oil prices, a rationalization of the tax system, and the continuing benefits of depreciation. By 2003, the Russian government was borrowing money in world markets long term at an interest rate of around 7 percent, indicating significant investor confidence. Most forecasts for Russia's economic growth were highly optimistic. But while Putin consolidated Yeltsin's economic reforms, he moved Russia backward in building democracy.

1.3 Plan of the Book

The chapters that follow describe the problems facing Russian reformers from the perspective of destroying old institutions and building new ones. These chapters were written at the time the problems were faced and usually published shortly afterwards. This is important. Many of the discussions of Russian reforms written in the late 1990s are after-the-fact evaluations, full of dubious counterfactuals and false analogies and written with the benefit of hindsight. Whatever are the faults of the chapters in this book, they analyze problems as my collaborators and I saw them either before the effects of policies became clear, or even before the policies themselves were put into place.

Chapter 2 describes the problems of Gorbachev-era partial reforms and the dysfunctionality of the resulting combination of plan and market. It shows how severe shortages result from partial liberalization of a planned economy.

Chapters 3 and 4 present what from the political perspective was unquestionably the most important reform in Russia in the 1990s: the mass privatization program. Chapter 3, written shortly after the program got underway, describes its goals and strategies, as well as the relationship between private ownership and other institutions of a market economy in Russia. Chapter 4 evaluates small-scale privatization and documents the crucial role of new people, as opposed to incentives, in securing the restructuring of small shops. Chapter 5, published in 1996, is perhaps the most ideologically charged in the book. It makes the case for depoliticization of economic life as the principal goal of reform and argues against the approaches that emphasize greater state control during the transition.

The next three chapters, all written in the mid-1990s, describe the evolution of the relationship between the state and private business in Russia following privatization. Chapter 6 documents the consequences of the disorganization of the Russian state—corruption and the harassment of small business—using a survey of shopkeepers in Moscow and Warsaw. Chapter 7 describes and explains one major consequence of predatory state policies toward business: the rise of the unofficial economy. Chapter 8 discusses some possible strategies for the reconstruction of law and order and the establishment of an effective public legal system in place of private enforcement of property rights and contract. These three chapters illustrate at least some of the challenges of building new institutions from the rubble of a collapsed state.

Chapter 9, written in the late 1990s, describes the problems of Russian federalism. Following Riker's (1964) classic work, it argues that a viable federalist structure must combine economic decentralization with political centralization—an arrangement Russia lacked through most of the 1990s. The reform of the federal system in the direction of greater political centralization has been one of Putin's first steps.

Many of the views expressed in these chapters have been criticized, sometimes severely. Although this is not the place to respond to all criticisms, one strain of thought has kept reappearing since Russia's transition began and reflects perhaps the deepest disagreement among economists about the strategy of transition. Numerous critics of Yeltsin's reforms, as well as of the views I have expressed in my writings, maintain that Russia's reformers were laissez-faire ideologues. According to these critics, the difficulties of Russian transition have stemmed from this strict adherence to "market fundamentalism."

This line of argument has been advanced by a distinguished succession of writers. In the early 1990s, it was eloquently presented by the Russian politician and economist Grigory Yavlinksy (Yavlinsky and Braguinsky, 1994); Chapter 5 is in part a response to his writings. On July 1, 1996, a group of important Soviet and American economists, including Nobel laureates Kenneth Arrow, Lawrence Klein, and Robert Solow, published a letter in a Russian newspaper condemning President Yeltsin's economic reforms for their neglect of the state in transition. The letter was printed two days before the runoff in the presidential elections, and was widely interpreted as an endorsement of the communist presidential candidate Zyuganov, many of whose ideas the letter echoed. Most recently, another Nobel laureate, Joseph Stiglitz, produced a virulent attack on Russian reforms along similar lines (Stiglitz, 2002).

Stripped of its vitriol, this line of criticism of Yeltsin's reforms contains three strands. First, the argument holds that the reformers, as "market fundamentalists," ignored the role of public institutions, such as law enforcement agencies and competition authorities, in the successful functioning of a market economy. Second, critics argue that these market-supported institutions should have been created before any radical steps such as privatization were taken. Third, and most broadly, the critics wanted the Russian government to have taken a much more active part in the economic transition. As stated in the 1996 letter by the Nobel laureates, "The Russian government must play a much more important role in the economy, as in such modern mixed economies as the United States, Sweden, and Germany. The government must play a central co-ordinating role in establishing the public and private institutions required for a market economy to function" (Intriligator, 1997).

With respect to the first claim, that the reformers and their advisors simply ignored institutions, the chapters in this book speak as clearly as I believe is possible. Nearly every essay—written from the early to the late 1990s–speaks about the creation of institutions, from corporate governance, to antitrust, to a legal system, to a viable federal structure.

With respect to the second claim, namely that institutions must come first, the critics appear to neglect both history and logic. Many market-supporting institutions, including the antimonopoly and the security commissions, were created in Russia either before or during the privatization program, and many relevant commercial laws were passed at around the same time. But creating pro forma institutions is only the first step. Institutions of a market economy acquire their governance role only when they interact with actual firms, entrepreneurs, and investors. In every country, this process is a tug of war between private attempts to capture the regulators through lobbying and bribes and the pressure on regulators to serve the public interest. As in most other countries, Russia's new regulatory institutions were often corrupt and ineffective— and it is surely wrong to say that having more of them, or having them earlier, would have helped markets to function. Over time, these institutions were improving, as they often do as countries and markets develop. The demand for institutions first—before private property or markets—misses the logic of institutional evolution in Russia or any other country.

But it is the third criticism, the demand for a powerful and coordinating state, that most profoundly misses the logic of the transition from communism. It is not only that the empirical evidence assembled over the past decade shows decisively that aggressive state intervention and regulation in developing and transition economies leads to little but corruption, suppression of new business formation, the expansion of the unofficial economy, and the stifling of economic growth. The experiences of Germany, the United States, and Sweden are of virtually no relevance, since these are wealthy countries with long-standing democracies and effective accountability of the state to voters. Even in these developed economies, the effectiveness of regulation has often been questioned. But the notion that regulation that works in Sweden can be transplanted to Russia, Argentina, or Malaysia without breeding corruption and abusive interventionism is breathtakingly far-fetched.

Perhaps more importantly, the demand for a more interventionist state in transition economies misses the fundamental point that the creation of institutions of democracy and a market economy is a political goal that is inseparable from the need to eliminate the mechanisms of communist control. Russia was not just building the institutions of democracy and a market economy; it was also destroying the institutions of communism. The remnants of a powerful coordinating state were not just unhelpful in this institutional replacement, they actively resisted it! There could be no democracy and market economy in Russia while the people and the institutions of the old coordinating order retained power. Indeed, what Yeltsin cared about the most was to make sure that Russia could never go back to communism, and to get that assurance he had to replace the institutional foundations of the old regime. Some countries in transition, such as Belarus, Kazakhstan, and Uzbekistan, have tried to maintain a central coordinating role of government, but they simply replaced the dictatorship of the Communist Party with personal dictatorships of their new leaders.

The last chapter of the book was written in 2004. It is a summary of where Russia ended up after the first decade of its transition. Its title became the title of this book: a decade after communism, Russia became a normal country.

— 2 —

The Transition to a Market Economy: Pitfalls of Partial Reform

In 1988, the Soviet Union began a program of partial economic reform. The government gave firms much more freedom to decide what to produce and to whom to sell their output. It also allowed workers to form private cooperatives and to lease capital from their firms. Such quasi-private organizations proliferated, accounting for 5 percent of employment by the end of 1990. At the same time the government retained ownership of almost all enterprises, and continued giving them state orders for much of their output. It also continued to regulate most prices, both at the retail level and between enterprises. In these respects, the reform was clearly only partial.

By mid-1991 it became clear that the partial economic reform had failed.[1] The gross national product (GNP) fell 2 percent in 1990 and 8 percent in the first quarter of 1991. The declines in output spread to almost all sectors. Consumer goods virtually disappeared from shelves. The number of deliveries unmet by enterprises skyrocketed, with almost 25 percent of firms failing to meet their contractual obligations. The economy seemed to be collapsing.

We show how the economic collapse can be understood in terms of coordination failures that were made much worse by partial reforms. Partial reforms encouraged the diversion of many essential inputs away from their traditional users toward private and other enterprises that were less constrained by arbitrarily regulated prices, and so could offer better

By Kevin Murphy, Andrei Shleifer, and Robert Vishny; originally published in *Quarterly Journal of Economics*, 107 (1992): 889–906. © 1992 by the President and Fellows of Harvard College and the Massachusetts Institute of Technology.

deals to suppliers. We present a model that illustrates how such diversion undermines planned allocation and how it can reduce output and welfare. Our economic argument can be summarized easily using an example from a market economy. Suppose that the state of Washington produces apples that are sold throughout the United States. Let the market-clearing price of apples be 15. Suppose first that all states impose the constraint on Washington apple producers that they cannot sell their apples above 10. The supply falls, and apples are rationed. Lines and speculation may follow as well.

Suppose, alternatively, that not all but only 30 states impose the maximum price of 10 on Washington apples. What happens then? The answer is that the states that imposed the price ceiling are in bad shape. The people in the unconstrained 20 states get all the apples they want at the price of 10, because they can effectively pay just a penny above the constrained price and get all the apples. They are even better off than they were under the free market equilibrium. In contrast, people in the 30 states with a price limit get only the remainder of the apples supplied at the price of 10, and so they experience a much more severe shortage than they did when all states had put on a price limit. When only a few states impose the maximum price, they hurt themselves as well as the producers, and benefit enormously the states that have not restrained prices, which simply free ride on them.

This example sheds light on the experience of state firms in the former Soviet Union after 1988. Traditional suppliers to many of these state firms broke their ties and sold or bartered the supplies to private or state enterprises that were able to offer better deals. The chief of a large oil distribution concern, for example, complained that refineries sold the oil to cooperatives that were then reselling it to consumers at triple the state price, with the result that officially designated users experienced acute shortages (*Sovetskaya Rossiya*, May 15, 1991). At the same time, state firms were unable to replace the diverted inputs because they had no access to markets. As a result, state firms often cut output, broke contracts themselves, and by doing so created further bottlenecks downstream. Like the U.S. states with price ceilings on apples, state firms that did not have the legal authority, financial resources, or barterable items to compete for inputs stagnated.

Section 2.1 presents our basic model of the effect on a socialist firm of introducing competition for inputs from a private firm. We show how such competition can reduce efficiency. Section 2.2 then extends the basic model, particularly to the case with tighter quotas for state firms relevant for China (Byrd, 1987). Section 2.3 asks what sectors private firms are likely to enter. Section 2.4 concludes the chapter.

2.1 A Model of Supply Diversion

We present a simple model of competition for inputs between a state firm and a private firm. In the model, a private firm should be interpreted broadly as any firm that can circumvent state price ceilings and outbid the traditional buyers in the competition for inputs. It can be a private cooperative, another state enterprise that can offer a higher price or bribe, or even a state enterprise that has attractive items to barter in exchange for inputs. The traditional state buyers often lose this competition for inputs because they lack financial resources or barterable goods, or, alternatively, are too closely monitored to risk paying more than the official price.

For concreteness, it is easiest to think of a specific stylized example. Think of the market for timber, and let there be two uses of timber: to construct boxcars and to build houses. Timber is produced in the state sector, which initially must deliver it to users at a price below the market-clearing price. Initially, both houses and boxcars are produced in the state sector as well, and the plan allocates timber between the two sectors. The reform enables "private" house builders to buy timber from the state timber sector at negotiated prices either legally or at a substantially lower expected penalty. The production of timber and of boxcars remains in the state sector. We are interested in how the production of houses and of boxcars is affected by the reform. We make six specific assumptions about the allocation of timber.

A1. The official price P of timber is below the market-clearing price: timber is rationed. This assumption is accurate in virtually all socialist countries. One reason for underpricing inputs is the desire of planners to stimulate the production of intermediate and final manufacturing goods. For example, paper is underpriced because the government is selling newspapers cheap, and timber is underpriced because housing is cheap. Also, many goods are underpriced in socialist countries because underpricing causes

rationing and so enables ministries to collect bribes from the rationed buyers (Shleifer and Vishny, 1992).

A2. The price P is what the buyers of timber actually pay. In particular, they do not pay bribes to get the scarce timber. In reality,
bribes of course are very common. However, not every firm is
willing or able to bribe the ministries, and hence bribes do not
allocate the inputs fully efficiently. We consider bribes in subsection 2.2.4.

A3. Producers of timber are on their supply curves and are not
compelled to produce more than they wish to at P. This assumption is appropriate for the situation after the reforms of
1988 that gave state firms more control over their choice of
output. In subsection 2.2.3 we consider the case in which the
timber industry is forced to supply more than it wants to at P.

A4. Initially, timber is rationed efficiently between the two sectors, so
that the marginal valuation of timber P^* at which aggregate demand for timber equals the supply at P is the same in the two
sectors. The assumption of efficient rationing is inappropriate if,
for example, the planners compel the timber industry to supply
all the timber the boxcar industry wants, with the residual going
to the housing sector. We modify this assumption in subsection
2.2.1.

A5. After the reform, the timber industry can choose to whom to
sell its output. This assumes more freedom than state firms have
in practice, but may well approximate the ex-Soviet situation, in
which plan enforcement has been lax after the reforms. In subsection 2.2.2 we consider what happens when the timber industry must deliver a quota to the boxcar industry.

A6. After the reform, the boxcar industry cannot bid more than P
for timber, but the housing industry can. This assumption captures the fact that, in the former Soviet economy, cooperatives
were often allowed to, and even required to, pay higher prices.
Even when prices are controlled and transactions occur through
barter and bribes, private firms often have greater financial resources and barterable goods than state firms do, and so can
outbid them. The assumption that the state buyers of inputs face
greater constraints on what they can pay than the private buyers
do is the essence of the model.

Figure 2.1 describes the allocation of timber before the reform. Panel A shows aggregate supply and demand for timber, panel B shows the demand by the boxcar sector, and panel C shows the demand by the housing sector. The demand curves by the boxcar and housing sectors can be thought of as marginal value product schedules in these sectors. Under our rationing rule, the timber industry delivers Q_b (plan) to the boxcar sector and Q_h (plan) to the housing sector at the price P per unit, and its output is the supply at P.

When partial reform allows house builders to buy timber from the state timber industry at a negotiated price, the problem becomes identical to that in the example of the Washington apples, in which the boxcar industry corresponds to states with a price limit, and the housing industry to the states without such a limit. After the reform, the housing industry buys all the timber it wants at a price epsilon above P. The boxcar industry, in contrast, gets only what is left over from the unchanged quantity supplied at the price P. In equilibrium the housing sector expands until it gets all the input it wants at the subsidized price; the boxcar industry contracts because it does not get its timber and the total supply of timber stays constant (Figure 2.2).

Figure 2.2 shows the welfare consequences of allowing the private firm to buy timber. First, for the boxcar sector the shadow value (value marginal product) of timber rises sharply because deliveries fall by the amount Δ, equal also to the rise of deliveries of timber to the housing

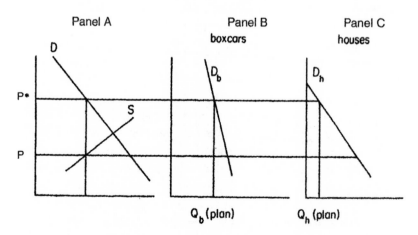

Figure 2.1 Efficient rationing of timber

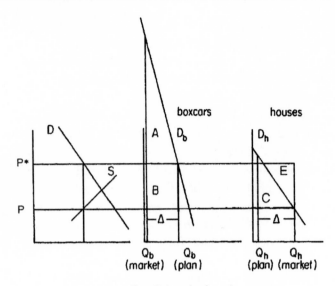

Figure 2.2 Liberalizing the housing sector

sector. As a result, the boxcar industry loses consumer surplus corresponding to the triangle A. In addition, the state (or the boxcar industry) no longer collects the surplus resulting from underpricing timber by P^*-P on the Δ units: area B. On the other hand, the consumer surplus of the housing sector rises by triangle C as it can get all the timber it wants at P. The overall welfare falls since C is strictly smaller than B. The welfare loss is the sum of A and the triangle E. The reason for the welfare loss is that we started from efficient rationing and ended up with less efficient rationing whereby the marginal valuation of timber is much higher in the boxcar industry than in the housing industry. In this model, partial reform reduces welfare because it diverts resources from higher to lower value use.

When is the welfare loss the largest? First, the more elastic the demand for timber by the housing sector, the more extra timber it buys, the more deliveries to the boxcar sector fall, and the greater the welfare loss. The misallocation of timber rises the most when the private firm can expand the most. Second, the less elastic the demand for timber by the boxcar sector, the greater the consumer surplus loss from the reduction in the deliveries of timber to that sector, and so the greater the total welfare loss. The misallocation is greatest when the state boxcar sector really needs the timber but cannot get it.

For several reasons, the case of elastic demand for timber in the free sector, and inelastic demand in the state sector, is realistic. First, private firms have the *ability* to enter sectors that require fairly little capital and complementary inputs. Second, private firms have the *incentive* to enter precisely the sectors in which shortages leave much room to expand. As a result, entry will occur where the demand for inputs is elastic. In contrast, the sectors remaining in state hands have a large amount of fixed capital and require a variety of complementary inputs. Once the capital is in place and the complementary inputs are delivered and cannot be resold, the demand for any other input in this sector becomes very inelastic. In addition, the demand for boxcars is likely to be inelastic because the boxcars might be needed as further inputs in production and few substitutes may be available. Both of these factors make the demand for timber by the boxcar sector inelastic. This combination of elasticities yields the maximum misallocation of resources, since the sector from which timber is diverted values it much more than the sector that gets it.

The misallocation of resources is obviously the consequence of the fact that some, but not all, resources can move to the private sector. If capital and other inputs from the boxcar industry moved into the private sector as well, and this industry could compete for timber, then timber would be allocated efficiently at the market-clearing price. The reason for large inefficiencies is that the state firms cannot sell some of their factors of production, such as capital and centrally distributed inputs, but cannot compete for the complementary inputs either.

In the former Soviet Union, some adjustment to this problem took the form of leasing. State enterprises were allowed to lease some of their plant and equipment to their employees who formed cooperatives. This practice became common. Unfortunately, the state constrained leasing arrangements, in part because of monitoring problems. The government could not make sure that the state firms did not simply neglect the plan and gave cooperatives extra use of the equipment, particularly in exchange for bribes. As long as the movement of capital into the private sector was restricted, the mismatch of resources persisted.

This simple model helps explain how partial economic reform has led to significant input diversion from state firms, a breakdown of economic coordination, and sharp output declines in many sectors. In fact, the model suggests how every firm can simultaneously experience a shortage of some input, since the state sector is probably short of inputs that got competed away, while the private firms are short of capital that they cannot bid away from the state firms. Moreover, the strong complementarity of inputs can explain how moderate amounts of diversion can have large effects on output.

The commodities that were most commonly diverted from downstream producers in the former Soviet Union were raw materials, such as timber and oil, and fairly universal intermediate goods, such as steel pipe and cement. These goods could be resold easily at market prices, and in fact many commodity exchanges specialized in making markets in them. As a result, diversion was widespread.

Another important form of input diversion is that of human capital into private activities. As some of the best employees either quit the state enterprises to work for themselves, or else even retain their state jobs without showing up, the state sector loses another critical input it cannot easily replace, namely qualified labor. Such diversion is very costly as well.

Even when the state can effectively demand a fixed quantity of inputs from the upstream industry, quality is much harder to monitor. As a result, higher-quality inputs would be sold to the private firms, with those of lower quality delivered to the state sector. This too could result in a welfare loss if the state sector has an inelastic demand for quality. This mechanism has been important in agriculture and construction industries, in which the higher quality of private sector output in part reflects the higher quality of diverted inputs.

In the model, the diversion of inputs from the state sectors, or the reduction of the quality of inputs delivered to the state, reduces welfare because the value of state output is high. This assumes, perhaps incorrectly, that the demand curve for timber in the state sector reflects social preferences. For example, the state might be producing boxcars that no one wants, or wasting timber on defense in a situation of severe shortage of consumer goods. In this case, true demand for these goods is much lower than state demand, and the efficiency loss from the diversion of inputs from the state sector may actually be an efficiency gain. This point should not be taken too far, however, since many goods are produced by state monopolies, and the disruption of production by these monopolies can lead to genuine economic hardships.

2.2 Alternative Assumptions

2.2.1 Inefficient Rationing to Start

Assumption A4 says that the government rations timber efficiently between the boxcar and the housing sectors. This assumption ensures that
the total value of output strictly falls after a partial liberalization. A more
plausible assumption is that the state favors the industrial sector, such as
boxcars, in its rationing scheme.

The simplest way to model this is to assume that, before liberalization,
the boxcar sector gets all the timber it wants at price P and the housing
sector gets only the rest of the supply (Figure 2.3). The marginal valuation
of timber is therefore lower than before in the boxcar sector and higher
than before in the housing sector, where shortages are extreme. After
partial liberalization, when the housing sector can bid what it wants to
for timber but the boxcar sector cannot, the final allocation becomes the
opposite of the planned allocation. The housing sector now gets all it

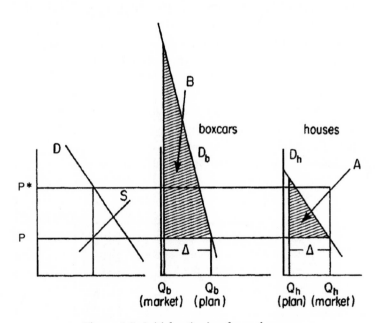

Figure 2.3 Initial rationing favors boxcars

wants at price P and the boxcar sector gets the residual. Because timber is underpriced, too many houses are now being built, and there is a severe shortage of boxcars (assuming that the demand curves measure true social valuations).

The gain to the housing sector is the consumer surplus gain, given by triangle A. The loss to the boxcar sector is the consumer surplus loss, given by triangle B. The net welfare gain is the difference between these two triangles. If the demand for timber by the housing sector is elastic, but that by the boxcar sector is inelastic, then triangle A is smaller than triangle B. When a fixed amount of timber moves from the sector with an inelastical demand to a sector with an elastic demand, the overall welfare (or value of output) falls. The reason is again that resources are misallocated because all the capital and complementary inputs in the boxcar sector are standing idle. In this case as well, partial reform reduces welfare.

2.2.2 State Use of Quotas: The Best Case

The key assumption that drives our welfare results is A6, namely that the timber industry has complete control over whom to sell its output to. In many cases, it is more plausible to assume that the state uses quantity controls to force the delivery of timber to the boxcar industry at price P. For example, the state might demand that a fixed quota of timber be supplied even at the rationed price. Consider a case in which the boxcar sector got all the timber it wanted under rationing, and assume that even after the liberalization of the housing sector the state can still enforce the delivery of that same amount of timber to the boxcar sector. In the best case for quotas, the timber sector delivers its lowest production cost units to the boxcar sector, and then sells what it produces afterwards to the housing sector at an equilibrium price. This case in presented in Figure 2.4.

The quota in this case improves welfare relative to liberalization with no quota. As long as the quota is met, there is no change in the allocation to the boxcar sector, and the output in that sector stays constant. After the quota for timber is delivered, it flows to the highest value use, and so the supply of timber to the housing sector equals demand. The market clears at some price above P. With a quota, consumer surplus equal to triangle B in Figure 2.3 is no longer lost, although the welfare gain in the

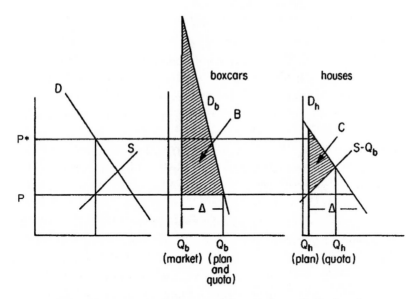

Figure 2.4 Quota for boxcars and increased supply for housing

housing sector is now given by a smaller triangle C. Since we have assumed that in Figure 2.3 triangle B is larger than triangle A, that is, demand in the boxcar sector is less elastic than that in the housing sector, it must be that C is smaller than B. The quota improves welfare. The strictly enforced quota prevents the highly valued timber in the boxcar sector from being diverted to the housing sector.

The case with the quota sheds light on an important difference between partial reforms in the former Soviet Union and those in China. China has pursued partial reforms of the sort described here, except that the central government maintained extremely strict enforcement of state quotas and allowed firms to sell only the units above the state quotas to private buyers. As a result, the government managed to contain the supply diversion problem. The Soviet government, in contrast, while nominally retaining delivery quotas for state enterprises, substantially relaxed plan enforcement. To a significant extent, this relaxation can be explained by the decline of the power of the central government and of the Communist Party, which historically have done most of the enforcing. As a result, diversion of inputs was not controlled in the former Soviet Union.

This difference between the ability of China and the former Soviet Union to control the amount of input diversion resulting from partial reform might explain why such reform has worked so well in China and so badly in the former Soviet Union. Unlike the Soviet economy, which collapsed as a result of partial reform, the Chinese economy showed a large increase in growth. The difference between the experiences of the two countries also suggests that partial reform does not succeed without continued coordination through planning. If such coordination cannot be sustained, prospects for partial reform are dismal.

The government of the former Soviet Union had responded to supply diversion as predicted by the theory, although not nearly as effectively as the Chinese government. Specifically, it created special police forces with the authority to inspect the inventories of the cooperatives and confiscate illegally purchased goods. The government also restricted trading cooperatives, which buy inputs at low cost and resell them at higher prices. Finally, the government restricted cooperatives from participating in international trade, another lucrative area for arbitrage. These bans precluded the diversion of underpriced inputs from buyers who valued them but had no ability to pay. These increases in state policing might seem inconsistent with the spirit of liberalization, but make perfect sense once it is recognized that incentives to divert inputs to alternative users rise sharply when these users are private moneymaking firms that can pay market prices.

2.2.3 State Use of Quotas: The Worst Case

The critical assumption we made is that the timber firms met the quota to the boxcar industry using the lowest marginal cost timber, and then produced more timber for the free market. As a result, the housing industry faced a timber price equal to the marginal cost, which led to an efficient output level conditional on the quota. Such a rosy scenario does not obtain if some of the efficient producers escape the quota and sell only to the housing industry. In fact, the most efficient producers have the greatest incentive to sell to private firms, since they are earning the highest profits from these sales. When the low marginal cost units are not delivered to the state sector and the state uses quotas, the marginal cost of the units delivered to the state may be much higher than the price, creating a new inefficiency.

In the extreme case, suppose that the most efficient producers escape the quota, and sell to the housing industry all they want at a price epsilon above *P*. The remaining timber producers meet the quota at *P*. These producers are obviously off their supply curves, and meet the quota only for fear of penalties (Figure 2.5). The government has to cover their losses. Since the quota is met, the boxcar sector does not lose the consumer surplus *B* as it did without the quota. The housing sector expands greatly, since it pays the price *P* for its timber, and so gets an additional consumer surplus equal to triangle *A*, just as it did without the quota. However, the timber industry is now selling this extra output going to the housing industry at a price below the true marginal cost, leading to a loss of producer surplus given by triangle *E*. It is clear from Figure 2.5 that the quota increases welfare if the supply curve of timber is more elastic than the demand curve for timber by the boxcar industry, that is, if $B > E$. If the supply of timber is highly inelastic, because, for example, current capacity is limited, then the quota reduces welfare. Welfare gains from a quota are much larger when the quota is imposed on the efficient producers.

This argument suggests an important cost of using quotas when private house builders can get timber at the rationed price. House builders are getting timber at a price below its true marginal cost, as they are forcing the extra production of timber to meet the boxcar quota at a high marginal cost. This inefficiency is smaller than the inefficiency in the absence

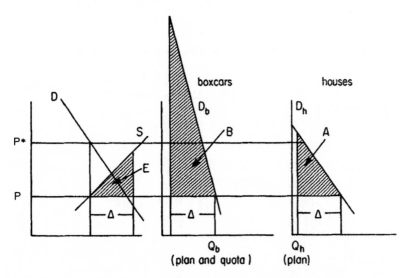

Figure 2.5 Quota for boxcars and increased supply of high marginal cost units

of a quota if the supply of timber is more elastic than the demand for timber by the boxcar industry.

In general, there is likely to be a negative correlation between the efficiency of the enterprise and the ability of the planners to monitor it. Large, strategic state enterprises tend to be most closely supervised by the planners, but also are likely to be the least efficient. In contrast, some of the smaller enterprises may be more efficient, but much harder to monitor. As a result, the planners are most likely to extract the input quotas from the inefficient producers, while the efficient ones sell their output to the private firms. The consequence is the inefficient production of marginal units by closely monitored firms. This view of quotas suggests even more strongly why the policing by the state of deliveries rises precisely at the time of liberalization: the most efficient enterprises are likely to try the hardest to avoid the quotas.

2.2.4 Bribes

We have assumed in our basic model that price P is what the consumers of timber actually pay under rationing. At that price the marginal valuation of timber under rationing, P^*, is higher than P in both industries. In practice, this usually means that the timber ministry will collect bribes from the producers eager to get the timber. Assume for simplicity that the timber firms get only P and therefore produce the same supply as before.[2] Then $P^* - P$ per unit goes to the ministry in the form of bribes, and the equilibrium output remains the same as under rationing. The total price to both the boxcar and the housing industry will be P^*, the sum of the official price and the bribe. At that price the total demand is equal to the supply at P.[3]

What happens to this industry after partial reform depends on whether the ministry or the timber firms have the property rights over the timber output. Suppose first that the timber firms continue to get P for timber, but the ministry can now openly negotiate timber prices with the housing firms and keep the profits, while continuing to take bribes from the boxcar firms. In this case, partial reform does not change the allocation of inputs. The boxcar industry continues to pay the official price P plus the bribe of $P^* - P$ for timber, while the housing industry switches to paying P^* openly. The allocation stays the same, except that the ministry collects some of the profits officially rather than as bribes. If the official profits are taxed while bribes are not, however, the ministry will try to keep the official price of timber down to P for both buyers and to continue charging bribes. In this case, bribes prevent the detrimental consequences of partial reform on the allocation of inputs because they effectively enable the boxcar producers to compete for the inputs through bribes.

Suppose alternatively that the ministry loses the property rights over timber, so that the timber firms now receive the revenues from the sale of timber to the housing sector. Assume first that the price that the timber firms get from selling to the boxcar sector stays at P. In this case, as in our basic case, the housing industry diverts all the timber it wants at price P from the boxcar industry. Timber in that industry continues to be allocated through bribes, and the full price to those who get it rises, but since the bribes go to the ministry rather than to the timber firms, the latter prefer to sell to the housing industry for P plus epsilon. Partial reform in this case has all the same adverse consequences that it had without bribes.

This result assumes unrealistically that the ministry stands idle as the value of the bribes it is collecting deteriorates. More realistically, the ministry responds to the loss of bribe income by raising the price paid to the timber firms, since that raises the value of bribes. As a result, the housing industry too must pay more for timber. In equilibrium the housing industry pays some price $P' > P$, and the boxcar industry pays P' plus the market clearing bribe to its ministry. Moreover, because the price rises, the supply of timber rises as well. In this case as well, the distortion is reduced relative to the case with no bribes, since competition forces the ministry to raise the official price of timber and to reduce its diversion from the boxcar industry to the housing industry. Because bribes effectively enable the boxcar industry to compete for the inputs, they reduce the costs of partial reform. However, since marginal valuations of timber diverge in the two sectors even with bribes, bribes do not completely eliminate the costs of partial reform.

In this analysis we have assumed that the market for timber clears through bribes. In reality, however, some firms are not well enough connected to pay the bribes; some might be afraid of criminal repercussions, and some might be too uninformed to know how the market works. These firms are particularly hard hit by partial reform, because they lose their inputs and are not able to get them back. In sum, bribes reduce the distortions caused by partial reform by effectively providing the mechanism for state firms to pay more for their inputs. However, only in extreme circumstances do bribes completely eliminate these distortions.

2.3 Which Sectors Do Private Firms Enter?

So far, we have specified the sector that private firms enter exogenously. It is also interesting to ask which sectors are most attractive to private firms, and therefore where entry is the most energetic and extensive. Private firms enter the sectors in which they can expand and make money. The key attractions for entry are large unmet demand, availability of inputs such as capital and materials, and the low price of inputs. The last point implies, in particular, that private firms are likely to enter sectors in which the inputs are most severely underpriced by the state, so that they can obtain them at the lowest prices relative to values.

This fact raises a major problem for partial reform, for inputs are the most valuable on the margin where they are the most underpriced. If the price of timber is low, it is in short supply and has a high shadow value. The short supply makes entry attractive to the private firms, which enter and divert some of that supply of timber to their own use. The incremental producer surplus to the private firms is directly proportional to underpricing. The implication of this result is that private firms are likely to enter precisely where they can do the most damage in terms of diverting inputs from competing state sectors. Private firms are likely to enter sectors in which the inputs are most scarce, and so create the largest resource misallocation as a result of their entry.

The result that private firms may enter where they do the most damage seems counterintuitive. In a market economy, private firms enter and buy up only the resources that they value more than the firms they are diverting the resources from. Here, in contrast, prices are distorted, and so private firms buy even the inputs they value less than the state firms that are not getting these inputs. The trouble is that state firms cannot compete for these resources, and so are not getting them even if they value them more. In an economy with distorted prices, much of what the firm gains from entry is rents redistributed from other firms. As a result, private gains may be positive and social gains negative. This critical difference between a socialist and a market economy explains how entry can reduce welfare.

This observation also sheds light on the difference between a private firm entering a socialist economy, as we have here, and a socialist firm entering a market economy. By a socialist firm we mean one that produces a certain possibly inefficiently high output level on state orders and can afford to lose money thanks to state subsidies. A socialist firm entering a market economy buys inputs that are priced correctly. As a result, unless it has a strong effect on the prices of these inputs, it will not create large distortions in other sectors of the economy. Moreover, the state firm does not have an incentive to expand solely because its inputs are underpriced. When a socialist firm expands beyond the efficient level, it buys correctly priced inputs and loses money, which puts a check on its expansion. In contrast, a private firm in a socialist economy has a very strong incentive to expand precisely because it is buying underpriced inputs and so, assuming that demand is elastic, makes more money as it expands. Because inputs are priced correctly in a market economy, the socialist firm does not expand on the margin where it creates the greatest negative externality, whereas a private firm in a socialist economy does. This result perhaps explains why having a few state firms in a market economy, as is common in Western Europe, is not nearly as damaging as a small dose of the market can be to a socialist economy.

2.4 Conclusion: Implications for Reform

Our discussion suggests that partial reform is fraught with pitfalls. When some, but not all, resources are allowed to move into the private sector, and state prices remain distorted, the result may be a significant disruption of the state sector. The reforms in the former Soviet Union illustrate the mistakes emphasized in this chapter. In 1988 the government legalized some private enterprises, such as cooperatives, and substantially liberalized plan enforcement, allowing state enterprises more discretion on what to do with their outputs. At the same time, the arbitrary schedule of official prices between state firms was largely retained. The result has been that only some resources moved to the private sector, but the ones that did often created bottlenecks and shortages in the state sector. By destroying the traditional coordination mechanisms in the economy, without substituting true markets, partial reform contributed to the collapse of output.

The most natural implication of the analysis in this chapter is that the price reform should take the form of a big bang, with all prices being freed at once. Such a radical price liberalization would obviously eliminate the problems that we are discussing. The model also suggests some pitfalls of partial reform that at least in principle could be contained. The Chinese government, for example, has managed to control the diversion problem by strict enforcement of delivery quotas between state enterprises. Such controls require a much stronger government than Russia had in 1991. Fortunately, the Russian government moved to an almost complete price liberalization in early 1992.

— 3 —

Privatizing Russia

Mass privatization was surely the defining feature of Russian economic reform in the 1990s. This chapter, originally written in 1993, describes the privatization program. It presents the ideas underlying the program, the design of the program itself, the results of its implementation, as well as some of the challenges related to corporate governance and enterprise restructuring in Russia. Since the paper was written, the program was completed, in the summer of 1994, and a great deal has been written about its outcome and consequences (see, for example, Boycko, Shleifer, and Vishny, 1995). The present chapter eliminates some of the material from the original paper that has become outdated and briefly updates some of the numbers.

The first section describes our general approach to privatization as depoliticization. We argue that, in most countries, politicians try to influence firms to address political objectives, such as overhiring or locating in particular areas. Firms' managers extract subsidies from the treasury in return for their cooperation. The result of this politicization of firms is inefficiency in public enterprises. We argue that privatization is just one of several steps that make it more expensive for politicians to influence firms. As such, privatization reduces the amount of inefficiency that firms accept to satisfy politicians, but it does not make firms fully efficient.

In the second section, we argue that creating product market competition, improving corporate governance, and eliminating political control

By Maxim Boycko, Andrei Shleifer, and Robert Vishny; originally published in *Brookings Papers on Economic Activity*, 2 (1993): 139–181. © 1993.

of capital allocation are other important steps that make political influence more expensive. An important message of the second section is that debates about whether privatization, corporatization, or any other single measure is sufficient to make firms efficient miss the point: these are all partial measures of depoliticization.

The third section briefly describes the political goals of privatization. Like all other major reform measures, privatization is fundamentally a political phenomenon, designed to produce a realignment of political forces in a country.

In the fourth section, we discuss the design of the Russian privatization program in light of the objective of depoliticization. In particular, we discuss why Russia opted for voucher privatization, rather than for a Polish-style mutual fund scheme. We also show that, quite aside from its objectives, the Russian program was to a large extent shaped by the political constraints on what was feasible.

The fifth section presents the basic facts about Russian privatization and addresses an important puzzle that the evidence raises, namely the remarkably low valuation of Russian firms in the marketplace.

In the sixth and seventh sections, we look beyond privatization and ask what other mechanisms can reduce political influence on firms. The sixth section briefly describes the dismal state of product market competition in Russia. The seventh section examines governance of firms through equity ownership. We present survey evidence suggesting that privatization in Russia is leading to very significant ownership by managers and workers and to some ownership by large outside shareholders. Although some management and outsider ownership is a reason for optimism, the extent of insider entrenchment raises concerns about future restructuring.

3.1 Privatization as Depoliticization

To focus on the goals of privatization, it is useful to start by asking what is wrong with public enterprises and why. On the question of what is wrong, there is much agreement: public enterprises are inefficient. They employ too many people, produce goods that consumers do not need, locate in economically inefficient places, do not upgrade their capital stock, and so on. While these problems are particularly severe in Eastern Europe, public enterprises throughout the world are conspicuous for their inefficiency as well.[1] This observation is no longer controversial.

The question of why public enterprises are inefficient is harder to answer. Standard public finance starts with the assumption that governments maximize social welfare and views public enterprises from this vantage point. In particular, public enterprises are supposedly productively efficient and in fact remedy monopoly and externality problems caused by private firms (Atkinson and Stiglitz, 1980). As a positive theory of public enterprises, this one fails miserably. More recent work has stayed with the assumption of benevolent government, but argued that public enterprises are inefficient because the government is poorly informed about their efficiency and so rationally subsidizes them to pursue uncertain projects (Laffont and Tirole, 1993; Dewatripont and Maskin, 1990). These theories might explain why governments subsidize highly uncertain research and development projects or defense contracts. It does not, however, make much sense as an explanation of the dramatic inefficiency of public agriculture, coal mining, and other relatively routine production. The high costs and inefficiencies of such firms are public knowledge, yet the government still does not insist on their restructuring.

An alternative theory argues that public enterprises are inefficient because they become the means by which politicians attain their political objectives (Boycko, Shleifer, and Vishny, 1996). Excess employment, location in economically inefficient places, and underpricing of output all help politicians get votes or avoid riots. For example, it is plausible to argue that the principal objective of the Russian communists was to secure their own survival against (perceived) external and internal threats. Many features of the communist economy follow from this assumption. Russian state enterprises produced so many military goods because the politicians cared about security and not about social welfare. The government lavished capital on military firms at the expense of consumer product firms for the same reason. The communist government invested resources in public health, but without including health care for the elderly, because it needed healthy soldiers, not because it was humanitarian. The communist government asked firms to overemploy people because it insisted on full employment to prevent social unrest that would threaten its control. The government created large collective farms to control peasants and so avoid the perceived threat from them. State firms produced large farm machinery to ensure that only these large state farms could survive. Thus, a simple view of political objectives can go some way toward explaining many of the inefficiencies of the Soviet economy. The examples can be multiplied and extended around the world. Public enterprises are inefficient because their inefficiency serves the goals of politicians.

Except in a pure command economy, managers need not automatically do what politicians want them to do. Instead, managers and politicians bargain over what the firm does. Managers' objectives usually are closer to profit maximization than are those of politicians, if only because managers want to maximize resources under their control. To convince managers to pursue political objectives, politicians subsidize firms. In return for those subsidies, managers hire extra people, locate in economically inefficient places, and so on. The relationship between politicians and managers is best described as a bargain: managers might be the ones who come to the politicians and beg for money, threatening to lay off workers if they do not get funds. But this works only when politicians care about employment. Because politicians want something other than profits from firms, bargaining between managers and politicians results in payments from governments to firms (subsidies or soft budget constraints) in return for the desired inefficiency.

This framework has an obvious implication for privatization and other restructuring policies. Specifically, the objective of these policies must be to change the terms of trade in the bargain between politicians and managers, making it more expensive for politicians to buy inefficiencies with subsidies. To do that, the cost to the politician of finding a dollar of subsidies must increase, the ability of that dollar to buy extra inefficiency must fall, or both. When subsidies become more expensive and less effective, managers will do less to cater to the objectives of the politicians, and the firm will begin to restructure. In this chapter, we consider privatization and other policies from this perspective of depoliticization.

The first question to ask is whether restructuring actually requires privatization, that is, change in the ownership of cash flows of state firms. It is sometimes argued that all that is really necessary is to change control from politicians to managers: in other words, to corporatize state firms.[2] Once control changes, cash flows ran remain publicly owned as long as managers have some incentives to maximize profits. These might come from incentive contracts for the managers, from product market competition, or from hard credit policies; we discuss these issues later. Indeed, in Poland, many state enterprises began to restructure in the regime of product market competition and stricter oversight by banks without privatization (Pinto, Belka, and Krajewski, 1993). This evidence suggests that privatization of cash flows is not necessary for restructuring when control is removed from politicians.

The depoliticization model outlined above suggests that corporatization is one of the key steps that make subsidies less effective. By shifting control from politicians to managers, corporatization enables managers to extract more surplus in the bargain with politicians. Whereas before corporatization, politicians could order firms, for example, to employ extra workers, after corporatization, they must pay them to do so, which is more expensive. Because corporatization raises the cost to politicians of getting firms to cater to their wishes, it stimulates restructuring. But how much restructuring it stimulates depends on other factors determining the costs of political influence. For example, in Poland after stabilization, the combination of corporatization and tight budgets significantly reduced subsidies to firms and stimulated restructuring. In Russia, monetary policy was not as tight, and hence the effectiveness of corporatization by itself would likely be much lower, because politicians control enough money to influence firms. More generally, corporatization has often failed to lead to significant restructuring because politicians have attempted to regain their control over firms.[3] In a country such as Russia, where the mechanisms of political influence are numerous and the politicians' demand for influence is high, corporatization by itself is a rather weak measure.

Of course, everywhere in the world politicians try to exert influence over private firms by offering them procurement contracts, regulatory and tax breaks, and outright subsidies in return for meeting political objectives. So what does privatization accomplish that corporatization does not? How does privatization depoliticize firms?

First, when managers and outsider shareholders receive substantial cash flow rights, they now care about the forgone profits from failing to restructure and as a result the cost of convincing firms to be inefficient in the process of pursuing political objectives rises. This incentive effect makes it more expensive for politicians to get what they want, and hence can accelerate restructuring. Second, in many cases, the mechanisms for political influence over firms are dismantled when firms are privatized. For example, after privatization, ministries are abolished. This change both eliminates one political constituency that wants to control the firm (the ministry) and makes control by politicians operationally more difficult. Third, privatization creates a political constituency of owner-taxpayers who oppose government interference in the economy because it raises their taxes and reduces their profits; this contributes to depoliticization through a political mechanism, rather than an economic one. For all these reasons, privatization by itself is a critical strategy of depoliticization and hence restructuring.

3.2 Beyond Privatization

Important as privatization may be for depoliticization, it is not sufficient. Politicians try and often succeed in getting private firms to pursue political objectives as well. In Russia, privatized firms still receive subsidies in exchange for keeping up employment. In Italy, many private firms continue close relationships with politicians. Other measures promoting depoliticization must complement privatization. We examine three critical strategies: competition policy, equity governance, and capital allocation.

Throughout the world, product market competition plays a critical role in depoliticizing firms. When firms face efficient rivals, they must either be efficient themselves to survive in the marketplace or become subsidized. But keeping an inefficient firm in a competitive market from going bankrupt is much more expensive for a politician than keeping afloat an inefficient monopoly that can waste large monopoly rents before it begins to lose money. Unfortunately, politicians realize that competition raises the cost to them of exerting influence, and they often restrict product market competition by political action. First, politicians often protect domestic firms from both foreign and domestic competition, which of course leaves them with rents that can be dissipated on politically desirable activities. Second, bankruptcy procedures are often politicized, and hence inefficient firms are "rehabilitated" rather than allowed to go bankrupt. But when politicians fail to undermine competition, restructuring benefits come quickly. Poland and the Czech Republic have made great strides in depoliticizing firms by creating a competitive marketplace, both by encouraging domestic competition and opening to international trade.

The second important depoliticization mechanism is equity governance: giving equity ownership to active decision makers. Equity governance of necessity entails significant management ownership. It is also fostered by significant shareholdings by large investors—also referred to as core investors or active investors—who can put pressure on managers to restructure and to resist pressures from politicians.[4] The reliance on core investors for governance has characterized privatization programs in France, Mexico, and, more recently, the Czech Republic.

The third key depoliticization mechanism is replacing political allocation of capital with private allocation. As long as the allocation of credit in the economy is politicized, the firms that cater to politicians, rather than to shareholders, obtain credit. Bankrupt firms simply seek debt relief from the politicians and satisfy political objectives in return. Even managers with incentives either through their own ownership or through pressure from large shareholders cater to politicians in exchange for credits and subsidies. The success of restructuring relies critically on depoliticizing credit policies.

This necessitates two things. First, it requires eliminating soft credits and government subsidies, which have historically been politicians' most effective mechanism of control. But politicians cannot be controlled unless money is controlled. Hardening the budget constraints of firms requires macroeconomic stabilization. Second, depoliticization of finance requires that capital be available on commercial terms. Although some restructuring can occur without much new investment (firms can lay off some employees, change their product mix using the existing equipment, reduce waste in inventories, and so on), substantial restructuring usually requires capital. But depoliticization of capital allocation is usually opposed by politicians, who try to control credit policies through bankruptcy regulation, control of banks, and inflationary finance. Although getting private capital allocation to replace political capital allocation may be the hardest task, it is perhaps the most significant for eventual depoliticization of firms.

To summarize, restructuring the Russian economy requires depoliticization of firms. This strategy must be pursued on many fronts, including privatization, competition policy, corporate governance, and capital allocation. To assess the likely success of Russian privatization, we need to look at progress on all these fronts.

3.3 Political Goals of Privatization

Even though the ultimate economic objective of privatization is restructuring, privatization is always and everywhere a political phenomenon. The goal of governments that launch privatization is always to gain support for the reformist (or conservative) politicians. Mass privatization fits this mandate particularly well because it is perceived by the general populace as the only part of the economic reform that can unambiguously benefit them. Unlike price liberalization, monetary tightening, and reduction of government spending, all of which impose painful costs on some people, privatization allocates shares to the people for free or at low prices—typically a popular measure. The political support for privatization might even spill over to other reforms, such as stabilization. By creating a class of supporters of reform and reducing the power of its opponents, privatization can change the political balance in the country.

The need to gain support for reform is the political argument for privatizing rapidly. If privatization is slow, the benefits to the population are by definition small, and hence the political capital they buy the reformers is small as well. Fast privatization is privatization that offers large political benefits from the start, which is exactly what a reformist government needs. Critics of fast privatization have argued that it creates fast unemployment and thus drains the government budget (Aghion and Blanchard, 1993). This can produce both political opposition and economic problems for further privatization. This argument overlooks two essential points. First, privatization in Eastern Europe is inherently very slow. Slowing it down further beyond what internal political forces accomplish will stop it altogether. Second, and more important, rapid privatization buys political benefits and thus allows reforms to deepen.

3.4 The Russian Privatization Program

The Russian privatization program was designed to meet the objectives discussed in the preceding section.[5] Yet it was also designed in an extremely hostile political environment. As a result, the program had to accommodate the political and economic demands of various stakeholders in state firms, so as to get their support or at least preclude active opposition. The principal stakeholders included enterprise managers and employees—whose lobbies controlled the parliament and who themselves effectively controlled state firms in the transition—and local governments, who gained much of the political influence over firms that the center lost. The second part of this section explains how these constraints shaped the privatization program.

3.4.1 Description of the Program

As a first step, the program divided firms into those that would be sold primarily for cash by the local governments and those that would go into the mass privatization program. In this way, most small shops and some smaller enterprises were immediately allocated to the local governments, which demanded the revenues from small-scale privatization as their major concession.

As a second step, the program divided larger firms into those subject to mandatory privatization, those subject to privatization with the permission of the privatization ministry (GKI), those requiring government approval for privatization, and those whose privatization was prohibited. Mandatory privatization included firms in light industries, such as textiles, food processing, and furniture. Firms requiring GKI approval tended to be somewhat larger firms, yet not operating in any of the important strategic industries. Major firms in most strategic industries, such as natural resources and defense, could be privatized only with the agreement of the entire government. Given the antireformist composition of the government in 1993, this restriction meant that these firms in general could not be privatized. Even if some part of their equity could be privately owned, control always remained with politicians. Finally, some firms, including those involved in space exploration, health, and education, could not be privatized at all.

As a third step, all large and medium-sized firms (except those in the last list) were to be corporatized. That is to say, they were to re-register as joint stock companies with equity owned by the government, adopt a corporate charter, and appoint a board of directors. Initially, the board would include representatives from the property fund (the government's selling agency), the management, the workers, suppliers, and customers. The corporatization decree, signed by President Yeltsin in June 1992, was correctly viewed as the first major step toward subsequent privatization of state firms.

Once a firm corporatized, its managers and workers got to pick among three privatization options. The first option (variant 1) gave workers 25 percent of the shares of the enterprise for free, yet made these shares nonvoting. Top managers could purchase 5 percent of the shares at a nominal price. In addition, after privatization, the workers and the managers could get an additional 10 percent at a 30 percent discount to book value through something that resembled an employee stock ownership plan (ESOP). The second option (variant 2) gave managers and workers together 51 percent of the equity, all voting, at a nominal price of 1.7 times the July 1992 book value of assets. This, of course, represented a very low price relative to the market value of these assets in a highly inflationary environment. Workers could pay for these shares in cash, with vouchers (to be discussed later), or through the retained earnings of the enterprise, and could pay over some relatively short period of time. As in the first option, an additional 5 percent of shares could be obtained by managers and workers at low prices through an ESOP. Finally, a third option (variant 3), imposed by the managerial lobby in the parliament, allowed the managers to buy up to 40 percent of the shares at very low prices if they promised not to go bankrupt. For a variety of reasons, this option was seldom used.[6]

Once the managers and workers selected their benefits option, they could submit a privatization plan that described how the rest of the shares were to be sold. Although some enterprises were subject to mandatory privatization, in practice, the filing of privatization plans was almost always voluntary. The principal way in which the sale of shares took place in Russia was through auctions of shares for vouchers. Every person in Russia was offered a privatization voucher for a small fee, and most people picked them up. The voucher had a denomination of 10,000 rubles, was supposed to expire at the end of 1993, and was freely tradable.[7] This voucher could then be used as the sole allowable means of payment in auctions of shares of privatizing enterprises. Each privatizing enterprise entered into its individual voucher auction in the city where it was headquartered; systems were built to enable people to buy shares of firms located in other cities. Bidding in these auctions was very easy: the principal type of bid was to submit the voucher and to get however many shares it bought at the equilibrium price. Because vouchers were tradable, some investors acquired blocks of vouchers and bid for large blocks of shares. In a typical company, up to 30 percent of the shares were sold in voucher auctions, although smaller stakes were sold in "strategic" enterprises that were privatized.

Voucher privatization was clearly the defining feature of the Russian program. It was chosen over the alternative mass privatization scheme using mutual funds for four reasons, listed in order of increasing importance.[8] First, in Russia a mutual fund scheme would be too difficult to implement technologically. Second, it was hoped that vouchers would more actively involve people in privatization by giving them a choice of what to invest in, and hence make privatization more popular to the public than a mutual fund scheme, which does not involve choice. Third, a mutual fund scheme that imposed large shareholders on managers would have created serious opposition from the managerial lobby, which would have made implementation of the program difficult. Fourth, there was a great concern in Russia that large state-sponsored mutual funds owning large stakes in Russian companies would become politicized and hence unable to enforce restructuring policies. For these four reasons, Russia gave up the instant large shareholder advantage of Polish-style mutual funds and opted for a voucher privatization program.[9]

3.4.2 The Program in Light of the Constraints It Faced

The design of the program clearly reflected the political constraints. Most important stakeholders received major concessions. To begin, local governments gained control over small-scale privatization, as well as most revenues from it. They would have received revenues from large-scale privatization as well, except that the means of payment were vouchers. Most important, voucher auctions were run locally, which gave local governments some limited opportunity to exclude undesirable outsiders. Because of these concessions, local governments in most cases did not resist privatization, although many would have preferred cash to voucher payments.

Workers in enterprises being privatized received the most generous concessions of any privatization in the world. They have gotten either 25 percent of the firm for free (plus an ESOP) or 51 percent (plus an ESOP) at a discount. Moreover, they get to choose the privatization option that the firm chooses in a vote. With the benefit of hindsight, workers' benefits in the Russian privatization appear very high and may have adverse consequences for governance, as discussed below. It is important to realize, however, that at the time the program was proposed, the groups in the parliament demanding total worker ownership appeared to present the greatest threat to privatization. Only by making a coalition with those groups by offering significant worker ownership could the reformers succeed in defeating the managerial lobbies that opposed privatization.

Concessions to the managers do not appear large on the surface, but in truth they were enormous. Although managers' direct ownership stake was only 5 percent in variant 1—perhaps higher in variant 2—in many cases, managers bought additional shares cheaply in voucher auctions or in the aftermarket from employees. As a much more important concession to the managers, the privatization program did not impose large shareholders on the firm, so managerial independence in Russia was much greater than elsewhere in Eastern Europe. In the Czech Republic, firms got core investors as part of privatization, and in Poland they were expected to get mutual funds as blockholders. Because major shareholders were not forcibly imposed on the privatization process, managers tacitly gained a major concession, reflecting their parliamentary influence, as well as their de facto control of enterprises. Insistence on core investors would have aroused strong opposition from managers and made privatization impossible, especially because privatization in Russia was effectively discretionary.

While granting concessions to many important groups, the Russian privatization failed to address the wishes of the central bureaucracy. The result has been that the bureaucracy fought privatization every step of the way. Bribing the bureaucracy is one of the greatest challenges of any economic reform.

In short, the Russian privatization program represented a political compromise reflecting the existing property rights and political influences in the country. The real question was whether, nonetheless, privatization would lead to restructuring. We turn to this question next.

3.5 The Progress of Russian Privatization

Between October 1992 and January 1993, 150 million Russians could pick up their vouchers at their local savings banks. The fee for the voucher was only 25 rubles (5 cents at the prevailing exchange rate). Because, as we explained, privatization in Russia was much more populist than in the Czech Republic, the idea of charging a reasonable participation fee ($35 in the Czech Republic) to eliminate marginally interested citizens was rejected. By the end of January 1993, almost 97 percent of vouchers had been distributed.

Voucher auctions began in December 1992, when eighteen firms were sold in eight regions, and continued uninterrupted until June, 1994. "Altogether, over 14,000 firms went through voucher auctions in 20 months, corresponding to roughly two-thirds of the qualified universe of companies. About 97 million vouchers were accepted in these auctions (out of the total of 144 million), with almost all the rest being used up in closed subscriptions and small-scale privatizations" (Boycko, Shleifer, and Vishny, 1995, p. 105). By the end of the program, roughly two-thirds of Russia's manufacturing employment came from privatized firms.

Over the 20 months of privatization, the market price of the voucher fluctuated between $4 in the winter of 1993 and $20 in June of 1994. Even under the assumption that the price of a voucher was $20, the implied value of the Russian industry was only $12 billion, below that of one large U.S. company at the time, such as Kellogg or Anheuser-Busch. One way to calibrate the prices of manufacturing companies is to note that U.S. manufacturing companies sold at market values of about $100,000 per employee. Russian manufacturing companies, in contrast, sold at market values of about $200 per employee, a 500-fold difference!

What might explain such a low price level of Russian assets? The first hypothesis is that most of these firms really are worthless, because they have a very outdated capital stock. We submit, however, that this hypothesis goes only part of the way in explaining the pricing. Consider the following rough calculation [as of 1993]. At the purchasing-power-parity value of the dollar of about 300 rubles, Russian manufacturing wages average about $200 per month, about one-tenth of Western manufacturing wages. If the value of the Russian companies were in the same proportion to wages as in the West, then these companies should be worth about one-tenth of what their Western counterparts are worth. On this calculation, the value ratio of 500 still seems implausible.

The low quality of Russian assets thus fails to explain their low market value by a factor of 50. Additional explanations are needed. One line of argument is that private wealth in Russia is limited, and hence the low value of assets is explained by this low value of private wealth, which translates into the low value of the voucher. This theory is implausible once it is realized that there was perhaps $15 billion of capital flight from Russia in 1992.[10] Moreover, foreigners could participate freely in voucher auctions, which again raises the available pool of capital. The capital shortage story cannot plausibly explain the low valuation.

The plausible explanations fall under a general category: expropriation of shareholders by stakeholders. That is, although assets themselves have some value, the part of the return to these assets expected to accrue to outside shareholders after the stakeholders have taken their own cut is very small.

Three important types of stakeholders take a cut. The first are employees. As one very progressive Russian manager has put it, the goal of his privatized company is to raise its efficiency and make profits so that it can increase wages. Many Russian firms continued to pay for kindergartens, hospitals, schools, and other services for their workers after privatization.

The second important set of stakeholders is managers, who expropriate shareholder wealth through asset sales to their own privately held businesses and other forms of dilution. This theft by managers is probably the principal reason for the remarkably high capital flight from Russia. Shareholder rights in Russia are not protected, and few companies expect to pay dividends in the near future, leaving more for managers to take.

The last stakeholder responsible for reducing firm value to outside shareholders is the government, which expropriates firm value through taxes, regulations, restrictions on product mix and layoffs, custom duties, and many other interventions, including potential nationalization. The fear of government expropriation is often referred to as political instability, and surely explains some of the low value to outside shareholders. Of course, expropriation of shareholders by the government is nothing other than continued politicization of now-privatized firms. Evidently, the Russian market estimates that such politicization is likely to continue: among them, the three types of stakeholders will grab about 98 percent of shareholder wealth.[11]

In sum, voucher auctions have moved a substantial part of the Russian industry into the private sector, even though the implied asset values were very low. The next question is whether rapid privatization is likely to lead to restructuring.

3.6 Product Market Competition

In Section 3.2, we argued that privatization is only one of several steps needed to depoliticize Russian firms. In the next two sections, we discuss the other steps, beginning with product market competition. As we argued above, product market competition is extremely important in raising the cost to politicians of influencing firms. For this reason, competition strategy, including facilitation of entry and openness to imports, has been a critical reform strategy in Poland and the Czech Republic. Unlike these countries, Russia has not had much success with competition as a de-politicization strategy, both because it started out with an extremely uncompetitive economy and because policies failed to foster competition.

Russia inherited from central planning a highly uncompetitive economy. To facilitate central control, most industries were highly concentrated.[12] Import penetration in most sectors has been extremely low, and trade collapsed with the collapse of the communist trading block. Finally, central planners established rigid supply chains and built a transportation and storage system to match these rigid supply chains. As a result, most Russian firms, even if they were not unique producers of particular goods, bought their inputs only from specifically designated suppliers and sold their outputs only to specifically designated customers. No competition worked or could easily begin to work in most goods markets.

Of course, competition policy could address these problems. Unfortunately, in Russia, such policy has done the reverse. Moscow bureaucrats—whose personal financial concerns have not been allayed by privatization—have plotted to resurrect their ministries in the form of trade associations and financial-industrial groups, so as to facilitate both collusion and subsidized finance from the central bank. To this end, they have tried to consolidate, rather than break up, firms. Nor is there much talk about opening up foreign trade and stimulating competition in this way: existing firms rarely fail to get protection. Even at the local level, where competition could probably be the single most reliable strategy of depoliticization, politicians have restricted it. Many local governments have already taken action to protect incumbent firms from entry through licensing and other anticompetitive practices. The Russian antimonopoly committee has been captured by the interests of bureaucracy and managers fearing competition. It has no interest in breaking up large firms or encouraging entry. It has shown a strong interest in preventing privatization of those firms with market power (that is, most firms) on the grounds that it is easier to regulate prices of state firms. In fact, the antimonopoly committee argued for the consolidation of firms into monopolies so as to make price regulation easier. Finally, privatization of transport, which may be the single most effective procompetition strategy, has been slow in most regions.

Moreover, competition is most effective when companies that lose money actually go bankrupt. The Russian bankruptcy law, written under close supervision of the managerial lobby, allows for effectively permanent "rehabilitation" of bankrupt companies under existing management. In part as a response to this law, and in part as a consequence of a long history of borrowing from the government, Russian companies rarely repay their debts. As long as debts and negative cash flows do not result in hardships for the management but simply lead to getting help from the government, depoliticization will remain an elusive goal.

This leaves us with a fairly pessimistic view of the role of product market competition in depoliticizing Russian firms in the near future, despite the fact that free trade, free entry, and other policies promoting competition have been essential in depoliticizing firms in Eastern Europe. While we argue below that other depoliticization strategies have worked better in Russia, competition policy remains a gaping hole in the reforms.

3.7 Corporate Governance through Equity Ownership

In discussing equity governance, we will distinguish between management and outside shareholder ownership. As we argued in the second section, management ownership works as a governance device when managers refuse to cater to the preferences of the politicians. Ideally, managers must have high ownership stakes, yet at the same time not be completely entrenched, so that outside investors can oust them when they fail to maximize profits. To begin, we briefly discuss the evolution of management ownership in Russia.

Systematic data on management and other shareholder ownership in Russia do not exist. Two researchers working at GKI, Joseph Blasi and Katharina Pistor, have conducted small surveys of firms that ask managers about the ownership structure of their firms. The data in these surveys are self reported and hence in some cases may be incorrect. Nonetheless, the overall results present a very clear picture.

Specifically, between closed subscription, ESOPs, and subsequent acquisition of shares, managers and workers together end up owning an average of 70 percent of the company. Of that, about 17 percent on average is owned by the management team, of which about 7 percent on average (and less than 3 percent if one company is excluded) is owned by the CEO. The ownership of the additional shares is divided between outsiders and the property fund (the government), with the outsiders owning an average of 14 percent and the property fund owning an average of 16 percent.

The evidence suggests that management teams end up owning considerably more than they get in the closed subscription. They usually get 5 to 10 percent of the shares of their companies from the combination of the subsidized distribution and shares they get through the ESOPs. Managers usually try to enhance their ownership stake by buying more shares both in the voucher auctions and from workers. Sometimes the managers get loans from the company to supplement their stakes. In the end, managers end up with much higher ownership than they got in the closed subscription.

High as the managerial ownership of cash flows is, it probably underestimates their degree of control. Indeed, managers in most companies aggressively consolidated their control beyond that warranted by their ownership of shares by getting workers' voting support either informally or through formal trust arrangements. In several takeover situations, managers succeeded in keeping their jobs only because of worker support. In many companies, managers actually encourage workers to buy more shares to consolidate their own control.

This emerging picture of workers as allies of the managers—who not only fail to provide any monitoring of the managers, but actually contribute to their entrenchment—is unique in Russia. In Poland and elsewhere in Eastern Europe, workers' collectives often counterbalance managers' control—although not necessarily with the best results for restructuring. In Russia, in contrast, workers' collectives appear to be passive, although of course this passivity might be a reciprocation for highly accommodating managerial practices. Thus, although worker passivity allayed the fears of many who worried about worker control, the price managers pay for worker support may well be the slowdown of restructuring. The greatest fear is that when credit constraints begin to tighten, workers will become natural allies of politicians in preventing restructuring and thus will disrupt depoliticization of firms.

In sum, Russian managers emerged from privatization with quite substantial ownership of cash flows. They also emerged with a tremendous amount of control, particularly because of their influence over workers' collectives. In smaller companies, this ownership structure may well be efficient because it provides managers with a strong incentive to maximize profits, as long as they are not captured by workers' collectives. In the largest companies, however, some external checks are needed on managers to prevent their entrenchment and capture by politicians.

Of the 14 percent of the shares owned by outside investors, about 9.5 percent is owned by blockholders whom managers were willing to identify to the interviewer. Thus, in this sample, blockholders acquire almost two-thirds of the shares that outsiders get in the voucher auctions. (Recall that managers and workers also participate actively.) This evidence underscores the importance of voucher tradability for the formation of blockholdings in Russia. Accumulating blocks of vouchers and then bidding them in a voucher auction is the principal strategy by which potential large investors can get their blocks. Without voucher tradability, the only strategies for accumulating large blocks would be to start an investment fund, which some large blockholders are clearly doing, or to buy shares in the aftermarket, which is very difficult. The creation of a liquid market for vouchers has enabled Russian privatization to do what for political reasons it could not accomplish directly: to create core investors for many major companies.

Who are these large blockholders in Russia? They appear to be of three types. The first are private voucher investment funds that were created following the Czech model. These funds collect vouchers from the population in exchange for their own shares and then invest them through voucher auctions. Most Russian funds appear disinterested in corporate governance, but some have acquired large stakes in several companies and have actively challenged the management.

The second type of large investor consists of wealthy individuals and private firms that made their fortunes in the last few years in trade and other commercial activities. These investors often have the financial and perhaps even the physical muscle to stand up to the managers.

The third category of large investors is foreigners. To them, the market prices in voucher auctions present a major attraction. At the same time, they do not usually openly challenge the managers, for fear of a political reaction. Indeed, they usually acquire their stakes through Russian intermediaries. Foreign investors are still insignificant relative to other large shareholders, but they might come to play an important role in restructuring.

Anecdotal evidence suggests that large shareholders often try to use their votes to change company policies, although less often to change management. So far, corporate managers have resisted these challenges fiercely and rather successfully. Managers threaten the workers with dismissals if they do not support the incumbent and appear to be getting the critical worker support. But managers also physically threaten challengers at shareholder meetings, rig shareholder votes, illegally change corporate charters (from one share–one vote to one shareholder–one vote, for example), refuse to record share trades in corporate share registers, and so on. Most of these activities are not reported in the press. The current situation is best described as a stalemate: large outside shareholders are clearly posing a challenge to the existing management, but management, in turn, often with the support of the workers, has managed to repel most threats. The market for corporate control in Russia is very lively; it remains to be seen whether it is effective enough to get restructuring going.

In sum, the transition from political to private governance is clearly very painful. Politicians do not give up their control over enterprises very easily. They have resisted privatization from the start, and they are still trying to bring firms under the control of industry associations and financial–industrial groups. Moreover, the residual equity stakes that remain in the hands of property funds may well be used in the future to reassert political control over enterprises.

As political governance recedes, it is replaced to a significant extent by managerial control. Such control is better than control by politicians because managers with significant ownership stakes have more interest in value maximization and restructuring. Nonetheless, in many cases, managerial ownership needs to be supplemented by large outsider ownership to put pressure on the managers and workers' collectives to restructure. As of now, large outside shareholders face tremendous resistance from both managers and politicians in exercising their control rights. Still, they remain the most effective source of external governance in Russia. In the future, their role will increase when they become a source of capital and not just oversight.

3.8 Conclusion

This chapter presented a view of privatization as a step in the depoliticization of firms—the severance of public influence on private enterprises. We focused on three aspects of change in the way firms are run and financed that could influence the success of depoliticization: privatization itself, competition policy, and equity governance. We then evaluated Russian privatization from this vantage point.

In some respects, Russian privatization was a great success. Firms were privatized at a breathtaking pace. Equity governance mechanisms emerged very rapidly, and some of them, particularly large shareholder activism, were shaking up Russian firms. The population approved of privatization and actively participated in the process.

But without question, the greatest impact of Russian privatization has been to undermine the influence of the old-line politicians. The fundamental open question about privatization and other reforms in Russia is whether the days of these politicians are really over.

— 4 —

How Does Privatization Work?
Evidence from the Russian Shops

A number of recent studies have testified to the benefits of private as opposed to state ownership of firms. One research strand compares private and state firms engaged in the same line of activity, such as air transport or railroads, and finds the former to be more efficient (see Vining and Boardman [1992] for a survey). A second strand reveals the improvements in a given company's operations following privatization (Megginson, Nash, and van Randenborgh, 1994). A third strand documents the lower cost of contracting public services to private suppliers compared to providing it publicly (Donahue, 1989). This research makes a convincing case for the greater efficiency of private ownership.

It is less clear from the existing research exactly how private ownership leads to greater efficiency. One commonly accepted view is that private owners have stronger incentives than government appointees to maximize profits because they own equity and so bear financial consequences of their decisions. Empirically, however, the case for incentives as the reason for greater efficiency of private ownership has not yet been established.

A second theory suggests that privatization works insofar as it selects owners and managers who are better at running firms efficiently. Managers of state firms are selected for their ability to get along with politicians, address political concerns, and lobby for assistance. In contrast, managers of private firms are selected for their ability to run the firms efficiently. In the short run, entrepreneurs buy privatizing firms precisely

By Nicholas Barberis, Maxim Boycko, Andrei Shleifer, and Natalia Tsukanova; originally published in *Journal of Political Economy*, 104 (1996): 764–790. © 1996 by The University of Chicago.

to restructure them and increase profits. In the long run, privatization changes selection criteria for new managers from political acceptability to market skills. On that theory, privatization works when it brings such new and different people to run firms.

The two theories, of course, are not mutually exclusive, but it is useful to know how much explanatory power each of them has. To this end, we have designed and conducted a survey of 452 shops in seven Russian cities.[1] Of these shops, 413 were privatized in 1992 and 1993 and will be the focus of our analysis. In addition, we surveyed 38 state shops, and, by accident, one newly started private shop. The traditional Soviet shops were famous for their inefficiency. They stocked very few and very low quality goods, used much more space than they needed, provided horrible service, closed early, and hardly ever upgraded their appearance. All these shops needed restructuring, and they needed it fast. In 1992 and 1993, Russia privatized most of its shops. For this reason, the Russian shops present a good laboratory for testing theories of how privatization works.

The survey was conducted in 1992 and 1993, and asked questions on restructuring steps taken at these shops following privatization. The four restructuring steps that we analyze in this chapter reflect the most obvious changes that socialist stores needed: major renovation, change in suppliers to get different goods, increase in working hours, and employee layoffs. The survey also contained questions on changes in ownership and management and on the structure of shareholdings. Finally, the survey looked at the method of privatization. This information is used here to shed light on the theories of how privatization works.

Understanding how privatization works has some interest for at least three reasons. First, it may help shed light on the successes and failures of privatization. In many instances privatization of shops in Russia has led to no changes at all, and it is not obvious, at first sight, what exactly accounts for the failures. Second, the analysis may shed light on the two theories we outlined, namely incentives (Holmstrom, 1979) and human capital (Rosen, 1992). Third, the analysis in this chapter may help design future privatization programs and modify the ones that have already been put in place. If, for example, we discovered that incentives play a critical role, then transfer of state property to insiders, such as the workers and the managers, which is always politically the easiest, would be attractive as long as insiders received cash flow incentives. If, in contrast, the data showed that new owners are critical, then the design of a privatization program should focus on management turnover both in the process of and after privatization, which makes transfers to insiders look less attractive. In this case a good privatization program would rely on insider incentives to the smallest politically feasible extent, and would encourage competitive transfers of control via auctions and similar mechanisms.

Section 4.1 describes our survey. Section 4.2 presents basic empirical results on the effects of human capital and incentives of post-privatization restructuring of shops. Section 4.3 concludes the chapter.

4.1 Description of the Data

The analysis in this chapter is based on responses to a survey we conducted of managers of 452 shops located in seven Russian cities. The cities are in all parts of Russia; they include Krasnodar (49 shops), Moscow (47), Nizhny Novgorod (61), Omsk (102), Smolensk (80), Voronezh (43), and Yaroslavl (70). The privatized shops were selected randomly from a comprehensive list of such shops offered by privatization officials in that city; the state shops were selected randomly from a similar list of shops that have not yet been privatized. The survey was conducted between June 1992 and August 1993. The privatization of shops in Russia started in April of 1992, but almost 70 percent of the shops in our sample were privatized between October 1992 and March 1993. Because the survey was conducted so soon after the shops were privatized, we measured only the short-term restructuring effects of privatization. In the longer term, learning, product market competition, and further ownership changes might bring about further restructuring. Nonetheless, our approach is useful if one wants to understand how particular privatization strategies can have immediate effects.

Of the shops in the sample, 80 percent were food retail, 11 percent were other retail, and 9 percent were other services, such as barbers. Half of the shops had fewer than 20 employees, with an average of 25 employees. We have no reason to believe that our sample of privatized shops is in any way unrepresentative.

The Russian law provides for two methods of privatizing shops. The first is an auction, conducted either by outcry or as a tender, in which the party that offers the highest price wins. The second is a competition in which various participants submit bids and in which criteria other than price, such as preservation of shop profile or employment, can be used to determine the winners. In addition, in some cities, especially Moscow, shops were illegally privatized via a noncompetitive sale to their managers and workers. Most cities have used a combination of privatization methods, although proportions differed across cities. In our sample, 35 percent of the privatized shops were sold to the workers, 25 percent in auctions, and 40 percent in competitions, although the workers could have also won an auction or a competition. Both were highly competitive, with a median number of 11 participants.

Three quarters of the privatization contracts contained some restrictions on the future activities of the shop. Of the privatization contracts that had restrictions, 96 percent restricted the future profile of activities for three to five years (for example, a food shop could not be converted to an electronics shop for a certain period of time); 67 percent restricted layoffs, typically for only one year; and 12 percent required continued sale of goods to the poor at subsidized prices. Except for restrictions on layoffs and on prices to the poor, the vast majority of the surveyed shop managers did not consider the restrictions to be binding. In particular, as any recent visitor to Russia can testify, profile restrictions rarely bind because shops can always devote a small fraction of floor space to the original business and sell whatever they want in the rest of the space.

Our measures of shop restructuring were limited by two considerations. First, the survey had to be short, so that busy shop managers would agree to be interviewed during the business day. In fact, the survey contained 41 questions and took about half an hour to administer. Second, as we learned from pilot surveys, we could not ask questions about sales, profits, wages, or any other parameters that could be interpreted by shop managers as coming from the government tax authorities. These two considerations prevented us from asking detailed questions from which we could infer changes in shop productivity. Rather, we opted for asking whether shops undertook particular restructuring steps and for getting quick yes/no answers. The one exception to that is that we have a bit more information on how many suppliers' shops changed.

We focus on four measures of shop restructuring, which represent the most tangible steps that could be taken in the first few months after privatization. The first measure is whether the shop has made a major renovation (*kapitalny remont*), which a Russian manager would have clearly interpreted as a major redesign and rebuilding of premises.[2] Major renovation has the advantage of being a significant step, but it also has the problem of requiring capital. Since new owners might just have better access to capital, as opposed to better human capital, major renovation under new owners is not conclusive evidence of the importance of human capital for restructuring. Moreover, new owners may renovate shops simply to suit their personal tastes—much like new owners in the West renovate shops (or houses) that worked perfectly well under old ownership. In this case, renovation under new ownership would not be evidence of efficiency improvements. Our additional measures of restructuring do not suffer from these alternative interpretations.

The second measure is whether the shop has changed over half of its suppliers. The shift from the traditional state suppliers to new private, or even state, suppliers is a significant step toward increasing the variety and quality of goods sold in a shop. Moreover, changing suppliers does not require physical capital and is unlikely to reflect solely the tastes of the new owners. The third measure—which also does not suffer from the problems of the major renovation variable—is whether the shop stays open longer than it did before. Finally, the fourth measure, which is probably the least informative about restructuring, is whether a shop has laid off employees. Privatized shops often experience an increase in business, and thus absence of employee layoffs does not represent a failure to restructure. Moreover, given that the workers are at least partial owners in many cases, wages are very low, and politicians are extremely hostile to unemployment, layoffs in many cases are not the wisest restructuring strategy, quite aside from the fact that they are restricted.

In our sample of 452 shops, 14.5 percent of the shops made a major renovation. In addition, 44 percent of the shops have changed at least a half of their suppliers. The principal reasons given for changing suppliers were access to new goods (78 percent of the answers), better service (45 percent), and lower prices (52 percent). Only 32 percent reported being abandoned by the old suppliers. A quarter of the shops reported that all of their suppliers belonged to the private sector, and 40 percent stated that more than half of the suppliers were private. Only 15.9 percent of the shops reported staying open longer hours, although 73 percent said that the work was more intensive. Finally, 44 percent of the shops reported that employees were dismissed, whereas only 19 percent reported that managers were dismissed. Far and away the dominant reason given for worker dismissal was inadequate qualifications (45 percent). Only 3 percent of the shops stated decreased demand as a reason, and 15 percent mentioned increased productivity.

Before asking how privatization affects restructuring, we can use our small sample of 38 state firms to ask whether privatization affects restructuring. In our sample, 16 percent of privatized firms had a major renovation, compared to zero percent of state firms. The likelihood of major renovation indeed rises sharply as a result of privatization, confirming its validity as a restructuring measure. With other measures, the difference is not as drastic. The likelihood of changing more than 50 percent of suppliers is 43 percent for privatized firms and 49 percent for state firms. Among privatized shops, 16.2 percent reported longer hours, compared to 13 percent of state shops. Finally, 44 percent of privatized shops have laid off employees, compared to 47 percent of state shops. These results can be interpreted in two ways. They may be suggesting that capital renovation and longer hours are the better restructuring measures since they are more closely associated with privatization. Alternatively—and we tend to favor this interpretation based on our observations in Russia—these results may mean that badly done privatizations, of which there are many in this sample, may be no more effective in bringing about restructuring than state ownership.

Much of our analysis uses ownership information generated by the survey. We divided the potential owners after privatization into the workers, the old management, the new management, the outside investor (the latter could be a physical person and a legal entity). The difference between the last two categories of owners is not substantive, since there usually are entrepreneurs even behind legal entities who are buying the shops. Of the 413 privatized shops, 353 specified their ownership structure. In almost 70 percent of these shops, old employees and managers retained some ownership, whereas a new manager appeared as an owner in 6 percent of the shops, an individual outside investor in 14 percent, and a firm-investor in 29 percent of the shops. The ownership structures fell into three distinct groups. In 183 cases (52 percent of the total), the shop was owned entirely by the workers and old managers, some of whom won it in an auction or competition. In 107 cases (30 percent of the total), the shop was owned entirely by new managers and outside investors. Only 63 cases (18 percent) had a mixed ownership structure.

Among shops owned by their workers and old managers, managers on average owned 56 percent of equity, and workers owned 44 percent.

Among shops owned entirely by new people, the shop was almost always owned 100 percent by only one category of owner (the manager, the individual investor, or the firm-investor). In 6 percent of the cases, this owner was the new manager; in 89 percent of the cases, the owner is an outside investor; and in only 5 percent of the cases both the new investor and the new manager have ownership. Finally, in the residual category of 63 firms with both old and new owners, the dominant pattern was a combination of old workers and managers and an outside investor.

We use these ownership data in two ways. First, we apply them to define measures of change in human capital of the owners of the shop. We identify new human capital with having 100 percent of the shop owned by a combination of a new manager, individual investor, and legal entity-investor. That is, we conclude that decisions are made by individuals with a different human capital only if employees and old managers have no ownership in a shop. According to this measure, 30 percent of the shops were run with new human capital. We have experimented with defining new human capital if new people own 50 percent of the shares; the empirical results were similar but weaker.

We try to distinguish new ownership from new management. In this survey, management change is identified by an affirmative answer to the question of whether the shop had management layoffs. This measure is not perfect, since it points to new management not only when the top manager was replaced by an outsider, but also when the top manager stayed but some of his subordinates were laid off, or when the top manager was laid off and replaced by his deputy. However, this is the only measure of new management we have. In our sample, management was changed at least partially in 19 percent of the cases. There is a substantial overlap between ownership change and management change. In fact, management changed in 39 percent of the cases where ownership changed, but in only 11 percent of the cases where ownership did not change. As we mentioned, management layoffs did not necessarily lead to entirely new blood at the helm. In 31 percent of the cases in which a manager was laid off, the firm was still entirely owned by old managers and workers, whereas in 59 percent of the cases it was owned entirely by new people. Keeping this reservation in mind, we examine the effect of new management on restructuring.

The second purpose to which we put the ownership data is to test incentive theories. For that, we simply use information on management ownership and outside investor ownership. Interestingly, it appears that new managers were very rarely given ownership stakes. There are only six cases of new managers who are the sole owners, and seven cases of new managers who own shares together with investors. These facts are surprising if ownership incentives were needed to motivate managers.

A fundamental problem we need to address is that the acquisition of shops by new owners, as well as the actual distribution of equity, might be endogenous: new owners and the distribution of equity might be selected optimally according to privatizing shops' needs. For example, if only some shops need major renovation, and only new owners can provide capital for such renovation, then new owners would acquire only the shops that require renovation, creating a spurious correlation between new ownership and restructuring. Similarly, the distribution of equity might be endogenously determined by the characteristics of a given shop (see Demsetz and Lehn, 1985). If this endogeneity problem drives our results, we cannot draw conclusions about the roles of human capital and equity incentives for restructuring.

To address this problem, we use the method of privatization and a measure of whether the shop was sold together with its premises as instruments for change in ownership and management, as well as for equity stakes. The idea is that the method and the procedure of privatization were determined before the actual winners emerged. These may be bad instruments if, for example, only the shops that needed restructuring were put up for auction, and hence were likely to get new owners. However, it is very difficult to argue that our instruments do not work for supplier change and longer hours as measures of restructuring, since the method of privatization was in all likelihood not determined with these restructuring steps in mind. Thus, for at least some of our restructuring measures, we have adequate instruments to test the theories.

Finally, our hypotheses on the determinants of restructuring presume that the ownership structure and human capital allocation emerging from privatization matter. But if privatized shops can always be resold, or equity stakes can always be redivided, then as long as privatization puts the shop in the private sector, who owns it does not matter. A consequence of this view is that some firms do not restructure not because they have managers with wrong human capital or bad incentives, but because it does not pay to attract managers with good human capital and incentives to these shops. Fortunately for our research, this view is inconsistent with the facts. As of the time of the surveys, resale of Russian shops was virtually impossible, and never happened in our sample. When shops were turned over to their workers, the contract typically restricted resale explicitly, allegedly to prevent speculation. Even in arms-length privatizations, restrictions on land and real estate transfers prevented resale of shops. For these reasons, the ownership structures and human capital allocations that emerged from privatizations were not necessarily efficient and could not be easily altered. As a result, the theories we look at are actually testable with the data we have.

In sum, we have some measures of shop restructuring and its potential determinants. We also have some instruments for these determinants. In the next section, we examine empirically the hypotheses concerning the role of human capital and incentives in restructuring.

4.2 Evidence

This section is divided into three parts. First, we provide a simple overview of the results using conditional means of our restructuring variables. Second, we present Ordinary Least Squares (OLS) regressions of our restructuring variables on measures of human capital change and incentives. Although our dependent variables are discrete, we use OLS with heteroskedasticity-corrected standard errors rather than probits to make the comparison of regressions and instrumental variable results easier. We have performed probits as well (and reported them in an earlier draft of the chapter); the implied probabilities from probits are extremely close to OLS parameter estimates. The last subsection presents the instrumental variable estimates of the effects of human capital and incentives on restructuring.

4.2.1 Overview

The empirical work in this chapter uses a somewhat smaller sample of firms than some of the raw statistics we described. The reason is that we need privatized firms for which we have data on both ownership change and management layoffs. We are also restricted by incomplete responses to the questions about restructuring. With these cuts in the sample, we have 331 privatized shops for which we have data on renovation, 336 with data on supplier change, 334 with data on increases in hours the shop is open, and 266 with data on employee layoffs and on employment restrictions. In these four samples, major renovation occurs in 13.6 percent of the shops, a change in suppliers in 45.2 percent, increase in hours in 16.5 percent, and a layoff in 46.2 percent, respectively.

Table 4.1 presents the probabilities of restructuring as a function of its potential determinants. The likelihood of renovation in firms without complete ownership change is 10 percent, compared to 22 percent for firms with complete ownership change. Similarly, complete ownership change raises the probability of a change in suppliers from 38 to 62 percent, and that of an increase in hours from 15.5 to 19 percent. In contrast, complete ownership change has no effect on the likelihood of layoffs. Management change sharply raises the likelihood of renovation, supplier change, and shop hours increase. It also raises the likelihood of layoffs considerably, although this result may simply mean that managers are laid off at the same time as the workers. The importance of management and ownership change for restructuring is the key result of this study.

Next, we divide shops into those in which the manager share is above the median of 23 percent and those in which it is below the median. Higher management ownership raises the likelihood of renovation, store hours increase, and layoffs, but not of supplier change. When we divide shops into those with zero and positive outside investor ownership, we find that positive investor ownership raises the odds of renovation and supplier change, though not of longer hours. In contrast, layoffs are more likely when outside investors own no shares. One problem with looking at conditional means is that higher management and investor ownership may be correlated with the presence of new managers and owners, who have an effect on restructuring because of their human capital.

Table 4.1 also shows that when the shops are auctioned or sold in a competition with criteria other than price alone, the likelihood of restructuring measures other than layoffs is higher than when they are sold to the old managers and workers at a low price. In the following, we argue that the use of the auction method encourages restructuring in part because it facilitates human capital turnover.

4.2.2 Human Capital: OLS Results

The initial tests of the human capital theory are presented in Table 4.2. We estimate regressions with four dependent variables: the renovation

Table 4.1 Probability of restructuring

Variable	Renovation ($N = 331$)	Supplier Change ($N = 336$)	Longer hours ($N = 334$)	Employee layoffs ($N = 226$)
Unrestricted mean	.136	.452	.165	.462
Complete ownership change:				
No	.103	.385	.155	.464
Yes	.216	.619	.188	.458
Management layoffs:				
No	.107	.407	.125	.397
Yes	.262	.651	.339	.766
Management ownership:				
< 23%	.109	.488	.145	.351
> 23%	.163	.417	.184	.570
Outside investor ownership:				
= 0	.114	.369	.166	.549
> 0	.163	.557	.163	.345
Shop owns its premises:				
No	.113	.453	.152	.505
Yes	.182	.451	.191	.362
Competitive sale method				
No	.120	.306	.144	.517
Yes	.135	.521	.174	.421

Unconditional and conditional means of four measures of restructuring: renovation, one if capital renovation was done, and zero otherwise; supplier change, one if more than 50 percent of the suppliers were changed, zero otherwise; longer hours, one if longer hours were worked, zero if not; and employee layoffs, one if layoffs were made, zero otherwise. Complete ownership change is one if 100 percent of the owners are new to the firm, zero otherwise. Management layoffs is one if managers were laid off, zero otherwise. Management ownership is the percentage of the shop owned by the management, whether old or new. Outside investor ownership is the percentage of the shop owned by outsiders, whether physical or legal entities. A shop is sold in a competitive sale method if it is sold by auction or competition.

Table 4.2 Restructuring as a function of human capital change

Variable	Renovation (N = 331)			Supplier change (N = 336)			Longer hours (N= 334)			Employee layoffs (N = 266)		
	1	2	3	4	5	6	7	8	9	10	11	12
Constant	.265	.255	.238	.601	.597	.560	.317	.249	.260	.744	.641	.650
	(.067)	(.071)	(.070)	(.079)	(.082)	(.083)	(.067)	(.065)	(.066)	(.095)	(.098)	(.099)
Date	−0.016	−.014	−.014	−.022	−.019	−.019	−.016	−.012	−.012	−.020	−.014	−.014
	(.006)	(.006)	(.006)	(.007)	(.007)	(.007)	(.006)	(.006)	(.005)	(.009)	(.008)	(.008)
Complete ownership change	.104		.071	.223		.178	.024		−.033	0.250		−.093
	(.045)		(.051)	(.058)		(.071)	(.046)		(.045)	(.068)		(.080)
Management layoffs		.130	.087		.210	.125		.192	.200		.322	.329
		(.060)	(.088)		(.068)	(.103)		(.064)	(.099)		(.074)	(.102)
Complete ownership change × management layoff			.028			.033			.009			.050
			(.124)			(.139)			(.130)			(.149)
Layoff restrictions										−.172	−.142	−.122
										(.065)	(.063)	(.065)
Adjusted R^2	4.31	4.49	4.88	6.24	4.73	6.78	1.85	5.69	5.25	4.14	9.96	9.74

Note: OLS regression estimates of the probability of four measures of restructuring as a function of the date since privatization and variables indicating human capital change. The measures of restructuring are renovation, one if capital renovation was done, and zero otherwise; supplier change, one if more than 50 percent of the suppliers were changed, zero otherwise; longer hours, one if longer hours were worked, zero if not; and employee layoffs, one if layoffs were made, zero otherwise. Date is the number of months after June 1992 that privatization occurred. Complete ownership change is one if 100 percent of the owners are new to the firm, zero otherwise. Management layoffs is one if managers were laid off, zero otherwise. The employee layoff regressions also control for layoff restrictions, one if restrictions were reported, zero otherwise. Heteroskedastocity-consistent standard errors are in parentheses.

dummy, the change of more than half the suppliers dummy, the longer store hours dummy, and the employee layoffs dummy. The independent variables are the date of privatization relative to June 1992, in months (which can be negative), the complete change of ownership dummy, and the management layoff dummy. In the layoff regressions, we also control for layoff restrictions. We attempted to control for the city, the size of the shop, and the sector of the shop in the regressions, but these controls did not matter and so we did not use them in the results reported in this section and elsewhere in the chapter.

Table 4.2 shows that restructuring takes time. Waiting one month gives a 1.4 to 1.6 percentage points higher probability of renovation, a 1.9 to 2.2 percentage points higher probability of a change in suppliers, a 1.2 to 1.6 percentage points higher probability of longer store hours, and a 1.4 to 2.0 percentage points higher probability of layoffs.

Table 4.2 also shows that shops with completely new owners have a 10.4 percentage points higher probability of renovation than shops without completely new owners, a large difference given that the overall likelihood of renovation in this subsample is only 13.6 percent. The comparable number for new managers is an even higher 13 percentage points. Both of these effects are statistically significant. In the third column, we include both new management and new ownership dummies as well as the interaction term. The incremental effect of new ownership on renovation when there is no management change is 7.1 percentage points, and is not significant. The incremental effect of new management on renovation when there is no ownership change is 8.7 percentage points, and is not significant either. However, the total effect of new management and ownership on the probability of renovation is 18.5 percentage points, with a t-statistic of 2.4. New human capital, measured by the combined management and ownership change, has a large effect on restructuring.

The increase in the probability of changing more than half of the suppliers when owners change is a highly significant 22 percentage points, which is also quantitatively substantial given that the overall probability of supplier change is 45 percent. The increased probability of a change in suppliers when managers change is an also significant 21 percentage points. When we include both dummies and an interaction term in the regression, we continue getting a significant 17.8 percentage points effect of new ownership without management change, but an insignificant 12.5 percentage points effect of new management without ownership change.

The combined effect of new ownership and management is 33.6 percentage points, with a t-statistic of 4.2. Thus new owners together with new managers sharply raise the likelihood of changing more than half of the suppliers.

For supplier change, we actually have more data, since we allowed shop managers to choose from four categories: changing no suppliers, changing more than 90 percent of suppliers, changing about 25 percent of suppliers, and changing about 50 percent of suppliers. We have estimated the supplier change regression in Table 4.2, as well as all the subsequent supplier change equations, using a more continuously defined measure of supplier change. In terms of both parameter estimates and statistical significance, the results were similar to those we report.

The increase in the probability of longer hours is a statistically insignificant 2.4 percentage points and a statistically significant and large 19 percentage points when management changes. When both variables are included in the regression, the effect of new ownership is negative and insignificant, but the effect of new management is still a significant 20 percentage points. The combined effect of new human capital is 17.5 percentage points, with a t-statistic of 2.2.

The results are very different for employee layoffs. New ownership does not increase significantly the likelihood of layoffs. Perhaps the most plausible reason is that outside investors primarily buy shops in order to expand operations. In contrast, new management does increase the likelihood of layoffs by more than 30 percentage points (which is large relative to the mean probability of layoffs of 44 percent). This result is highly statistically significant, but has two interpretations. First, new managers may be more likely to lay off workers than old managers are. Second, old managers might get fired together with the workers, in which case management turnover is correlated with but does not cause employee layoffs. This difficulty of interpretation renders layoffs the least useful restructuring variable. The regression with both new ownership and new management confirms the insignificant net effect of the former and the significant net effect of the latter. The total incremental effect of new ownership and management is 29 percentage points, with a t-statistic of 3.1. The total effect comes from new management and hence has an ambiguous interpretation. Layoff restrictions do reduce the probability of layoffs by 12 to 17 percentage points, depending on specification.

In sum, new human capital, as measured by new ownership or new management, matters for restructuring, as measured by major shop renovations, supplier changes, and store hours increases. The effects of these changes in human capital are quantitatively large and generally statistically significant. The results are more ambiguous for layoffs. The results are consistent with the human capital theory of how privatization works. Specifically, when new people acquire and control the shops, restructuring follows. In contrast, when old managers stay, as in the case in which shops are turned over to them and the workers, much less happens. Privatization works through turnover of human capital at the helm.

There is an alternative interpretation of the evidence on renovations, namely that new owners have money or access to loans, rather than skills, and hence can afford to renovate. Old managers and employees, in contrast, face capital market constraints. This story has undoubtedly some truth to it, but it does not explain the evidence on supplier changes and longer store hours, neither of which requires money, but both of which are more likely with new owners. We thus continue to favor the human capital interpretation because it can explain the results for all three restructuring measures.

The more troublesome alternative story is that new ownership and management are endogenous. The shops in which the benefits of restructuring are the highest are the ones that attract new owners and managers. In contrast, the shops that do not need restructuring simply go to the managers and the workers. On this interpretation, shops with new owners restructure not because these owners have human capital suitable for restructuring, but because they are selected to be different shops. We take up this alternative story later in this section.

4.2.3 Incentives: OLS Results

Table 4.3 examines the effect of incentives on the likelihood of restructuring. As before, we run OLS using four measures of restructuring—renovation, change in suppliers, longer store hours, and employee layoffs—controlling for the date of privatization, which again shows up with both statistically significant and substantively large coefficients. We use two measures of incentives: total management ownership and total outside investor ownership. In layoff regressions, we control for restrictions on layoffs.

The likelihood of renovation is not significantly increased by higher management ownership. The coefficient in the regression with management ownership alone is in fact negative. When outside investor own-

Table 4.3 Restructuring as a function of cash flow incentives

Variable	Renovation (N = 353)			Supplier change (N = 340)			Longer hours (N = 338)			Employee layoffs (N = 266)		
	1	2	3	4	5	6	7	8	9	10	11	12
Constant	.393	.362	.304	.719	.607	.474	.257	.324	.151	.671	.786	.707
	(.076)	(.069)	(.090)	(.082)	(.077)	(.101)	(.066)	(.065)	(.077)	(.110)	(.093)	(.123)
Date	-.023	-.023	-.022	-.023	-.024	-.023	-.015	-.016	-.014	-.019	-.019	-.018
	(.006)	(.006)	(.006)	(.007)	(.007)	(.007)	(.005)	(.006)	(.005)	(.009)	(.008)	(.008)
Management ownership	-.000		.001	-.001		.003	.002		.003	.002		.002
	(.001)		(.001)	(.001)		(.001)	(.001)		(.001)	(.001)		(.002)
Outside investor ownership		.001	.001		.002	.003		-.000	.001		-.001	-.001
		(.000)	(.001)		(.001)	(.001)		(.000)	(.000)		(.001)	(.001)
Layoff restrictions										-.127	-.131	-.121
										(.068)	(.068)	(.068)
Adjusted R^2	4.34	4.99	5.06	2.41	5.74	6.48	3.43	1.75	4.66	5.39	5.20	5.18

OLS regression estimates of the probability of four measures of restructuring as a function of privatization and variables measuring cash flow incentives. The measures of restructuring are renovation, one if capital renovation was done, and zero otherwise; supplier change, one if more than 50 percent of the suppliers were changed, zero otherwise; longer hours, one if longer hours were worked, zero if not; and employee layoffs, one if layoffs were made, zero otherwise. Date is the number of months after June 1992 that privatization occurred. Management ownership is the percentage of the shop owned by management, whether old or new. Outside investor ownership is the percentage of the shop owned by outsiders, whether physical or legal entities. The employee layoff regressions also control for layoff restrictions, one if restrictions were reported, zero otherwise. Heteroskedasticity-consistent standard errors are in parentheses.

ership is also included, the coefficient on management ownership becomes positive but still small and insignificant. The effect of outside investor ownership is also small and insignificant.

A better picture for incentives emerges from supplier change regressions. The coefficient on management ownership, when included alone, is again insignificant and "of the wrong sign." However, when outside investor ownership is also included, the regression implies a 3 percentage point rise in the probability of supplier change per 10 percentage point increase in management ownership. Outside investor ownership is statistically significant both when included alone and in combination with management ownership. In the latter specification, the parameter estimate suggests a 3 percentage point increase in the probability of supplier change per 10 percentage point rise in outside investor ownership. Outside investor ownership provides some incentives for supplier change, and perhaps management ownership does so as well.

The longer hours regressions also suggest some effectiveness of equity ownership. Management ownership raises the likelihood of an hours increase by 2 percentage points per 10 percent increase in ownership—a relatively large effect. Outside investor ownership, when included alone, has no effect on this measure of restructuring. When both ownership variables are included, both coefficients are positive and significant, although quantitatively the effect of management ownership continues to be much larger. This result is not surprising if store managers, rather than owners, are primarily responsible for keeping them open longer.

The evidence on employee layoffs is the least conclusive. There is a marginally significant but small effect of higher management ownership on the probability of layoffs, which becomes insignificant once outside investor ownership is controlled for. The coefficient on outside investor ownership is insignificant and has "the wrong sign." Cash flow ownership does not provide a strong incentive to lay off people.

Although the results in Table 4.3 offer some support for the role of cash flow incentives in raising the probability of restructuring, their interpretation is ambiguous. Specifically, new human capital variables and ownership variables are probably correlated, and high ownership might proxy for human capital change. One way to address this problem in our data is by focusing on situations in which human capital is old. Specifically, we look at the subsample in which less than 50 percent of the shares are owned by new people *and* where managers are not laid off, and estimate the likelihood of restructuring as a function of old management ownership. These results, presented in Table 4.4, show no evidence of a significant positive effect of higher management ownership on the likelihood of renovation, supplier change, or increase in store hours, and a negative effect on layoffs. This result, in our opinion, is a setback for the view that equity ownership incentives, without human capital change, promote the restructuring of shops. What explains these results? We are aware of five possible interpretations.[3]

First, it is possible that, in shops, managerial effort is observable by owners, and hence there is no reason to rely on equity ownership as an incentive device. The fact that, when new owners hire new managers, they don't give them any equity is consistent with this view. Shops thus

Table 4.4 Restructuring as a function of management ownership subsample: no complete ownership change and no management layoffs

Variable	Renovation ($N = 172$)	Supplier change ($N = 174$)	Longer hours ($N = 174$)	Employee layoffs ($N = 143$)
Constant	.263	.456	1.866	.472
	(.095)	(.132)	(.088)	(.188)
Date	−.016	−.014	.008	−.019
	(.007)	(.010)	(.006)	(.012)
Management	−.000	.001	−.002	.001
ownership	(.001)	(.002)	(.001)	(.002)
Layoff				.117
restrictions				(.085)
Adjusted R^2	2.44	.14	1.30	1.83

OLS regression estimates of the probability of four measures of restructuring as a function of the date since privatization and management ownership, a variable measuring cash flow incentives within a subsample in which no managers were laid off and people new to the shop own less than 50 percent of the shop. The measures of restructuring are renovation, one if capital renovation was done, and zero otherwise; supplier change, one if more than 50 percent of the suppliers were changed, zero otherwise; longer hours, one if longer hours were worked, zero if not; and employee layoffs, one if layoffs were made, zero otherwise. Date is the number of months after June 1992 that privatization occurred. Management ownership is the percentage of the shop owned by management, whether old or new. The employee layoff regressions also control for layoff restrictions, one if restrictions were reported, zero otherwise. Heteroskedasticity-consistent standard errors are in parentheses.

do not provide a useful laboratory for testing the role of equity incentives. Although this view has some merit, we are not entirely convinced. The so-called sponsors who are the owners of shops are often entrepreneurs operating in many diverse lines of business. They are unlikely to keep an eye on managers intensively enough to completely forswear the use of equity incentives.

Second, incentives may take the form of ex post settling up rather than ex ante ownership. The owner and the manager might simply reach an understanding that, if a shop does well, the owner will reward the manager. We are not fully persuaded by this argument either. After all, many of the new shop owners have earned their money in semi-legal activities, and their reputations are not pristine. To a manager, equity should be a safer bet. Moreover, even if owners use other incentives, management equity ownership should provide, on the margin, an extra incentive for restructuring.

Third, it is possible that, by focusing on share ownership, we are looking at the wrong margin of incentives. Even if ownership incentives are strong, shops controlled by insiders may be less likely to restructure simply because the effort cost of restructuring is too high for the workers, and they would rather continue their old working habits unless forced to restructure by the new owners. Under this theory, new owners restructure not because they have the appropriate human capital, but because they do not fully bear the cost of higher worker effort. Thus, even if new owners pay higher wages for getting more work out of the old employees, they still can extract some of the rents from the workers. Because the workers pay the full effort cost of restructuring, they do not have an incentive to restructure when they share control. This argument is similar to that made by Shleifer and Summers (1988) in the context of hostile takeovers.

This theory faces both theoretical and empirical difficulties. To get people to work harder, new owners must pay higher wages, and so face the same cost of extracting higher effort as worker-owners do. If the workers were getting such large rents from their jobs before privatization, they would have tried to stop privatization of their shops, or quit after new owners gained control. If anything, the evidence seems to be the reverse: resistance to small-scale privatization is low and few people quit (or are laid off) after new owners gain control. This theory also has trouble explaining why the old managers are not more likely to restructure when their ownership increases, even though the cost to them of extracting rents from the workers stays constant while benefits rise.

The fourth interpretation of the share ownership evidence is that equity incentives are not nearly as important as new human capital for the restructuring of shops. The old managers simply do not have the skills to restructure, at least in the short period of time over which we observe these shops. Even with incentives, you cannot teach an old dog new tricks.

Finally, the fifth possibility is endogeneity. In the case of ownership, this explanation would argue that shops are heterogeneous, and different ones require different management and outsider ownership to provide optimal incentives. In a cross section, then, there is no necessary relationship between equity ownership and performance, similar to the argument made by Demsetz and Lehn (1985). Below, we deal with the possibility of endogeneity of new owners and equity ownership.

4.2.4 Human Capital and Incentives: Two-Stage Least-Squares Results

In this subsection, we try to address the selection argument. This argument is based fundamentally on unobserved heterogeneity of shops. It states that new owners and equity shares are selected endogenously to suit different needs of different shops. New owners and managers appear only in shops that need restructuring, and therefore the positive correlation between new ownership and restructuring is spurious. Optimal equity ownership differs across shops, and hence there is no obvious correlation between it and restructuring in equilibrium. Thus, all of our evidence can be explained by these selection arguments.

Before we test the selection argument empirically, we stress that we find it ex ante quite unconvincing, for several reasons. First, even if one believed that new owners are selected endogenously for some shops, there is a question of *why* new owners are needed for restructuring of these shops. After all, insiders could always buy the shops a lot cheaper. One possibility is that new owners provide capital for restructuring, which is needed only in some shops, and which old owners do not have access to. But this possibility is inconsistent with our evidence that new owners are also more likely to change suppliers, and to keep the shops open longer— the two restructuring strategies that do not require capital. An alternative possibility is that new owners are selected into shops that need restructuring because these owners have the appropriate human capital. This possibility is consistent with our view.

Second, it is not clear to us, based on our experience in Russia, that the new owners actually do get the shops that need restructuring most. If anything, the shops that benefit the most from restructuring are the ones that workers and managers would lobby the hardest to keep for themselves. In the city of Moscow, such lobbying turned privatization of shops into outright giveaways to the insiders, and Moscow surely has some of the most valuable shops, which can benefit enormously from restructuring. The selection argument, then, is less appealing than it seems initially.

Nonetheless, we try to address this argument empirically as well. To this end, we use three instruments for the potentially endogenous variables: a dummy equal to one if the shop was sold in an auction, a dummy equal to one if the shop was sold in a competition, and a dummy equal to one if the shop was sold together with its premises. These variables are likely to be correlated with ownership and management change, as well as resulting ownership structure. The question is: Are they also uncorrelated with the unobserved urgency of restructuring shops? For the case of capital renovation, one could argue that we do not have adequate instruments. To attract new owners to those shops that need capital renovation, local officials might put up these shops for auctions and competitions, as well as include the premises in the privatization package. In this case, our instruments are correlated with the unobserved need for renovation. However, this argument is implausible for the longer store hours and supplier change variables. Local officials are unlikely to select for auctions the shops that could benefit from staying open longer, or need to change some suppliers, and the shops that need capital renovation the most are unlikely to be the very same shops that most urgently require other restructuring measures. Thus, for supplier change and longer store hours, we do have theoretically plausible instruments.

Table 4.5 presents the results of the first-stage regressions. The method of privatization has a very large and statistically significant effect on all the dependent variables: complete ownership change, management layoff, management ownership, and outside investor ownership. Shops privatized through an auction or competition are more likely to change owners and managers, and to have low management and high outsider owner-

Table 4.5 Predicting human capital change and ownership

Variable being instrumented	Complete ownership change (N = 327)	Management layoffs (N = 327)	Management ownership (N = 331)	Outside investor ownership (N = 331)
Constant	.108	.264	47.144	1.208
	(.058)	(.074)	(4.432)	(5.486)
Date	−.013	−.021	−.124	−.198
	(.006)	(.006)	(.372)	(.521)
Shop owns it premises	.109	.050	−9.166	15.156
	(.048)	(.045)	(2.797)	(4.332)
Auction dummy	.488	.266	−20.726	51.336
	(.056)	(.058)	(3.933)	(5.256)
Competition dummy	.387	.108	−24.241	49.500
	(.045)	(.041)	(2.745)	(4.264)
Adjusted R^2	23	10.9	21.1	32.5

First-stage results from a two-stage least-squares procedure in which the variables measuring human capital change and the cash flow incentives are regressed on four instrumental variables. Complete ownership change is if 100 percent of the owners are new to the firm, zero otherwise. Management ownership is the percentage of the shop owned by management, whether old or new. Outside investor ownership is the percentage of the shop owned by outsiders, whether physical or legal entities. The instrumental variables are date, the number of months since June 1992 that privatization occurred; a dummy variable taking the value one if shop owners own the premises; a dummy variable taking the value one if the shop was sold in an auction; and a dummy variable taking the value one if the shop was sold off in a competition. Heteroskedasticity-consistent standard errors are in parentheses.

ship, than shops turned over to the workers. These effects are not surprising, but suggest that we have good instruments.

More interestingly, the inclusion of premises in the privatization significantly raises the likelihood of complete ownership change, as well as reduces management and raises outside shareholder ownership. It has no effect on the likelihood of management layoffs. The inclusion of premises may offer the buyer of a shop better property rights than a lease from the local government, which is the principal alternative way to get access to space. This greater security of property rights might therefore attract new owners who want to invest in the shop, consistent with the theories of Grossman and Hart (1986). In fact, our survey investigated the issue of security of access to space a bit further. In the sample, 33 percent of the shops owned their premises, and the remaining leased them from the local governments. More than 97 percent of the shops said that the terms of the rent were defined, 67 percent reported the duration of leases of longer than 10 years, and 72 percent said that their leases contained an option to buy. At the same time, 29 percent of the shops said that their rent changed every month, and 37 percent indicated that the rates of growth of rent were not defined, which suggests considerable residual power of the landlords. Although we cannot vouchsafe for the security of ownership of premises against regulatory expropriation by the bureaucrats, ownership still seems more secure than leasing. It is not surprising, therefore, that inclusion of premises attracts new owners, who own a great deal of equity and give little to their managers.

Table 4.6 presents the second-stage results of the instrumental variable procedure. The magnitude of the effect of ownership change on the probability of renovation increases, although the effect is no longer statistically significant. The effect of management change on renovation remains marginally significant.[4] The effects of new ownership and new management on supplier change and increase in store hours are quantitatively larger than in OLS, and still statistically significant. Complete ownership change raises the likelihood of supplier change by 56 percentage points, and of longer hours by 17 percentage points. The corresponding effects for management layoffs are 115 percentage points and 57 percentage points, respectively. The instrumental variable evidence thus confirms that new human capital encourages restructuring, consistent with our theoretical skepticism about the selection story.

Table 4.6 Two-stage least-squares estimates of the effects of human capital change

Variable	Renovation (N = 327)		Supplier change (N = 332)		Longer hours (N = 330)		Employee layoffs (N = 265)	
	(1)	(2)	(3)	(4)	(5)	(6)	(7)	(8)
Constant	.260	.164	.494	.206	.258	.088	.808	.928
	(.076)	(.108)	(.090)	(.161)	(.071)	(.107)	(.102)	(.174)
Date	−.017	−.010	−.021	.002	−.014	−.003	−.021	−.027
	(.006)	(.008)	(.008)	(.012)	(.006)	(.008)	(.009)	(.012)
Complete ownership change	.129 (.091)		.557 (.116)		.172 (.094)		−.187 (.181)	
Management layoffs		.360 (.194)		1.158 (.328)		.572 (.213)		−.379 (.336)
Layoff restrictions							−.129 (.074)	−.193 (.074)

Second-stage results of a two-stage least-squares procedure in which four measures of restructuring are regressed on fitted values of the explanatory variables. The measures of restructuring are renovation, one if capital renovation was done, and zero otherwise; supplier change, one if more than 50 percent of the suppliers were changed, zero otherwise; longer hours, one if longer hours were worked, zero if not; and employee layoffs, one if layoffs were made, zero otherwise. The explanatory variables are date, the number of months after June 1992 that privatization occurred; complete ownership change, one if 100 percent of the owners are new to the firm, zero otherwise; and management layoffs, one if managers were laid off, zero otherwise. The employee layoff regressions also control for layoff restrictions, one if restrictions were reported, zero otherwise. Heteroskedasticity-consistent standard errors are in parentheses.

Table 4.7 presents the second-stage regressions for the equity ownership variables. As in Table 4.3, some, though by no means all, of the coefficients on the incentive variables are significant either statistically or substantively. However, we have the same problem as in Table 4.3 of high outside investor ownership, and low management ownership, being correlated with new owners and managers. Consequently, we need to look at the instrumental variable results for the subset of shops that did not change owners and managers, as in Table 4.4. This is possible to do because in many cases insiders won an auction or a competition. Indeed, the first-stage regression shows that, in this subsample, management ownership is lower in shops privatized through auction or competition, as well as in shops that own their premises. The second-stage results, presented in Table 4.8, are similar to those in Table 4.4. They show no significant effects of (predicted) management ownership on the probability of any restructuring measure we analyze. This evidence, as before, is not supportive of the importance of equity ownership by the old managers for the restructuring of privatized shops.

In sum, the two-stage least-squares results confirm the OLS evidence that human capital change stimulates restructuring, but the effect of equity incentives in our data is not nearly as clear.

4.3 Conclusion

The principal message we draw from our empirical evidence is that restructuring requires new people, who have new skills more suitable to a market economy. A secondary message is that, without new people, equity incentives for old people might not be particularly effective in bringing about significant change. These messages, of course, are subject to several caveats. First, we surveyed the shops only a few months after they were privatized, and more restructuring was sure to come later. Moreover, the beneficial effects of equity incentive might take longer to work than those of new human capital. Second, equity incentives might not be the only, or even the dominant, form of incentives for shop managers. Ex post settling up and other pay-for-performance arrangements, such as bonuses, might be more common in shops. Third, the results for shops may not extend to industrial firms, especially since the latter rely less on ex post settling up and more on managerial equity ownership. All these criticisms have some validity, especially in suggesting caution in interpreting our results on incentives. Nonetheless, these criticisms do not significantly detract from the central positive message of the importance of new human capital for restructuring. In fact, to the extent that appropriate human capital is more essential for complicated industrial firms than for small shops, the central conclusion of this chapter might be even more compelling for industrial firms.

Much of the design of privatization programs, including the work of some of the present authors on the large-scale privatization in Russia (Chapter 3), has focused on cash flow incentives. In many cases, insiders were given substantial ownership stakes in the privatizing firms. One reason for this was the political requirement to buy insider support for

Table 4.7 Two-stage least-squares estimates of the effects of incentives

Variable	Renovation (N = 331)			Supplier change (N = 336)			Longer hours (N = 334)			Employee layoffs (N = 265)		
	(1)	(2)	(3)	(4)	(5)	(6)	(7)	(8)	(9)	(10)	(11)	(12)
Constant	.362	.272	−.225	.957	.538	−1.205	.370	.279	−1.171	.607	.777	−.775
	(.083)	(.071)	(.552)	(.110)	(.083)	(1.121)	(.087)	(.066)	(.878)	(.191)	(.096)	(2.239)
Date	−.018	−.018	−.015	−.028	−.026	−.016	−.016	−.016	−.008	−.017	−.018	−.013
	(.006)	(.006)	(.007)	(.008)	(.007)	(.015)	(.006)	(.006)	(.011)	(.009)	(.009)	(.016)
Management ownership	−.002		.010	−.008		.036	−.002		.030	.004		.032
	(.002)		(.011)	(.002)		(.023)	(.002)		(.018)	(.004)		(.045)
Outside investor ownership		.001	.006		.004	.022		.001	.015		−.001	.013
		(.001)	(.005)		(.001)	(.011)		(.000)	(.009)		(.002)	(.021)
Layoff restrictions										−.103	−.126	.027
										(.088)	(.079)	(.257)

Second-stage results of a two-stage least-squares procedure in which four measures of restructuring are regressed on fitted values of the explanatory variables. The measures of restructuring are renovation, one if capital renovation was done, and zero otherwise; supplier change, one if more than 50 percent of the suppliers were changed, zero otherwise; longer hours, one if longer hours were worked, zero if not; and employee layoffs, one if layoffs were made, zero otherwise. The explanatory variables are date, the number of months after June 1992 that privatization occurred; management ownership, the percentage of the shop owned by the management, whether old or new; and outside investor ownership, the percentage of the shop owned by outsiders, whether physical or legal entities. The employee layoff regressions also control for layoff restrictions, one if restrictions were reported, zero otherwise. First-stage results are shown in Table 4.5. Heteroskedasticity-consistent standard errors are in parentheses.

Table 4.8 Two-stage least-squares estimates of the effects of incentives

Variable	Subsample: no complete ownership change and no management layoffs			
	Renovation ($N = 172$)	Supplier change ($N = 174$)	Longer hours ($N = 174$)	Employee layoffs ($N = 143$)
Constant	−.060	1.599	1.644	.647
	(.305)	(.612)	(.331)	(.544)
Date	−.010	−.032	.012	−.022
	(.008)	(.016)	(.008)	(.015)
Management	.006	−.022	.003	−.004
ownership	(.006)	(.012)	(.007)	(.014)
Layoff				.149
restriction				(.128)

Second-stage results of a two-stage least-squares procedure in which four measures of restructuring are regressed on fitted values of the explanatory variables, within the subsamle in which no managers were laid off and people new to the shop own less than 50 percent of the shop. The measures of restructuring are renovation, one if capital renovation was done, and zero otherwise; supplier change, one if more than 50 percent of the suppliers were changed, zero otherwise; longer hours, one if longer hours were worked, zero if not; and employee layoffs, one if layoffs were made, zero otherwise. The explanatory variables are date, the number of months after June 1992 that privatization occurred; management ownership, the percentage of the shop owned by the management, whether old or new; and outside investor ownership, the percentage of the shop owned by outsiders, whether physical or legal entities. The employee layoff regressions also control for layoff restrictions, one if restrictions were reported, zero otherwise. First-stage results are shown in Table 4.5. Heteroskedasticity-consistent standard errors are in parentheses.

privatization, on the argument that even insider-dominated privatization is better than state ownership. But another reason was the idea that when insiders get ownership incentives, they become more interested in restructuring because they can benefit from higher profits. In the Russian and other recent privatizations, considerable effort was made to bring in large outside investors to provide both oversight of the managers and new ideas and capital. Nonetheless, in the vast majority of cases insiders retained control.

If our results on human capital can be generalized to large-scale privatization, they suggest that continued control by old managers presents a problem for restructuring, and that more attention should have been paid to management turnover as opposed to shareholder oversight over the existing managers. To some extent, large investors have begun to force old managers out: by some estimates, this happened in 10 percent of first shareholder meetings in Russia. Moreover, many old managers have been given enough wealth that they can afford to retire in peace and let a new generation take over. This, however, is probably not enough. Further reforms should facilitate director retirement (with large golden parachutes) as well as forced removals through proxy fights, bankruptcies, and other aggressive corporate control mechanisms. If privatization were designed from scratch, these strategies should have received more attention than they have.

A more general lesson of this limited study of Russian shops is that the success of reform depends significantly on the speed of turnover of political and economic leadership. Freely operating financial markets and governance mechanisms speed up this process in firms, whereas frequent elections do so in political markets. This view also points to the importance of developing new human capital through training.

In conclusion, we want to emphasize that our finding that skills may matter more than incentives is relevant for labor markets in general. Recent research in labor economics, especially in the analysis of executive pay, has stressed incentives and ignored "slotting" people into jobs[5] (Jensen and Murphy, 1990). If finding the right person for the job is much more important than offering incentives on that job, then Jensen and Murphy's and other results of little responsiveness of pay to performance are not surprising. The diversity of people and of their talents would dominate the differences in productivities, much as it does in the Russian shops. At least when we started this project, this conclusion was by no means obvious.

— 5 —

Origins of Bad Policies:
Control, Corruption, and Confusion

Many, if not most, economic policies pursued by governments around the world reduce public welfare. Governments routinely start, and fail to end, inflations, introduce regulations with costs that vastly exceed their benefits, fail to provide protection to private property, and get involved in an ever-increasing set of activities they cannot properly run. The question is, Why? What are the origins of bad economic policies?

Economic theory has offered some persuasive answers to this question. Buchanan and Tullock (1962), following in the footsteps of the *Federalist Papers,* have argued that democratic majority rule can lead to inefficient policies that redistribute resources from the minorities to the majorities. Stigler (1971) argued, in contrast, that organized minorities often gain control of economic policies, and convince the government to pursue highly inefficient policies that redistribute resources from the public as a whole (majority) to themselves. Still other economists attribute bad economic policies to government mistakes.

This chapter does not have much new to contribute theoretically to this work. Rather, it tries to develop some of the standard ideas in a bit more detail using the examples of policies toward property rights that have been discussed and pursued in Russia in the early 1990s. Few of these policies have reflected the will of the majority, since Russia's youthful democracy is not yet especially responsive to public concerns. Excessive pensions, minimum wages, and other middle-class benefits are yet to hit Russia in the same way as they have hit developed countries or

By Andrei Shleifer; originally published in *Rivista di Politica Economica,* 86 (1996): 103–123. © 1996.

even Eastern Europe. As a result, the federalist concerns about populism and majority rule are not of much relevance in the analysis that follows. However, many of the policies considered and pursued in Russia reflect the power of lobbies, so the Stiglerian analysis is highly relevant. In addition, the so-called policy mistakes are highly relevant, and I devote most of this chapter to the analysis of such mistakes.

For my purposes, it is useful to distinguish three sources of bad policies. The first is the politicians' desire to control property so as to use it to gain political support. For example, politicians often prefer political control over firms in order to force these firms to hire extra people who would then support these politicians with votes or political services (Chapter 3). The second source of bad policies is politicians' interest in personal income, namely bribes (Shleifer and Vishny, 1992, 1993). Both control and corruption are best understood in a Stiglerian framework, in which politicians pursue bad policies to appeal to particular concentrated interests. Finally, the third critical reason for bad policies is the confusion of politicians—their using wrong models of the economy, and even more important of the government, in making policy proposals. Confusion of policy makers is universal, yet I will argue that it has presented absolutely devastating problems for transition economies. My goal is to illustrate the role of these three sources of bad economic policies in the case of Russian policies toward property in the last few years and to suggest strategies to improve the quality of economic policy making during transition.

The next two sections deal with control and corruption relatively briefly, as these issues have been discussed extensively elsewhere. Section 5.3 focuses on the role of confusion. In addition to a few straightforward examples, I discuss in some detail a number of economic policies proposed by one of Russia's leading reform politicians (Yavlinsky and Braguinsky, 1994). This example dramatically illustrates the policy predicament of many transition economies. Section 5.4 concludes the chapter. Although the examples in this chapter come predominantly from Russia, I believe that the analysis is highly relevant to many developing, as well as developed, economies.

5.1 Control

Throughout history, politicians have tried to control productive assets through public ownership or regulation. Historically, such control brought sovereigns income that would have been difficult to obtain through taxation alone (Ekelund and Tollison, 1981; Tilly, 1990). Sovereigns established quasi-public monopolies to collect rents from consumers, regulated trade to charge fees, and claimed ownership of natural resources to raise funds for the state. These funds were then used to support the sovereigns' lifestyles, as well as to wage wars, which took up the vast majority of public budgets. The sovereign was typically too weak, and his vassals too strong, to raise all the desired revenues through taxation of income or wealth (De Long and Shleifer, 1993).

With the growth of democratic government throughout the world, the need to control property to raise revenue has diminished, as the state has generally become powerful enough to satisfy its needs through taxation. Instead, control over property has become a way for politicians to direct its use to win elections. For example, many countries nationalized bankrupt industries, such as coal and steel, to prevent significant unemployment and win votes. More generally, politicians often control firms to force them to hire extra people and pay higher wages, with the idea that the beneficiaries will vote for the politicians, work on their campaigns, or even threaten and intimidate their opponents. Grossly overstaffed European state airlines and steelmakers, third-world parastatals in all sectors, and municipal government enterprises in the United States all illustrate how control over firms brings politicians support from their employees as well as from the trade unions. Without direct control, politicians could not get such inefficient employment and wage levels out of private firms, except by making politically unacceptable transfers from the public to the private sector.

Although employment and extra wages paid to political supporters are the most common political benefits accruing to politicians controlling firms, there are many other benefits as well. For example, politicians controlling banks can direct these banks to lend money to political allies (witness Credit Lyonnais' loans to the friends of the socialist party). Control over food distribution has enabled African politicians to extract resources from farmers, and to transfer them to political allies, including city dwellers (Bates, 1981). Control of the railroads allows politicians in many countries to provide free transport to specific population groups whose support they seek. More generally, control over all productive assets in the economy has been the principal mechanism of controlling population pursued by communist regimes around the world: it enabled them to ignore the consumers, build up the armies, and deprive their opponents of any means of subsistence.

The behavior of Russian politicians following the collapse of communism illustrates how bad economic policies—some proposed and some actually pursued—are governed by politicians' preference for maintaining control over productive assets. The collapse of the Communist Party deprived politicians of their control over firms, since the Communist Party served as the traditional enforcer of that control through central planning and the power to fire and hire managers. This control reverted to managers and employees of former state firms, as well as to outsiders who received shares in privatization. Not surprisingly, politicians have fought this loss of control tooth and nail, by both opposing privatization and promoting policies reestablishing political control.

One unfortunate illustration of this phenomenon is the failure of land privatization in Russia, where the agricultural interests have successfully prevented the breakup and privatization of collective farms. The effect is that agriculture remains highly inefficient and dependent on government subsidies, which in turn allows the directors of collective farms to maintain their control over the farm workers and to deliver farmers' votes for the agrarian party that lobbies for and gets the subsidies. In cities as well, the local governments have maintained control over registration and transactions in land, which has enabled them to keep control over much of small business that has no choice but to cater to the local politicians (as well as bribe them, see below). Control over land and real estate has been a critical source of political power for both national and local politicians.

With respect to industrial assets, a dramatic attempt by the traditional politicians to maintain control has been the repeated introduction of proposals to form financial–industrial groups. When defending these proposals, the industrial ministers usually referred to the Japanese keretsu and Korean chaebol. In practice, they wanted to maintain control over firms by putting together whole industries into organizations that would be controlled by the former ministries, with powers to coordinate major production and investment decisions. The ministries offered firms a key service—lobbying for cheap state credits—in exchange for the political support for the preservation of these ministries. If adopted, this policy would have frozen the former state firms in the position of gross inefficiency and dependence on the government for survival. Fortunately, unlike in the case of land, these mechanisms of political control of firms have not succeeded in Russia, largely because of the popular appeal of the privatization program and the desire of enterprise managers to free themselves from the ministries.

The inefficiency of communism, and of state production more generally, vividly illustrates the enormous costs of political control of business. The fundamental question, then, is one of how these costs can be reduced. One commonly advocated approach is to rely on bureaucratic reform, which would replace the existing political control by that of publicly spirited, efficient bureaucracies that are free of political influence. There are a small number of such allegedly efficient and publicly spirited bureaucracies in the West (for example, Electricité de France, perhaps BBC), as well as in rapidly growing East Asian economies, such as Japan, Korea, Taiwan, and Singapore, although even in those countries public interference in business has been extensively criticized. Unfortunately, in countries with weak and corrupt governments, and traditionally parasitic rather than public-spirited bureaucracies, the inefficiencies of public control cannot be eliminated unless bureaucracy is radically reformed. Without a dictatorship or a foreign occupation, there are no good ideas for how to reform bureaucracy. Good public control, therefore, is usually not a viable option.

In these circumstances, political control needs to be reduced rather than upgraded. The principal policy for reducing political control of assets is privatization. Privatization deprives politicians of their control over firms, and also makes it more difficult for the politicians to persuade firms through subsidies to serve political goals. In Russia, privatization went a long way toward freeing firms from political influence by turning firms over to their managers, employees, and outside investors. As a result, most of the industrial ministries have either disappeared or lost much of their power. In other countries of the world as well, including those in Western Europe, privatization helped to weaken or destroy much of the political influence on firms, as well as some of the institutions through which this political influence is maintained, such as the labor unions. The result is that bad policies—such as the maintenance of extra employment or the provision of politically desirable product mix—have receded and efficiency of the economy has begun to improve. The accumulating evidence from Russia as well as Western Europe indeed shows that the efficiency benefits of privatization have been substantial, largely because of the decline of political influence over firms (see Megginson, Nash, and van Randenborgh, 1994; Lopez-de-Silanes, 1997; and Boycko, Shleifer, and Vishny, 1995 for some of the evidence on the benefits of privatization).

5.2 Corruption

Political benefits are not all that politicians derive from controlling productive assets. The other important benefit is bribes. When politicians have the power to control the decisions of firms, to regulate them, or to issue them permits to pursue new activities, they can collect bribes in exchange for less intrusive control, regulatory relief, or fast issuance of permits. Politicians readily take advantage of these opportunities. Many of the laws and regulations that politicians put in place have little social benefit, but facilitate the collection of bribes in exchange for relief from these very laws and regulations. The bad policies are put in place because they enhance politicians' personal incomes when private agents pay bribes to escape these policies. (In some countries, some corruption is legalized, and hence the word "bribes" is not used. For example, in the United States, politicians receive campaign contributions in exchange for favors that in other countries bring bribes).

Again, examples abound throughout the world. Many countries have customs regulations that are sufficiently complex and inconsistent as to make imports and exports that do not violate these regulations impossible. Trading companies then simply pay bribes to customs officials to get on with their business. Even if a shipment does not violate any of the regulations, the customs officials have the authority to take long enough to ascertain this fact that it is easier to pay a bribe to let the goods move. Many of the shortages of goods in communist Russia were created through underpricing explicitly to provide bribe income to the officials allocating these goods.

Economic transition, and the resulting need for a new legal and regulatory structure, presents politicians with a broad range of new opportunities for bribe-seeking policies. Three examples will suffice, but they can be multiplied. When Russia created a new national antimonopoly committee to deal with the problems of market power, the first act of this Committee was to create a list of firms it classified as monopolies. Once the list was put in place, the Committee could claim jurisdiction over pricing and other policies of these firms. Some major national enterprises appeared on this list, but many small local businesses, from bakeries to bathhouses, also appeared as local monopolies. Firms immediately began to pay bribes to the local antimonopoly officials just to get themselves off the list.

The federal bureaucracy charged with the creation of a private land market began its activities by claiming monopoly over the registration of all land plots and land transactions. Very few rules were put in place by the bureaucracy obligating the officials to actually do anything. Not surprisingly, the local employees of this bureaucracy were often bribed by private parties that had no ability to do anything except with a registration. It is not clear that the registration system that was put in place had any purpose other than to provide income for the officials.

Another famous example of a bad policy designed to enrich the officials is oil export quotas that are allocated by government fiat rather than auction. These quotas give the government officials in charge of allocating them enormous power to favor one oil company over another, and to charge for the favors. Not surprisingly, the relevant officials strongly oppose not only the elimination of the quotas but even attempts to auction them off.

Dealing with corruption is often difficult. One approach—similar to privatization—is to reduce the role of government in the economy by eliminating regulations and perhaps even whole agencies that have the power to write them. But this approach goes only so far, since in many instances transition economics need laws and regulations for markets to function. Having no government at all is not an answer to this need. Another approach is bureaucratic reform. Again, the problem is that only a few political leaders without dictatorial power have enough authority to reform the bureaucracy. In effect, a major revamping of government—including both the people and the rules by which it functions—is needed (Klitgaard, 1995). In a country such as Russia, no leader has such authority at the moment, and therefore top-down bureaucratic reform is not imminent.

The best available strategy for controlling corruption in the short term is probably the democratic process, since voters do not like corruption. Elections can work in two ways. First, corrupt officials often, though not always, lose them. Second, at some point in time elections can bring in leadership that is prepared to undertake government reform. In this way, the structure of government, and not just the people, will change through the electoral process. Democratization is thus an essential element of eliminating corruption, but it is not a fast process.

The importance of substantial turnover of existing politicians through the democratic process should not be underestimated. Many of the politicians in power in Russia and other transition economies have taken bribes, and are beholden to the people who paid them. This is the reason these politicians are so afraid to lose office: they become useless to those who paid them, and hence vulnerable to exposure. A new cadre of politicians, not yet been compromised by corruption, is needed to control it.

5.3 Confusion

Politicians sometimes pursue bad policies simply because they are confused, in the sense of having a bad model of the economy or of the government. Confusion is fundamentally different from control and corruption, in the sense that the latter both serve politicians' self-interest whereas confusion often does not. Confused politicians maximize their welfare given their beliefs about the world, but end up worse off than they would have been if they used a more accurate, and publicly available, set of beliefs. Confusion thus refers to failure to use available knowledge.

The prevalence of confusion is not surprising, especially in transition economies. Economic models are quite difficult, and economists themselves often disagree on the right model of the economy. In fact, many distinguished Western economists have revealed the same confusion as some of the Russian politicians about transition. Moreover, many of the politicians in transition economies have developed their worldviews under communism. Like most other people, they have developed their models of the world based largely on their personal experiences, which in most cases did not include much exposure to markets. Even if these politicians were free thinkers under communism, they often have trouble understanding the market economy.

Confusion pervades economic policy making even in advanced market economies: witness President Reagan's expectation that tax cuts in the United States would increase revenue, or President Clinton's notion that government control of health care would make its provision more efficient. Nonetheless, several factors ameliorate the confusion of politicians in market economies. First, by definition, these politicians have personally observed market economies in action, and hence have formed their beliefs based on some observation of reality, in contrast to the politicians in postcommunist economies. Second, the marketplace of ideas is more open in market economies, and hence these politicians had more, though not necessarily enough, opportunities to disabuse themselves of their most egregious misconceptions. Of course, politicians in market as well as transition economies often make confused arguments because they lie to appeal to voters, even if they are not confused themselves. Still, as I show below, at least some of the confusions appear to be genuine.

Some of the examples from Russia are straightforward enough to require little comment. Gorbachev argued that the Communist Party—the essence of whose governance has been complete control over all aspects of life—would lead Russia toward some sort of a social market economy. He appeared to have little notion of the limits that market economies place on politicians, and of how fundamental these limits are for market economies to function. In privatization, many people in Russia have argued for turning firms into an equivalent of collective farms as a means of privatization, with worker control and no traded shares. The fact that such firms have failed in most countries because they could not make decisions, raise capital, or change management did not stop the argument. In the legal arena, Russia's Civil Code—written by the best legal minds of the communist era—holds shareholders in some cases liable for the debts of their companies. Despite explanations from French, German, Italian, and American experts that limited liability is essential for the ability of corporations to raise funds, the Russian lawyers refused to accept it, virtually destroying the hopes for foreign (or any other outside) investment in Russian firms. It is difficult to attribute this feature of the Civil Code to anything but confusion.

Last (but not least), Russia is not unique in the world in having suffered from the theory—advanced by the governor of its central bank among others—that inflation is a consequence of monopoly pricing and not money creation, and that regulation of monopolies and price controls can stop inflation even if money supply continues to expand. There are few theories in economics as well documented and widely professionally accepted as monetarism, particularly in the case of rapid inflation. Still, the alternative theory managed to get a lot of air. This and the previous arguments, of course, have been made by intelligent people, and many have led to disastrous economic policies.

There is another, much more subtle, class of ideas about transition economics that deal with the role of government in the transition. These ideas tend to be based on the economic model of a benevolent and effective government and to ignore the reality of actual governments in Russia and elsewhere. To illustrate this extremely common type of confusion about economic policy, I rely on an article by Yavlinsky and Braguinsky (1994). This article has three major benefits. First, the authors' vision of the proper nature of transition in Russia is very clearly described and so can be analyzed in some detail. Second, this article represents the case of a major Russian politician of reformist orientation clearly putting his views on paper, so that they can be discussed. Third, Mr. Yavlinsky is surely one of the most sophisticated and westernized politicians in Russia. He is both a leader of a reform faction, and a coauthor of the 500-day plan, a highly orthodox reform program proposed, but not accepted, in Russia in 1991.

One could argue that, as a politician, Mr. Yaviinsky might be misrepresenting his true beliefs to create a politically appealing platform. This is surely true. However, the fact that Mr. Yavlinsky took the trouble to publish his views in a professional journal likely to be read by at most a few dozen people suggests that he is not just campaigning. There are no political benefits to the publication of this article. It is much more likely that the article was published because Mr. Yavlinsky is anxious to convey to the academic world, and to record for posterity, his conception of economic transition.

The general theme of the Yavlinsky and Braguinsky article is to contrast two fundamentally different approaches to economic reform. The shock therapy approach they reject specifies that the transition to a market economy should be accomplished by freeing the activity of economic agents to the utmost possible degree and at the highest possible speed. Instead, Yavlinsky and Braguinsky (p. 111) advocate "an entirely new strategy of transition, one that would emphasize active government intervention in privatizing, developing national industry and providing financial backing for savings, investment and growth, which is the only way to ultimate financial stabilization." Indeed, the authors propose a transition strategy with extensive control of the economy. In the following

I describe their argument in some detail, both because of its intrinsic interest and because it reveals clearly how bad policies can come about.

Yavlinsky and Braguinsky (p. 93) begin with a perceptive, if not always accurate, analysis of the Russian transition, and in particular of the laissez-faire policies that were part of that transition. First, they criticize privatization on two grounds: the lack of a mechanism in the privatization program for replacing ineffective managers and the related slowness of post-privatization restructuring. Second, they claim that price liberalization in Russia was not complete and that therefore "policy design chosen in Russia in 1992 was a further increase in relative price distortions and conservation of an inefficient industrial structure" (p. 96). Third, they argue that stabilization policies have been ineffective because "it is impossible to attain macroeconomic stabilization prior to institutional, structural and other real adjustment." In particular, absent such adjustment, government subsidies to firms have to continue. Finally, they complain that free trade policies are deindustrializing Russia (pp. 102–103).

Although all these complaints have some plausibility, they are all basically false. Although privatization has not led to as fast a management turnover and restructuring as one would wish, the process of change has begun in hundreds of firms, and has surely been much faster than would have occurred under state ownership (see Boycko, Shleifer, and Vishny [1995] for an overview of the evidence). Although some price distortions in Russia remain, a significant rationalization of prices has actually followed price liberalization, with consumer prices actually clearing markets and energy prices reflecting more accurately its value in alternative uses. Far from increasing distortions, price liberalization has been the clear and unambiguous success of reforms. Nor is it accurate to argue that stabilization should come only after structural reforms. As Sachs (1995) shows, most reforming economies started with achieving macroeconomic stability, and implemented deeper reforms only after the government gained solvency and effectiveness. Finally, Russia and other transition economies desperately needed a rapid transformation of their productive activities from heavy manufacturing to consumer goods and services. To the extent that free trade accelerated this transformation, it surely helped Russia to move to markets faster.

But the inaccuracy of the Yavlinsky and Braguinsky criticisms is not really that important: it is common in Russia, as well as in politics more generally, to criticize what others have done regardless of merit. The real trouble comes from their alternative view of transition, "the policy-led transformation design." Here again they touch on several aspects of policy, each of which illuminates a widely shared confusion.

With respect to privatization, the authors argue that "the government should exercise its rights as the owner of state property for one last time, and it should satisfy that it is transferring property into the right hands" (p. 106). In particular, "establishing a system of specially designed long-term investment banks with technical and perhaps financial assistance from the West and especially Japan, would go a long way toward solving the problem" [of deciding what to do with firms]. In short, Yavlinsky and Braguinsky want the government to continue controlling firms, and to restructure them with the assistance of government-controlled investment banks. To be fair to the authors, this sentiment is not unique to them: it is shared by a variety of Western economists (see, for example, Mc-Kinnon, 1991; Tirole, 1991).

This strategy reveals a profound confusion about the effects of government control. As we argued earlier, politicians throughout the world have used their control over firms (either direct or through government banks) to keep defunct firms afloat, delay restructuring, maintain excessive employment, and otherwise promote politically undesirable inefficiencies. The idea of enhancing government control before privatization to promote restructuring simply flies in the face of all the evidence of the effects of such control. Moreover, the Yavlinsky and Braguinsky approach overlooks the basic fact that, by 1992, the government in Russia had lost much of its control over firms, which had reverted to their managers. The reason that the privatization program showed much accommodation of managers is precisely because they controlled firms already. In reality, the government in Russia owned very little, and to the extent that it tried to exercise its control, it was strictly detrimental to efficiency. Second, Yavlinsky and Braguinsky advocate a policy of government investment (p. 108). "Instead of just relying on market forces, the government should design a serious program of developing manufacturing industries on a new basis, and one of the priorities from the government side should be the basic infrastructure, roads, railways, communications facilities and housing." The issue of efficiency of government investment has been quite controversial even in some of the best-governed economies, such as those of East Asia (Young, 1995). In economies with weak and corrupt governments, such as Russia, investment projects inevitably support the least efficient industries, precisely the "prestige and military projects" that Yavlinsky and Braguinsky want to get away from. Even today, the government of Russia's effectively dead textile region (Ivanovo) is putting its last funds into building new textile factories, while the old ones are standing idle. The governor of Amur region (on the border with China in Southern Siberia, where hardly anyone lives) speaks of his plans to bring an automobile factory to the region. The history of the last 20 years of communism has revealed a great deal about the grotesque waste coming from investment projects pursued by the Soviet government.

On the question of monetary policy, Yavlinsky and Braguinsky are inconsistent. They first denounce premature macroeconomic stabilization, then suggest the urgent need for "a system of government and private long term investment banks" to make long term loans (to whom?). They also advocate "special savings deposits that are repaid in kind, for instance, in automobiles" (p. 110), a gimmick that they acknowledge has been already tried and failed. Finally, having aired these creative proposals for fighting inflation, they advocate the introduction of a new currency, which would be stable internationally and fully convertible, to be issued by "a specially created bank under the supervision of an international currency board." That is, in the end, Yavlinsky and Braguinsky want to turn to a hard core monetarist stabilization, whereby the government gives up control of its money supply. With respect to trade policy, they go back to the traditional "strategy of strengthening the competitiveness of national industry, including export and import subsidies where necessary" (p. 113). In practice, as world experience has shown, this means retention of the existing, grossly inefficient and uncompetitive industrial structure. Such policies have been discredited around the world, for solid empirical reasons.

Yavlinsky and Braguinsky conclude their paper with a memorable paragraph, worth quoting in full: "As we have shown time and again in this paper, in advising on Russian reforms, mistakes were made that even the most mainstream theorists could not have made if they had only cared to think. In the old days, engineers who constructed a railway bridge in Russia had to stand under it when the first train crossed. One should either stake one's life in this transformation or better do something else. Hence, in concluding this paper we risk going outside the usual academic style and ask all those advisers who care so little about the countries they try to help that they are unable even to theorize properly to stay at home" (p. 105). In other words, leave us to our own confusion.

The Yavlinsky and Braguinsky paper is depressing for a variety of reasons. It shows the extremely poor quality of understanding by even the best liberal Russian economists. Importantly, the errors that Yavlinsky and Braguinsky make have to do with failures to understand not basic economics but rather the nature of government in transition economies. The analysis raises serious questions about the likely quality of the Russian economic policy in the decades ahead. After all, Yavlinsky and Braguinsky are not far from the best policy analysts in Russia. Their paper shows how lucky Russia has been to have decent leadership in the first years of its transition.

Yet the real question, as always in Russia, is, What's to be done? How can the quality of economic thinking and policy making be improved? Part of the answer is surely the continuation of the attempts to persuade Russian policy makers about the wisdom of laissez-faire policies. Although they often have inaccurate models of the economy, many policy makers in transition economies are extremely intelligent. Some of them can be persuaded by logic and by references to the obvious successes of economic freedom in Western Europe, Latin America, and the Far East.

The trouble with persuasion is that its effects are fickle. Russian President Yeltsin shows considerable volatility in his beliefs. The results can be highly unfortunate. Even if a politician is permanently persuaded, in a democracy he can be easily replaced by another politician, with very different views and with an explicit agenda to change policies.

A bigger problem with the effectiveness of persuading politicians of the wisdom of laissez-faire policies is that such policies are broadly incompatible with their interest in control and corruption. Interventionist policies of the sort Yavlinsky and Braguinsky advocate typically go hand in hand with extraordinary discretionary power of the politicians, which gives them both the ability to generate political benefits through their control and access to bribes. One needs to go no further than to recall the emphasis on controlling trade and increasing government investment. To persuade a Russian politician of the wisdom of laissez-faire policies is to convince him to give up the benefits to which his predecessors have been accustomed since time immemorial.

All this suggests that persuasion is not enough. A much more fundamental set of changes is needed to reduce the level of confusion in public decision making. These changes are of two broad categories: democratization and the replacement of human capital. Neither will do enough on its own, but together, if they go far enough, they can spell a fundamental change in the quality of economic decision making—with respect to property rights as well as other issues—in both Russia and many other countries.

The principal benefit of democratization is that it shifts political power—and hence the attention of the politicians—from the established lobbies to new political groups and to voters. In particular, democratization usually reduces the benefits to politicians of allocating the society's wealth to the traditional political constituencies, such as defunct state firms and the military. Instead, politicians begin to pay more attention to voters (which is not always good, since it can lead to destructive populist policies—witness macroeconomic populism in Latin America or the growth of social spending in Eastern Europe) as well as to the new propertied classes, who often have a strong interest in macroeconomic stability and property rights reform. In addition, democratization is probably the single most effective strategy for combating corruption, since voters' anti-corruption sentiment is strong and fairly universal. Thus, although this is not always true, democratization generally makes laissez-faire economics a more likely outcome.

But democratization is probably not enough. Many traditional politicians are too closely tied to their traditional constituencies, as well as too deeply involved in corruption schemes to move to laissez-faire policies. This, combined with exceptionally poor training, makes it unlikely that they can be persuaded of the wisdom of markets. For economic policies in Russia to change, politicians need to change. In this respect, unfortunately, the prospects for Russia are considerably gloomier than they are for Eastern Europe, since Russia experienced much less turnover of its political elite when communism fell than did the East European countries. Even many of the so-called liberal economists and politicians in Russia are tied to the Gorbachev regime, which after all was only an enlightened communist regime. To make genuine progress with economic policy, Russia needs new and younger faces in its politics.

There is a striking parallel here between economic and political restructuring. A clear lesson of the Russian privatization is that new people, rather than new incentives for the old people, are responsible for enterprise restructuring. Firms that change are those run by new people (see Chapter 4). Casual evidence from industrial firms as well points in the same direction. New policies for the economy in this respect are similar to new policies for firms: they require new human capital, embedded in new people, to be successfully carried out.

But youth and novelty alone are not sufficient for enlightened views of the economy. Russia provides numerous examples of young politicians who begin with some interest in laissez-faire but then slide into policies more compatible with the existing political powers. Yavlinsky of course is one example, but there are even members of Yeltsin's initial reform team who turned to communist or pseudo-communist views. One of the most difficult problems is how to keep young, intelligent politicians from getting confused, or from switching their ideologies away from liberalism.

The only real answer is transfer of knowledge through education and training. Some education occurs by osmosis, as politicians and business people become exposed to more and more Western ideas. Other education, such as Ph.D.'s in economics or less time-consuming degrees, is obviously more expensive. Still, there are no real alternatives. The same approach in the long term is probably the best strategy for Eastern Europe and Russia as well. Unfortunately, this implies that, in the short run, these countries will be stuck with extraordinary policy volatility and with a great deal of confusion as to what the best strategies for transition really are. Unless these countries are lucky to get very good politicians from the start—as the Czech Republic was with Vaclav Klaus—their transition is going to be slow.

5.4 Conclusion

This chapter has described the three origins of bad economic policies: control, corruption, and confusion. It emphasized Russia, but with the hope that the reasoning elaborated here can be applied elsewhere as well. The fundamental conclusion of this chapter is that the battle against poor policies has to take place on all feasible fronts. The role of government in economic life has to be reduced; hence policies such as privatization are essential for reducing the damage from poor economic policies. Political institutions, and politicians themselves, need to be revamped and upgraded; hence the democratic process plays a crucial role in steadily removing bad politicians as well as improving the institutions. Finally, the knowledge and beliefs of the political elites need to be upgraded— hence the critical role of training and Western exposure more generally in the process of improving policy formation.

These are all slow, evolutionary steps. One could hope instead that the political process in Russia (and other countries) leads to the election of top leadership that really shakes up the political system; revamps institutions; brings new, more knowledgeable people into politics; and thus radically improves the quality of economic policy making. Although this can happen, it makes no sense to do nothing and just wait for the messiah. Given the enormously poor quality of economic policy making, the returns to even slow, evolutionary methods of improving policy formation can be very high. It is equally important to remember that the charismatic leaders who win on the platforms of radical political reform can change things radically for the worse, as well as for the better.

— 6 —

The Invisible Hand and the Grabbing Hand

In the 1990s, several East European economies went through radical liberalization. Among them, Russia and Poland adopted similar packages of reforms, including almost complete price and trade liberalization, macroeconomic stabilization (which Poland accomplished five years before Russia), large-scale privatization (which Russia did four years before Poland), and small-scale privatization. Although Poland started two years earlier, both reform packages were radical.

Despite the similarity of reform packages, the Polish economy responded much better to the treatment. By the mid-1990s, it was growing rapidly, while the Russian economy at best stopped shrinking. The formation and growth of small businesses was also more dramatic in Poland. According to the European Bank for Reconstruction and Development (EBRD, 1996), in 1995 Poland had about 2 million small private businesses, whereas Russia had only 1 million with a population almost four times larger. Even if we allow, as the EBRD does, that Russia had another 2 million unregistered private businesses, small-business formation is still more lethargic in Russia.

Why, despite similar reform packages, has the Russian entrepreneurial response been weaker? Using a pilot survey of shop managers conducted in Moscow and in Warsaw in the spring of 1996, we argue that a key reason for this outcome is there are very different relationships between government and business in the two countries. In the survey, we ask questions about the legal and regulatory environment in both cities. We

By Timothy Frye and Andrei Shliefer; originally published in *American Economic Review: Papers and Proceedings*, 87 (1997): 354–358. © 1997.

find that the regulatory, and to some extent the legal, environment is a good deal friendlier to business in Warsaw than in Moscow.

6.1 Government in Transition

There are three basic views of how bureaucrats and entrepreneurs interact during transition, as well as more generally. Under the invisible-hand model, the government is well organized, generally uncorrupt, and relatively benevolent. It restricts itself to providing basic public goods, such as contract enforcement, law and order, and some regulations, and it leaves most allocative decisions to the private sector. Many countries in Eastern Europe, particularly those hoping to join the European Community, have looked to this model in their reforms.

In the two alternative models, government plays a larger role. Under the helping-hand model, commonly invoked in discussions of China (Walder, 1995), bureaucrats are intimately involved in promoting private economic activity: they support some firms and kill off others, pursue industrial policy, and often have close economic and family ties to entrepreneurs. The legal framework plays a limited role in this model, because bureaucrats adjudicate most disputes. Bureaucrats are corrupt, but corruption is relatively limited and organized. An extreme version of this model, the iron-hand model, is found in Southeast Asian countries such as Korea and Singapore. In transition economies, however, the helping-hand model has been less prevalent.

In the final, grabbing-hand, model, government is just as interventionist, but much less organized, than in the helping-hand model. The government consists of a large number of substantially independent bureaucrats pursuing their own agendas, including taking bribes. While these bureaucrats adopt the helping-hand rhetoric, in reality they are scarcely guided by a unified public-policy stance, and they remain largely independent of courts, capable of imposing their will in commercial disputes, and empowered to impose on business a variety of predatory regulations. In the extreme cases, the government becomes sufficiently disorganized that it loses its ability to ensure law and order and to provide basic legal protections. As a consequence, contracts become privately enforced.

These three models of government are "ideal types," and all real governments are mixtures of the three. Our questions try to assess how close local governments in Moscow and Warsaw are to these "ideal types" by focusing on the legal and regulatory environment. Table 6.1 summarizes the predictions of the three models of government that we examine.

6.2 The Survey

In March and April 1996, we surveyed 105 small shops: 55 in Moscow and 50 in Warsaw. We chose Moscow and Warsaw for two reasons. First, both Poland and Russia pursued radical economic reforms. Second, private business in both countries is growing especially fast in the capitals, which also makes the comparison appropriate.

The shops were selected randomly from small-business directories (Business Karta Moskvi and Panorama Firmi) that include several thousand entries. The survey includes a mix of private and privatized retail shops, each with a staff of 5–50 employees. Most (62 percent) are food shops, but we also include barber shops, book stores, dry-cleaning establishments, and small department stores. On average, Moscow shops employ more workers than Warsaw shops (23.4 vs. 14.8, $t = 3.33$), which may be due to policies promoting very small businesses pursued by the Polish government. On average, Warsaw shops have been in operation for almost 4.5 years, and Moscow shops for 3.3 years ($t = -4.25$). This is consistent with Poland starting its transition almost two years before

Table 6.1 Economic role of the state during transition

Model	Legal environment	Regulatory environment
Invisible hand	Government is not above law and uses power to supply minimal public goods. Courts enforce contracts.	Government follows the rules. Regulation is minimal. Little corruption.
Helping hand	Government is above the law but uses power to help business. State officials enforce contracts.	Government aggressively regulates to promote some businesses. Organized corruption.
Grabbing hand	Government is above the law and uses power to extract rents. The legal system does not work. Mafia replaces state as enforcer.	Predatory regulations. Disorganized corruption.

Russia. On average, Moscow shop managers are slightly older (44 vs. 42 years old, $t = 1.18$) and have slightly more experience working in retail (16 vs. 14 years, $t = 0.98$), but slightly less experience as managers (8.7 vs. 10.5 years, $t = -1.02$), than their counterparts in Warsaw. Overall, we have broadly similar samples of shops in the two cities.

6.3 Results

Our questions on the legal environment address two issues: the effectiveness of court systems in dispute resolution and the role of protection rackets. Under the invisible-hand model, courts are effective in resolving disputes between private parties as well as between them and the government, and there is no room for protection rackets. Under the helping-hand model, courts play a smaller role, especially in disputes with the government, but the government is powerful enough to displace the rackets. Under the grabbing-hand model, government is ineffective in providing basic services, courts are ineffective in resolving disputes, and in the extreme, agreements are enforced privately. The questions in Table 6.2 look at these alternative predictions.

In both countries, courts are rarely used. Only 19 percent of shop managers in Moscow and 14 percent in Warsaw reported using them in the previous two years ($t = 0.66$). This may simply reflect the high costs of using courts in both countries. However, when asked whether they

Table 6.2 Legal environment

Question	Warsaw (N)	Moscow (N)	t
Used courts in the last 2 years?	0.14 (50)	0.19 (53)	0.66
Needed to use courts, but did not?	0.10 (50)	0.45 (53)	4.32
Can use courts against government?	0.41 (46)	0.50 (52)	0.86
Can use courts against business partner?	0.45 (38)	0.65 (52)	1.97
Contacted by racket in the last six months?	0.08 (50)	0.39 (54)	3.91
Does one need a roof/umbrella to operate?	0.06 (50)	0.76 (54)	10.10

Notes: The table presents the fraction of affirmative responses to questions in Moscow and Warsaw and the *t*-tests of differences in responses.

needed to use the courts but did not, 45 percent of Moscow managers answered yes, whereas in Warsaw, only 10 percent did ($t = 4.32$). Either Moscow shop managers have less faith in their courts, or they face more disputes that potentially require court intervention than do their counterparts in Warsaw.

When asked whether they "could use courts to defend their rights if the government grossly violated their property rights," 50 percent of Moscow respondents, and 41 percent of Warsaw respondents, answered yes ($t = 0.86$). Evidently, business people in both countries have significant skepticism about the independence and effectiveness of courts in disputes with the government. On the other hand, when "the government" is replaced with "a business partner" in this question, 65 percent of the Moscow respondents, and only 38 percent of the Warsaw respondents, answer yes ($t = 1.97$). One interpretation of this finding is not the greater credibility of the Russian courts, but the greater availability of alternative means of dispute resolution in Warsaw. Finally, we find that 57 percent of the Moscow shops have hired legal counsel, compared to only 36 percent of Warsaw shops ($t = 2.2$). This may reflect greater interest in litigation, but more likely, lawyers are needed in Russia to deal with bureaucrats. Overall, we find a good deal of skepticism about the legal system in both countries.

We also ask about private rather than public protection. In Russia, shop owners often pay private security agencies to protect them from crime and to help resolve disputes. This institution is known as "a roof" in Russia and "an umbrella" in Poland. We asked the respondents whether it is true that one cannot operate a store in their city without a roof (an umbrella). In Moscow, 76 percent answered yes, whereas in Poland only 6 percent did ($t = 10.10$). A related question is whether a shop manager has been contacted by the racket in the last six months. In Moscow, 39 percent of the respondents answered yes, whereas in Warsaw only 8 percent did. These data make clear that private enforcement of law and order plays a greater role in Russia than in Poland. Since the respondents in both cities are equally skeptical about courts, the likely reason for the higher incidence of protection rackets in Russia is the greater failure of simple police protection (order as opposed to law) in Russia.

The next set of questions deals with the regulatory environment and the closely related problem of corruption (Table 6.3). We begin with a naive question about the helping-hand model. We ask, "Does the local

Table 6.3 Regulatory environment

Question	Warsaw (N)	Moscow (N)	t
Local government helps small business?	Hinders: 5 No influence: 41 Helps: 4 (50)	Hinders: 8 No influence: 39 Helps: 6 (53)	−0.19
Time to register business (months)?	0.72 (47)	2.71 (51)	5.02
Inspections last year?	9.0 (49)	18.56 (55)	3.46
Percentage of shops fined by inspectors last year?	46 (49)	83 (52)	2.72
Number of different agencies conducting inspections?	2.65 (49)	3.58 (55)	1.84
How legally vulnerable do you feel on a scale 1 to 10?	3.6 (50)	5.1 (55)	3.91
How often does one need to bribe officials on a scale of 1 to 5?	2.21 (47)	2.9 (53)	2.52

Notes: The table presents responses about government regulation and corruption and results of *t*-tests of the difference between Warsaw and Moscow.

government hinder, have no influence on, or help small business?" The answer is basically the same in the two cities: it has no influence. At least in their stance toward small business, both countries are very different from the East Asian model.

We then ask several regulatory questions. When asked how long it took to register their businesses, Moscow respondents reported an average of 2.7 months, compared to 0.7 months in Warsaw ($t = 5.02$). When asked how many inspections they had last year, Moscow managers reported an average of 18.56, and Warsaw managers 8.99 ($t = 3.46$). Moscow shop managers are also more likely to be fined by inspectors than their counterparts in Warsaw: 83 percent reported having paid fines compared to 46 percent in Warsaw ($t = 2.72$). Fines are likely to be a good measure of regulatory burden, as well as a proxy for corruption.

One measure of the severity of the regulatory burden is how concerned the shop managers are about being in violation of some regulations. To get at this issue, we ask shop managers how "legally vulnerable" they feel, on a scale from 1 to 10. The mean answer in Warsaw was 3.6, compared to 5.1 in Moscow ($t = 3.9$), consistent with the greater regulatory burden in Russia. Another measure of regulatory burden is corruption, since a standard way to get around the difficult regulations, requirements, delays, and fines is to pay a bribe. We ask our respondents somewhat discreetly: How often does one need to bribe officials to do business in your city, on a scale from 1 to 5 (1, almost never; 2, rarely; 3, sometimes; 4, often; 5, almost always)? The mean response in Warsaw was 2.2, compared to 2.9 in Moscow ($t = 2.52$). We also explore the structure of corruption by asking how many different kinds of inspectors visited the shop. On average, 3.58 different agencies conducted inspections of Moscow shops, compared to 2.65 in Warsaw ($t = 1.84$). If we accept the Shleifer and Vishny (1993) view that the amount of bribes increases with the number of independent bribe-takers, this evidence points further to the greater burden of corruption and regulation in Moscow than in Warsaw.

In sum, our evidence indicates that shop owners in neither country are particularly keen on using courts, though the Russian respondents have a greater need for them. On the other hand, private protection is used much more extensively in Russia than in Poland. Regulations in Russia appear to be a good deal more oppressive to business than they are in Poland. This is reflected in some measures of regulation, in the greater legal vulnerability that Russian respondents feel, and in the greater burden of corruption in Moscow.

The more predatory stance of Moscow's government toward business is consistent with the greater dynamism of such business in Warsaw. One further finding corroborates this view. When asked to rate the problem of product market competition on a scale from 1 to 10, Moscow shop managers' average answer was 4.8, compared to 6.2 in Warsaw ($t = 2.3$). Evidently, the Polish shopkeepers have their rents extracted by competitors, while the Russians have rents extracted by bureaucrats.

6.4 Conclusion

We have presented some evidence from Moscow and Warsaw shops on their dealings with legal and regulatory institutions. Although neither government is an "ideal type," the evidence points to the relatively greater relevance of the invisible-hand model to describe Poland, and of the grabbing-hand model to describe Russia. The law enforcement and regulatory evidence in particular shows that Polish local governments are more supportive of business. This evidence is consistent with the greater energy shown by small business in Poland than in Russia despite similar economic reforms.

This conclusion suggests that, to understand transition experiences, it is not enough to know how much of a standard menu of radical reforms a country adopts. The regulatory stance that national and local governments take toward business can perhaps explain as much as the package of reforms. This conclusion also raises a broader question: Why do different governments follow such different models? We defer a discussion of this question to future work.

— 7 —

The Unofficial Economy in Transition

The economies of Eastern Europe and the former Soviet Union (FSU) escaped communism with a heavy burden. When central planning collapsed, they continued to suffer from widespread political control of economic activity. Such politicization had to be reduced significantly for small business formation and growth to begin. In recent years, some of these countries have succeeded much more than others in replacing political control with functioning market institutions. As this chapter shows, they are also the countries that have had the healthiest public finances and the smallest unofficial economies.

The politicization of economic life can usefully be thought of as the exercise by politicians of control rights over business. Such rights may include regulatory powers over privatized and private firms, the ability to regulate and restrict entry, control over the use of land and real estate that private businesses occupy, the determination and collection of taxes on businesses, the right to inspect firms and close them if regulations are violated, control over international trade and foreign exchange transactions, and in some cases, even the power to set prices. Typically, politicians use these rights to pursue their own interests, such as maintaining employment in certain firms, supporting politically friendly and punishing politically unfriendly entrepreneurs, and subsidizing their allies. Politicians also use these rights to enrich themselves by offering firms relief from regulation in exchange for bribes. Political control generally reduces the profitability of doing business, and

By Simon Johnson, Daniel Kaufmann, and Andrei Shleifer; originally published in *Brookings Papers on Economic Activity*, 2 (1997): 159–220. © 1997.

therefore adversely influences entrepreneurial activity and economic growth (De Soto, 1989).

During the transition from communism to capitalism, the adverse effects of political control on growth are manifested in a number of ways. Most directly, when profits or potential profits are taken away from firms through regulation, taxation, or corruption, entrepreneurs choose not to start firms or expand less rapidly than they might otherwise. But entrepreneurs have another option, namely, to operate unofficially. In many transition economies, a consequence of politicization has been the growth of the unofficial economy, in which firms can avoid taxes and regulations, though probably not bribes. Firms that operate unofficially use protection and other "public" services supplied by private—including criminal—organizations. In this chapter, we show that the politicization of economic life and the resulting reallocation of resources to the unofficial sector have profound effects on the structure of a transition economy.

Specifically, we show that the movement of production into the unofficial economy has significant consequences for public finance. Since firms in the unofficial sector largely escape taxation, the reallocation of resources into that sector undermines tax collections, and consequently the ability of the government to provide public goods to the official sector. Such public goods include law and order, effective tax and regulatory institutions, and relatively uncorrupt public administration. The lack of provision of such market-supporting public goods makes operating in the official sector even less attractive to firms, and can set off the collapse of public finances as more and more firms escape into the unofficial economy.

Economies find themselves in either of two very different equilibria. In the first, tax distortions and regulations are low, government revenues are high, the provision of public goods in the official sector is sufficient, and therefore the unofficial sector is small. In the second equilibrium, in the official sector taxes and regulations are prohibitive, public finances are precarious, public goods provision is inadequate, and as a consequence, much of the economic activity is concentrated in the unofficial sector.

Our work can be thought of as complementing Olivier Blanchard's (1997) analysis of transition economies, which highlights the creation of new private firms by entrepreneurs as the engine of growth. We focus on the political and institutional determinants of the entrepreneurial response, and in particular, on the allocation of resources between the official and the unofficial sectors. We are not the first to stress the role of depoliticization in transition or the importance of building market-supporting rather than market-distorting institutions.[1] In this tradition, our chapter focuses on the implications of excessive regulation and taxation for the government's budget and for the provision of public goods required by a market economy. We elaborate on the existing literature in two distinct ways.

First, we describe the role of the unofficial economy in transition and measure its size. The unofficial economy does not receive enough attention in recent studies of reform. Neither the World Bank, nor the European Bank for Reconstruction and Development (EBRD), nor the International Monetary Fund (IMF) offers systematic estimates of the unofficial economy.[2] Norman Loayza (1996) presents an early theoretical analysis of the unofficial economy and applies it to the Latin American experience, but does not measure the unofficial economy.

Second, we emphasize the public finance aspects of transition by focusing our empirical analysis on the consequences for the government's budget of the escape of new firms from the official economy, and on the provision of potentially beneficial public goods. Law and order is one key public good that can be measured empirically in transition economies, but we are more broadly interested in the financing of a range of market-supporting institutions, including regulatory agencies, a reasonably honest public administration, and so forth. We look at the relationship between taxes and regulations, government budgets, and the provision of public goods, and examine the consequences of the condition of public finances for the unofficial economy.

In the next three sections of this chapter we present a simple model, describe our data, and present the evidence on the effects of political control on the unofficial economy. The chapter concludes with a discussion of the reform agenda of countries in the former Soviet Union, as suggested by our empirical findings.

7.1 A Simple Model

Our model captures, in the starkest way, some of the ideas described above. We consider the allocation of labor between the official and the unofficial sectors of the economy. The government imposes taxes on the official sector and provides public goods from the tax revenues. These public goods, such as law and order, increase the productivity of firms in the official sector. The unofficial sector does not pay official taxes, but neither does it have access to the public goods provided by the government. Instead, it pays fees to private protection agencies to provide some public goods, such as protection from thieves and contract enforcement. The quality of that protection depends on the revenues raised by the private agencies. We examine the allocation of labor between the two sectors and its implications for tax revenues, law and order, and the efficiency of the economy.

Denote by t the generalized tax rate on output in the official sector. The generalized tax rate includes taxation, regulation, and corruption (that is, bribes). Taxes raise revenue for the government, but some of the generalized taxes, such as regulation and bribes, do not. For now, let t be the share of output that the government in various ways removes from each firm in the official sector and obtains for its budget. Let s denote the corresponding generalized tax rate in the unofficial sector, charged by the private enforcers of law and order, to whom we loosely refer as the mafia. Analogous to the official sector, collections from s enter the mafia's budget.

Let T be the tax revenue in the official sector, and S the tax revenue in the unofficial sector. Let Q be the quantity of the public good, such as law and order, in the official sector, and R the corresponding quantity in the unofficial sector. Here Q captures the public goods from which firms operating unofficially can be excluded. For instance, firms in the unofficial sector do not have access to police, courts, or administrative assistance from the government. In contrast, public services such as roads, health care, and education are accessible to all firms, even those in the unofficial sector, and hence Q does not properly capture these goods.

Let L be the aggregate labor force, and let the wage rate be normalized to 1. Finally, let F and I be the subscripts denoting the official and the unofficial sectors, respectively; so that L_F and L_I denote the labor employed, Π_F and Π_I the after-tax profits, and Y_F and Y_I the output in each sector.

Consider the official sector first. The production function is assumed to be given by

(7.1)
$$Y_F = QL_F$$

so that the quantity of the public good directly enhances the productivity of the official sector. As a consequence, after-tax profits are given by

(7.2)
$$\Pi_F = (1 - t)QL_F - L_F.$$

The tax revenue, T, is given by $T = tQL_F$. We assume that the supply of public goods is increasing and concave in tax revenue; that is, $Q = Q(T)$, with $Q' > 0$ and $Q'' < 0$. This does not mean that government resources are spent entirely on the provision of public goods; indeed, a large portion might be stolen or wasted. We only assume that at least some share of the marginal dollar is spent on public goods.

This assumption raises an important substantive point, namely, that the cost of providing market-supporting public institutions may be so low that even a nearly bankrupt government could afford an adequate level of provision. Our assumption that a decline in government revenue leads to a deterioration in the supply of public goods may, therefore, miss the mark. Indeed, in the Russian federal budget for 1995, only about 10 percent of the expenditure was, by its own definition, dedicated to "law and order." Nevertheless, we believe that our assumption is appropriate because, despite their enormous benefits, market-supporting public goods are often among the first to be cut in a transition economy when the budget deteriorates. In such a situation, the government is typically weak, disorganized, and torn in a variety of directions by powerful lobbies who apply pressure to maintain the level of much less socially useful expenditures, such as agricultural and industrial subsidies and defense spending. In contrast, expenditures on the essential and more purely public goods, such as law and order, science, health care, and education, suffer.

Importantly, we also assume that the government does not spend any of its tax revenue to fight the mafia or to restrict the movement of firms into the unofficial sector. The government and the mafia compete for business—and therefore for the revenue base—through the combinations of tax rates and public goods that they offer in their respective sectors.

From the government's budget constraint, one obtains $Q = Q(tQL_F)$. Eliminating Q from the right-hand side, we write $Q = q(tL_F)$. For q expressed only as a function of tL_F, it is easy to verify that $q' > 0$ and, in some cases, $q'' > 0$. This is the first possible increasing return in our model: as public good provision increases, so does the productivity of the private sector and the tax revenues that it furnishes, which finances a further increase in public good provision. The q function exhibits increasing returns if the government is sufficiently productive at converting revenues into public goods. For example, if $Q(T) = T\alpha$ and $\alpha > \frac{1}{2}$, then $q'' > 0$.

One can repeat the above line of reasoning for the mafia, which collects taxes from firms in the unofficial sector and produces public goods for the firms it protects. For the unofficial sector, $R = r(sL_I)$, where $r' > 0$ and, under some conditions, $r'' > 0$. We do not, however, focus on these particular increasing returns in either the official or the unofficial sector because it seems implausible that the marginal expenditure from the budget on market-supporting public institutions is so high.

Figure 7.1 presents the equilibria in the model. In equilibrium, the labor market clears, so that $L_I + L_F = L$. The figure graphs the tax revenue and quality of public goods against the share of the unofficial economy. The solid line shows that the higher is the share of the unofficial economy, the lower are the official tax collections, and hence the supply of public goods to the official sector. The dotted line—the firm mobility function—shows that the higher is the supply of public goods in the official economy, the fewer firms choose to operate unofficially. The dotted line generally cuts the solid line from below.

Tax revenue and public goods (T and Q)

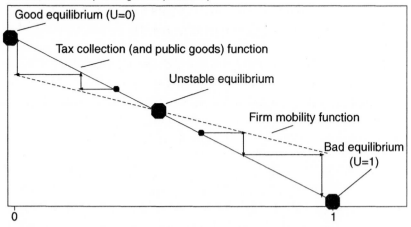

Figure 7.1 The unofficial economy and the collapse of public finances

In general, there are three equilibria in this model: one in which all resources are concentrated in the official sector, one in which all resources are in the unofficial sector, and a knife-edge equilibrium in which the two sectors coexist. The existence of the extreme equilibria is independent of the possible convexity of the q and r functions; that is, there is a second, and totally separate, source of increasing returns to sector size.

When all resources are concentrated in the unofficial sector, government tax collections in the official sector are zero, hence so is the amount of the public good supplied in that sector, as well as its productivity. As a consequence, all firms choose to stay in the unofficial sector. This equilibrium is stable. When nearly all firms are in the unofficial sector, government revenues do not suffice to provide the level of public goods needed to draw firms back into the official sector; in fact, more resources move to the unofficial sector. In Figure 7.1, this equilibrium is stable because the dotted line is above the solid line when all, or nearly all, of the resources are in the unofficial sector.

Similarly, if all resources are concentrated in the official sector, the tax revenues and public good provision in that sector are high enough that all firms choose to stay there. The equilibrium is stable because when only a few firms are operating unofficially, it is to the advantage of these firms to switch back and receive the public goods of the official sector. In Figure 7.1, the dotted line is below the solid line when the size of the unofficial sector is near zero. The forces causing the multiplicity of equilibria in this model are general, and are closely related to the idea of fiscal increasing returns of Blanchard and Lawrence Summers (1987), even though more realistic specifications would generate less extreme outcomes.

To examine the intermediate equilibrium, we compute the profits of the marginal firm, which is indifferent to being in the official or the unofficial sector. This firm takes aggregate employment in the two sectors, L_F and L_I, as given. Its marginal profit in the official sector is given by $(1 - t)q(tL_F) - 1$, and its marginal profit in the unofficial sector is $(1 - s)r(sL_I) - 1$. In equilibrium, it must be that

(7.3) $$(1 - t)q(tL_F) = (1 - s)r(sL_I).$$

For a given set of tax rates t and s, there generally exist L_F and L_I adding up to L that solve equation (7.3). However, this equilibrium is unstable. If, starting from this equilibrium, a firm tips over from the unofficial to the official sector, the resources of the official sector rise, hence so do tax collections and the quantity of public goods supplied and, finally, the productivity in that sector. More firms then switch into the official sector, and the intermediate equilibrium breaks down.

Although we have presented a static model, it can be given the "cobweb" dynamic interpretation suggested by the arrows in Figure 7.1. Suppose that an economy—perhaps for historical reasons or because of a good budget shock—ends up on the good side of the intermediate equilibrium, that is, at a point where the unofficial economy is relatively small and tax revenues are relatively large. Firms that are operating unofficially then recognize that the combination of taxes and public goods in the official sector is attractive enough for them to switch. As they move, tax revenues in the official sector rise, and hence so does the provision of public goods in that sector. As this happens, more firms operating unofficially switch, and so on, until this virtuous cycle leads to a fully official economy. Conversely, suppose that an economy ends up on the bad side of the intermediate equilibrium, with a relatively large unofficial economy and low tax revenues. Firms operating officially then recognize that they are better off in the unofficial sector and move. Their move has a deleterious effect on the budget and the provision of public goods in the official sector, which causes more firms to switch to the unofficial economy. This vicious cycle ends up at the extreme equilibrium where the whole economy is unofficial.

To interpret this model and its predictions, it is useful to think of an augmented framework in which, for reasons outside the model, some firms choose to operate in the official sector (for example, state firms or firms dealing extensively with the state) and others choose to operate in the unofficial sector (for example, firms that infringe on patents). In this case, the forces that we describe still operate, but both sectors coexist in equilibrium. What does the analysis say about such situations?

The key prediction of the model is the potential separation of economies into two distinct groups. In one, the government offers a sufficiently attractive combination of tax rates, regulations, and public goods that most firms choose to stay in the official sector. In this group, government revenues suffice to provide the public goods, and the unofficial sector is small because the government outcompetes it. In the other group, the government does not offer firms a sufficiently attractive combination of tax rates, regulations, and public goods to keep them operating officially, and hence many of them end up in the large unofficial sector, which offers a more attractive combination. The government budget in these countries does not suffice to offer more public goods, and hence the unofficial sector wins the competition for firms.

Our model does not make any immediate predictions as to which equilibrium is associated with higher output. However, if one makes the auxiliary but plausible assumption that the official sector is more productive at generating public goods, then the overall performance of economies with a small unofficial sector is superior. There are several reasons why the government may be more efficient at converting revenue into public goods: there are increasing returns to the production of some goods, such as defense and laws; the government already has some expertise at producing some of these goods; and private providers might not be able to commit credibly to long-term delivery of some services.

These are the very stylized predictions of a very stylized model. We evaluate these predictions empirically in the following sections. But first we revisit some of the key assumptions responsible for these results, in order to shed light on the theoretical generality of the conclusions.

7.1.1 Taxation, Regulation, and Corruption

The results are driven by the assumption that excessive taxes force firms out of the official sector. Taxation itself, however, has an offsetting benefit. At least on the increasing part of the Laffer curve, higher taxes raise more money for the government, some of which is spent on public goods. This is not the case with generalized "regulatory" taxes.

These are more detrimental to the official sector than high taxes proper, since they bring all the distortionary effects but no government revenue. If we included regulation in the model, the tendency toward bifurcation would be even stronger than it is now. In the empirical work, we consider both taxation and regulation.

The effects of corruption are somewhat different from those of taxation and regulation. Entrepreneurs generally pay bribes precisely to avoid paying taxes or following regulations, and therefore corruption reflects payments to evade government control. In general, the higher the level of taxation and regulation (t), the greater are the bribes that politicians can extract from entrepreneurs in return for excusing them from paying taxes or following regulations. Tax and regulatory burdens are therefore highly correlated with the level of corruption, which, in turn, can serve as a proxy for t. Similar to regulation, however, corruption does not raise any revenues for the government.

7.1.2 Who Sets Tax Rates?

In the model, we do not set up decision problems for the government and the mafia, and we treat the tax rates t and s as parameters. The choice of these parameters depends on the nature of competition between the government and the mafia, as well as the nature of competition inside the government (for example, between different levels) and inside the mafia (for example, between competing groups). If the government has access to a superior technology for producing public goods, it can always outcompete the mafia by setting t equal to s. The mafia may be at a further disadvantage if competing private gangs independently attempt to impose taxes on the same businesses, if the mafia cannot commit to not expropriating capital ex post, or if it cannot establish a reputation for the consistent provision of public goods such as contract enforcement. The government can also destroy the mafia, a point to which we return later. In short, the government has many advantages, which lead to its victory in most well-functioning economies.

In transition economies, it is less obvious that the government can always offer a better deal. First, the government often spends a lot of its revenues on activities other than the provision of public goods, such as subsidies to various unproductive activities or transfer payments. As a result, it might have a bigger leakage than the mafia. Second, the government might, for socially efficient reasons, choose to regulate more than the mafia does—for example, in regard to nuclear safety, pollution, or other externalities. Third, and perhaps most important, governments in some transition economies are disorganized and not in control of themselves. Consequently, t is not set by one unified government, but by a collection of agencies and levels of government that impose taxes, bribes, and regulations largely independently of each other. In this way, tax distortion in transition economies can be much higher than is optimal, which significantly undermines the government's tax revenues, and hence its ability to supply public goods. Moreover, to the extent that the mafia sets s in response to an excessive level of t, the mafia can adjust to out-competes the government, for example, by setting s much lower than t. The bad equilibrium, then, is a real possibility.

7.1.3 Government Does Not Restrict the Movement of Firms

A key assumption in our model is that entrepreneurs are free to switch resources from the official to the unofficial sector in seeking a better mix of taxes and public goods. But the government may be able to use political repression to punish anyone who leaves the official sector. It could use tax revenue to fight the mafia or, through raids and expropriation, it could directly penalize firms that are operating unofficially. Similarly, if the government is itself indistinguishable from the mafia, it may be able to impose high marginal taxes on both official and unofficial activities. A government that established itself as a successful repressive monopolist would charge high taxes, collect substantial revenues, and yet provide few public goods, instead using the revenues to line its own pockets and to fuel the machinery of repression. Although we do not model these pos-sibilities explicitly, Belarus and Uzbekistan, both highly repressive states, appear to be outliers in the data. The evidence on Belarus and Uzbekistan is consistent with the model of a repressive monopoly government that collects a lot of taxes but produces few public goods.

7.1.4 Labor Supply

One final assumption that warrants comment is that of fixed labor supply. In our model, entrepreneurs move between sectors in search of the best combination of taxes and public goods. Another response to poor gov-ernment performance is not to produce at all, or to produce in the house-hold sector, which uses no public goods and pays no taxes to either the government or the mafia. The introduction of elastic labor supply would strengthen our conclusion about the bifurcation of economies, because a government offering an unattractive combination of taxes and public goods would see its tax base further eroded by the withdrawal of labor supply. The introduction of elastic labor supply would also substantially strengthen our predictions concerning growth, since bad combinations of taxes and public goods would now lead not only to the reallocation of labor between the official and unofficial economy but also to a first-order reduction in output, as labor supply is reduced.

7.1.5 Summary

Broadly interpreted, our model has a number of empirical predictions. It suggests that in economies in which firms are free to move between the official and unofficial sectors, transition is likely to follow one of two paths. Some countries would be characterized by low burdens from taxes, regulation, and corruption; relatively high tax revenues; large quantities of public goods provided by the government; and small unofficial sectors. Other countries would be characterized by high burdens from taxes, regulation, and corruption; low tax collections; small quantities of public goods provided by the government; and large unofficial sectors. In our empirical work, we try to obtain some estimates of t and Q, as well as of the size of the official and unofficial sectors. Next, we examine the relationship between t and Q, on the one hand, and the size of the unofficial sector, on the other. We also examine the validity of the public finance mechanisms operating in our model; that is, the relationship between the tax and regulatory burden (t), the budget (T), and the supply of public goods (Q).

7.2 Data

In this section we discuss our data sources and explain how we use the available information to develop the measures of the unofficial economy and the indicators of reforms.

7.2.1 The Unofficial Economy

As used here, the "unofficial economy" constitutes activity that is not reported to the state statistical office. For obvious reasons, it is almost never reported to the tax authorities. Although our model refers to firms moving between the official and the unofficial sectors, in reality many firms operate in both sectors. An officially registered enterprise might produce and sell some of its output unofficially. It would thus avoid paying taxes and escape regulations related to the production of this output, but at the same time would not be able to rely on the government to enforce related contracts. Indeed, with respect to this unofficial output, the enterprise might pay bribes rather than taxes and hire private protection agencies to help with the contracts. In this way, the official and unofficial sectors are represented within a single firm, and not just across firms.

In the formerly communist countries, published GDP figures rarely capture any of this unofficial activity. We use data on total electricity consumption to compare unofficial activity across countries.[3] Electricity consumption offers a rough measure of overall economic activity; around the world, the short-run electricity-to-GDP elasticity is usually close to 1. Measured GDP, by definition, captures only the official part of the economy, so the difference between overall and measured GDP gives an estimate of the size of the unofficial economy.

Assuming a unit output elasticity may underestimate overall GDP and the size of the unofficial economy. First, there is some improvement in the efficiency of electricity use over time, particularly given the very low initial efficiency. Second, higher electricity prices reduce consumption per unit of output. Third, there may be a shift of the output mix away from electricity-intensive industries, both within existing enterprises and in the creation of new businesses, especially in services. Fourth, the underreporting of electricity consumption may increase, although the amount of electricity stolen is small and probably does not vary over time. However, a unit elasticity assumption would overestimate the overall size of a declining economy if electricity is used primarily for "overhead" activities, such as lighting buildings. Energy efficiency may also worsen owing to neglect of essential maintenance and some substitution of electricity for other energy sources (for example, switching from gas to electric heating). On balance, the unit elasticity assumption probably leads to only a small underestimate of total economic activity, particularly where there has been a significant adjustment in the relative price of electricity.[4]

Drawing on the work of Dale Gray (1995) and of Caroline Freund and Christine Wallich (1997), Daniel Kaufmann and Alexander Kaliberda (1996) develop a simple tiered classification of ex post output elasticity for electricity consumption. The "energy efficient" economies—the central and Eastern European countries, where energy price adjustments started earlier and have been more significant—are assumed to have an output elasticity of electricity consumption of 0.9 when their economies begin to grow again. The "energy neutral" economies—the Baltic countries, where price adjustment has taken place but started later—are assumed to have a unitary elasticity of electricity consumption. The "energy inefficient" economies—the rest of the FSU, where price adjustments started relatively late and have been much smaller-are assumed to have an output elasticity of electricity consumption of 1.15.[5] Relative to the unit elasticity assumption, these assumptions tend to reduce our estimate of the unofficial economy for the FSU and to raise it for Eastern Europe. In particular, they address the concern that because Eastern Europe has experienced much more rapid growth in services than the FSU, and services are not as electricity intensive as manufacturing, the estimates of the unofficial economy under the unit elasticity assumption would be biased upward for the FSU and downward for Eastern Europe. We have rerun our regressions using the unit elasticity assumption but have not found any notable differences. The regressions and figures presented in the following use electricity consumption data for 1995. We have also confirmed our results using 1994 data.

The difference between the change in electricity consumption and that in official GDP yields an estimate of the change in the size of the unofficial economy. To calculate the growth of the unofficial economy, one needs to have an estimate of its initial (pre-reform) size. We use the estimates cited by Kaufmann and Kaliberda, based on various studies, suggesting the following shares of unofficial activity in total activity for 1989: Bulgaria, 22.8 percent; Czech Republic and Slovakia, 6.0 percent; Hungary, 27.0 percent; Poland, 15.7 percent; Romania, 22.3 percent; and all the former Soviet republics, 12.0 percent (Kaufmann and Kaliberda, 1996). The fact that the share of the unofficial economy in the formerly Soviet countries is relatively low is probably attributable to much greater state repression of such activity in the FSU. The Czech Republic and Slovakia were also highly repressed under communism and also have a low initial share of the unofficial economy. In addition to estimating the size of the unofficial economy, we calculate the level of total GDP—official plus unofficial GDP. These numbers for total GDP do not rely on our estimates of the "initial" unofficial economy, but are derived by assuming that changes in electricity consumption equal changes in total GDP, applying the elasticity correction described in the text.

There are 25 "transition economies," but we are able to use electricity data for only 17: Bulgaria, the Czech Republic, Hungary, Poland, Romania, and the Slovak Republic in Central and Eastern Europe; Estonia, Latvia, and Lithuania in the Baltics; Russia, Ukraine, Moldova, and Belarus in the western part of the FSU; Azerbaijan and Georgia in the Caucasus; and Uzbekistan and Kazakhstan in Central Asia.

7.2.2 Measures of Reform

In examining the effects of political control on economic performance, we divide measures of policy into two categories. In the first category are proxies for t in our model, including measures of general liberalization, external liberalization (as a proxy for deregulation of foreign trade), privatization, deregulation, and the fairness of taxation. We also use corruption as a measure of t, since, as indicated earlier, they should be highly correlated. The second category includes direct measures of public goods in the official sector, Q. In particular, we focus on the legal environment in different countries, since this is an area in which firms in the official sector derive the benefits of government services to a much greater extent than do firms in the unofficial sector.

International organizations have attempted to measure t and Q for postcommunist economies. We use a variety of sources that evaluate reform from different perspectives. Here we briefly introduce the variables; more detail is provided in the Appendix.

We use a measure of internal price liberalization developed by Martha de Melo, Cevdet Denizer, and Alan Gelb. We use large-scale privatization, trade and foreign exchange system (external liberalization), extensiveness of legal rules, and effectiveness of legal rules from the European Bank for Reconstruction and Development.

We rely on the International Monetary Fund (IMF) for data on the budget deficit as a percentage of GDP. We have obtained the latest official IMF estimates through the end of 1996. We use official GDP data from the World Bank.

In addition to data provided by these international organizations, we use several independent assessments of the extent and nature of reform. For three years, 1995–97, the *Central European Economic Review* (CEER), published as a supplement to the *Wall Street Journal Europe,* has asked a panel of Western experts, primarily from the investment community, to rate reform in transition economies on various dimensions.[6] Each year's panel is different, as are the questions that it is asked. We look at the four measures that are relevant to our discussion: legal safeguards, crime and corruption, the tax fairness index (from the 1996 issue), and rule of law (from 1997). The tax fairness index is particularly important for the analysis that follows. It is designed to reflect both rates of taxation and fairness of administration. Conceptually, this is the proper approach. In terms of posted rates of taxation, Russia and other countries of the FSU are not much different from most of Eastern Europe.[7] However, it appears that tax administration is a good deal more capricious in the FSU, with different parts of government collecting taxes arbitrarily. The CEER panel deems that this leads to lower scores on tax fairness (or a higher "tax burden") in the FSU.[8]

The Heritage Foundation collects rankings of regulation.[9] We use the 1996 ratings (reporting primarily on 1995), which cover 20 transition countries, including 15 of the 17 for which we have reliable electricity data (that is, excepting Kazakhstan and Uzbekistan).

7.2.3 Control Variables

Undoubtedly, there are important structural differences between Central and Eastern Europe and the FSU that must be taken into account. Some of these differences are unrelated to the model. For example, the Soviet Union had a larger military–industrial production sector and its constituent countries suffered greater disruption to their trade following the fall of communism. Other differences may reflect heterogeneity in the model's parameters. For example, countries in the FSU may have an inferior technology for the production of public goods. Their much longer communist history meant that they did not have the commercial laws and other capitalist institutions developed during the 1920s and 1930s that Poland, Hungary, and the Czech Republic could go back to after the fall of communism. Such heterogeneity would lead to a dispersion of outcomes similar to that predicted by our model with multiple equilibria.

An obvious way to control for these differences is to add a dummy variable for belonging to the FSU. Both the heterogeneity model and the formal model detailed above predict that the FSU dummy is correlated with the share of the unofficial economy, and also that it reduces the partial correlation between that share and our measures of t and Q.

Empirically, we cannot distinguish these two models. However, it is important to emphasize that it does not much matter whether the data are generated by unmeasured heterogeneity between Eastern Europe and the FSU or by a model with multiple equilibria. Our model suggests that relatively small differences in initial conditions may be magnified by the mechanisms that we describe, leading to large differences in the size of the unofficial economy and in performance more generally. In our empirical work, we attempt to understand the relationship between taxation and regulation, the provision of public goods, and the size of the unofficial economy. The basic message of our story about the role of the unofficial economy in transition holds regardless of whether the FSU has ended up where it is because of bad history, bad policies, or bad luck.

The initial year of reform is taken to be the "year of most intense reform," as identified by Anders Åslund, Peter Boone, and Johnson, and is set equal to zero.[10] We determine the beginning of reform by substantial price liberalization, which, in effect, means that every country has started reform by 1994.

7.3 Effects on the Unofficial Economy

In this section, we examine the relationship between the tax and regulatory burden and the supply of public goods, on the one hand, and the size of the unofficial economy, on the other.

7.3.1 The Share of the Unofficial Economy

Table 7.1 shows the results of estimating the share of the unofficial economy *(U)* in total GDP, using the electricity consumption-based methodology explained above. The table reveals some interesting facts. The average unofficial share in East European countries starts in 1989 at 16.6 percent, peaks at 21.3 percent in 1992, and falls to 19.0 percent by 1995. By contrast, the average unofficial share in FSU countries starts at 12.0 percent and rises to 36.2 percent in 1994 before dropping to 34.4 percent in 1995. The upper panel of Figure 7.2 shows the pattern of the average share of the unofficial economy in Central and Eastern Europe, in the Baltics, and in the rest of the FSU over the period 1989–95; the lower panel of the figure compares the share of the unofficial economy in Poland and Russia over the same period. Between 1989 and 1995, the unofficial economy's share in both Poland and Romania fell by around 3 percentage points. In Russia and Ukraine, by contrast, the share of unofficial economy rose by 29.6 and 36.9 percentage points, respectively,

Table 7.1 The share of the unofficial economy (percent of total GDP)[a]

Countries	Unofficial GDP as a percentage of total GDP							1994 GDP index[b]		1995 GDP index[b]	
	1989	1990	1991	1992	1993	1994	1995	Official	Total	Official	Total
Eastern Europe											
Bulgaria	22.8	25.1	23.9	25.0	29.9	29.1	36.2	72.3	78.7	73.7	89.2
Czech Republic	6.0	6.7	12.9	16.9	16.9	17.6	11.3	81.0	92.4	84.3	89.3
Hungary	27.0	28.0	32.9	30.6	28.5	27.7	29.0	83.4	84.3	84.7	87.1
Poland	15.7	19.6	23.5	19.7	18.5	15.2	12.6	92.0	91.4	98.3	94.9
Romania	22.3	13.7	15.7	18.0	16.4	17.4	19.1	72.7	68.4	77.7	74.7
Slovakia	6.0	7.7	15.1	17.6	16.2	14.6	5.8	77.9	85.8	83.1	82.9
Former Soviet Union											
Azerbaijan	12.0	21.9	22.7	39.2	51.2	58.0	60.6	30.1	71.5	31.4	70.1
Belarus	12.0	15.4	16.6	13.2	11.0	18.9	19.3	62.5	67.8	56.1	61.2
Estonia	12.0	19.9	26.2	25.4	24.1	25.1	11.8	67.1	78.8	69.1	68.9
Georgia	12.0	24.9	36.0	52.3	61.0	63.5	62.6	15.6	37.6	16.0	37.6
Kazakhstan	12.0	17.0	19.7	24.9	27.2	34.1	34.3	51.0	68.2	46.5	62.3
Latvia	12.0	12.8	19.0	34.3	31.0	34.2	35.3	48.1	64.3	47.3	62.3
Lithuania	12.0	11.3	21.8	39.2	31.7	28.7	21.6	43.9	54.1	45.1	50.6
Moldova	12.0	18.1	27.1	37.3	34.0	39.7	35.7	41.7	60.9	43.0	58.8
Russia	12.0	14.7	23.5	32.8	36.7	40.3	41.6	51.3	75.5	49.1	74.0
Ukraine	12.0	16.3	25.6	33.6	38.0	45.7	48.9	44.2	71.6	39.0	67.0
Uzbekistan	12.0	11.4	7.8	11.7	10.1	9.5	6.5	85.0	82.6	84.0	79.0

a. Unofficial output is from Kaufmann and Kaliberda (1996), who base their calculations on electricity consumption data obtained directly from the World Bank: see text for details of their methodology. Total GDP is unofficial plus official GDP, where official GDP data are obtained directly from the World Bank's office of the Chief Economist.

b. 1989 = 100.

over the same period. In both Belarus and Uzbekistan, the share of the unofficial economy is low; it has hardly increased in Belarus and has actually declined in Uzbekistan. This is consistent with our notion that in these countries the state has suppressed the unofficial sector.[11]

Adjusting for the unofficial economy implies a substantial revision in GDP numbers for some countries, as is also shown in Table 7.1. For example, we estimate that Russian GDP in 1995 was actually around 75 percent of its 1989 level, rather than the 49.1 percent indicated in official

Unofficial/total GDP (percent)

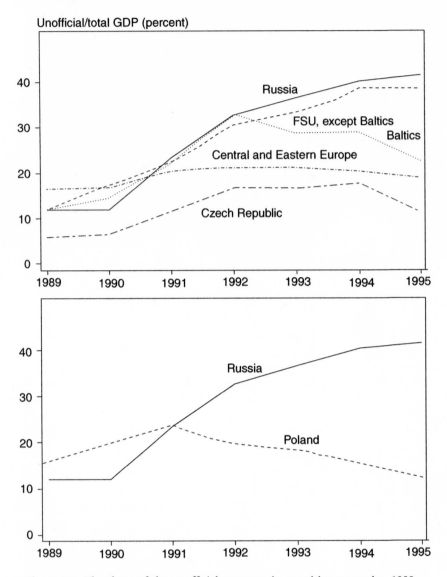

Figure 7.2 The share of the unofficial economy in transition countries, 1989–1995. *Source:* See Table 7.1.

statistics. The countries with the greatest drop in official GDP from 1989 to 1995 receive the largest upward correction in our total GDP estimates. For example, Georgian GDP in 1995 is estimated to be 37.6 percent of its 1989 level, not the 16.0 percent suggested by official statistics, while for Poland our estimate of total GDP (1994 or 1995 relative to 1989) is actually slightly smaller than the official number. The direction of the correction should be kept in mind when interpreting the empirical results below.

7.3.2 The Impact of Taxation, Regulation, and Corruption

Figures 7.3 and 7.4 offer a first look at the data. Figure 7.3 shows the share of the unofficial economy in total GDP and the Central European Economic Review's tax fairness index. In general, a lower tax fairness score is associated with a higher share of the unofficial economy, just as the model predicts. In Belarus and Uzbekistan, however, the government has been able to sustain low tax fairness without a large part of the economy moving into the unofficial sector. Similarly, Figure 7.4 shows

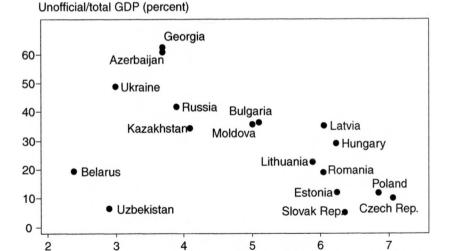

Figure 7.3 Tax fairness and unofficial output, selected transition economies, 1995. *Source:* Tax fairness ratings are from the *Central European Economic Review.*

Unofficial/total GDP (percent)

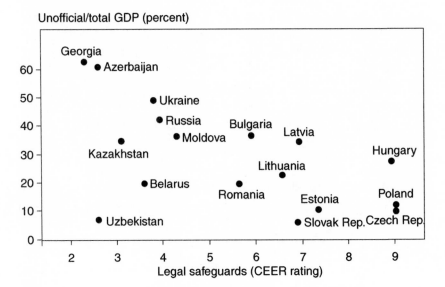

Figure 7.4 Legal safeguards and unofficial output, selected transition economies, 1995

that the quality of public goods (measured in this case by the CEER index of legal safeguards for investment) is higher where the share of the unofficial sector is lower. Again, Belarus and Uzbekistan are outliers: the quality of public goods is poor, but relatively little of their economies has switched into the unofficial sector.

Figures 7.3 and 7.4 suggest that our basic model does not adequately describe Belarus and Uzbekistan. The most likely reason is that the assumption of free mobility of economic activity between the official and the unofficial sectors is violated: the state has remained so repressive that entrepreneurs cannot switch into the unofficial sector. Figure 7.5 confirms this interpretation with data on the Freedom House indexes of rule of law and political process. Belarus and Uzbekistan—along with Tajikistan and Turkmenistan, which are not in our sample because of lack of electricity data—are by far the most politically repressed countries. To encompass them, we need to expand the model to allow for a state that represses the unofficial sector rather than competing with it. Below we continue to include Belarus and Uzbekistan in the graphs, but omit them as observations in our regressions.

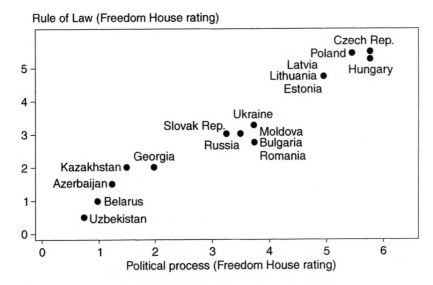

Figure 7.5 Political process and rule of law, selected transition economies, 1995. *Source:* Ratings from Freedom House.

Table 7.2 reports the results from regressions of the share of unofficial economy in total GDP on measures of state control over the economy (that is, our t variables) for a cross section of 15 countries. A negative coefficient implies that a lower t is associated with a larger share of the unofficial economy in total GDP. In each regression we control for whether a country was part of the FSU.

The first independent variable measuring state control is the World Bank measure of internal liberalization, which lies between 0 and 1. This variable is significantly correlated with the unofficial share of the economy. An increase of 0.1 in this index in 1995 reduces the share of the unofficial economy by around 13 to 16 percentage points.

The second independent variable, the EBRD's measure of external liberalization, runs from 1 to 5, although the countries actually lie between 2 and 5. This variable is also significant: a 1-point increase in this index reduces the share of the unofficial economy by 14 to 18 percentage points.

The third independent variable is the EBRD's measure of large-scale privatization, on a scale of 1 to 5. This policy variable is negatively correlated with the unofficial share of total GDP, and the coefficient suggests

Table 7.2 Regressing the share of the unofficial economy on measures of state control, selected transition economies[a]

	Internal liberalization	External liberalization	Large-scale privatization	Tax fairness	Crime and corruption	Regulation
	−135.6**	−17.9**	−10.7**	−11.3**	−5.1**	−11.3**
	(33.5)	(3.3)	(3.7)	(2.4)	(1.5)	(3.2)
Former	10.4	−8.7	14.2*	1	3.8	16.5**
Soviet	(5.9)	(6.9)	(6.6)	(6.4)	(7.8)	(6.1)
Union						
N	15	15	15	15	15	14
R-Squared	0.72	0.81	0.61	0.77	0.65	0.69

a. Dependent variable is unofficial GDP as a percentage of total GDP in 1995. All estimated equations include a constant. Sample comprises 15 countries: those listed in Table 7.1, excluding Belarus and Uzbekistan; regressions involving the regulation variable also exclude Kazakhstan.

*Denotes significance at the 10% level; **denotes significance at the 5% level. Standard errors are in parentheses.

that a 1-point increase in the score of large-scale privatization is associated with a 10 to 13 percentage point reduction in the share of the unofficial economy.

The fourth independent variable, the CEER tax fairness index, is also significant and has the predicted sign in the regression. As Figure 7.3 shows (Belarus and Uzbekistan aside), fairer taxes mean that a smaller share of the economy is unofficial.[12] This evidence supports the proposition that higher tax burdens drive firms into the unofficial economy.

The fifth and sixth independent variables represent two types of "taxation" that do not yield government revenues: corruption and regulation. Our proxy for corruption is the CEER index of crime and corruption, which ranges from 1 to 10. This measure is significant with the expected sign when used in the share regression. A 1-point improvement in the index—that is, a decrease in corruption—reduces the share of the unofficial economy by 5 to 6 percentage points.

Our proxy for regulation is the Heritage Foundation's regulation index. A 1-point increase in this index lowers the unofficial economy share by 11 to 14 percentage points. Figure 7.6 confirms the negative relationship between regulation and the share of the unofficial economy.

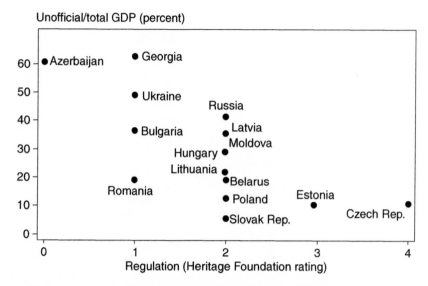

Figure 7.6 Regulation and unofficial output, selected transition economies, 1995. *Source:* Heritage Foundation.

7.3.3 The Impact of the Legal Environment

We use four measures of the legal environment. These can be thought of as proxying for Q in our model; that is, the supply of public goods to the official sector. The first two measures are evaluations by two different CEER panels of "legal safeguards for investment" and of the "rule of law." The third and fourth measures, from the EBRD, evaluate the countries in terms of the de jure extensiveness and the de facto effectiveness of legal systems in protecting investment.

While Figure 7.4 presents the relationship between the CEER measure of legal safeguards and the share of the unofficial economy, Figure 7.7 shows the relationship between the EBRD measure of legal effectiveness and that share. Together, these figures yield two conclusions. First, across most countries, there is a negative relationship between the supply of law and order to the official economy and the relative size of the unofficial economy. Second, Belarus and Uzbekistan are again exceptions, with low provision of public goods and yet low shares of the unofficial economy. As above, we omit these two countries from the regressions.

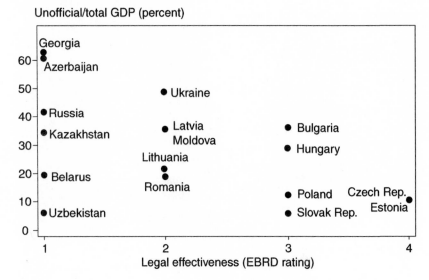

Figure 7.7 Legal effectiveness and unofficial output, selected transition economies, 1995. *Source:* European Bank for Reconstruction and Development.

Once again, there are sharp differences between Eastern Europe and the Baltics on one hand, and the rest of the FSU on the other. Eastern Europe and the Baltics have significantly higher scores on legal environment. In the CEER measure of the rule of law, only Bulgaria of the East European countries has a lower score than the highest scoring FSU country outside of the Baltics, Moldova, and the difference is very small. The difference in the CEER measure of legal safeguards is even more striking (see Figure 7.4): the lowest score among the East European and Baltic countries is 5.6 (Romania) and the highest score within the FSU, excluding the Baltics, is 4.3 (Moldova).

Table 7.3 shows the relationship between the four measures of the legal environment and the share of the unofficial economy in 1995. A higher score means a better environment for official business. In Table 7.3, all the measures have the predicted sign and are significant in explaining the unofficial economy share. This is strong support for the theoretical prediction that the unofficial economy is larger where public goods are poorer in the official sector and, in particular, where the rule of law is weaker. Controlling for initial share, a 1-point increase in the index of legal safeguards (which ranges from 1 to 10) is associated with a 7.3

percentage point fall in the share of the unofficial economy; a change in the rule of law index has a slightly smaller effect. The indexes of legal effectiveness and extensiveness have a similar size effect, although it is hard to compare precisely because they range from 1 to 5.

7.3.4 The Relationship between Taxation, Government Spending, and the Quality of Public Goods

Our model is based on public finance mechanisms that relate tax revenue (T) and the provision of public goods (Q). As such, it makes other predictions in addition to those tested in Tables 7.2 and 7.3. First, tax revenues should be lower when the tax burden is excessive, as measured by a low tax fairness score. Second, if tax revenues and government spending are strongly positively correlated, then lower tax revenues should be associated with a lower supply of public goods. In this subsection, we briefly examine the evidence bearing on these predictions.

Figure 7.8 confirms that with the exception of Belarus and Uzbekistan, tax revenue (as a percentage of total GDP, which includes the unofficial economy) improves with tax fairness. Equivalent 1994 data indicate that both tax revenue and tax fairness are high in the Czech Republic and Poland. From Figure 7.8, Russia has an intermediate tax fairness score,

Table 7.3 Regressing the share of the unofficial economy on legal environment indicators, selected transition economies[a]

	Legal safeguards	Rule of law	Legal effectiveness	Legal extensiveness
	−5.5**	−5.1**	−11.0**	−3.2
	(1.7)	(1.4)	(3.9)	(7.0)
Former Soviet	3.3	8.8	6.7	16.4
Union	(7.9)	(6.4)	(7.9)	(11.5)
N	15	15	15	15
R²	0.65	0.68	0.60	0.35

a. Dependent variable is unofficial GDP as a percentage of total GDP in 1995. All estimated equations include a constant. Sample comprises 15 countries: those listed in Table 7.1, excluding Belarus and Uzbekistan; regressions involving the regulation variable also exclude Kazakhstan.

*Denotes significance at the 10% level; **denotes significance at the 5% level. Standard errors are in parentheses.

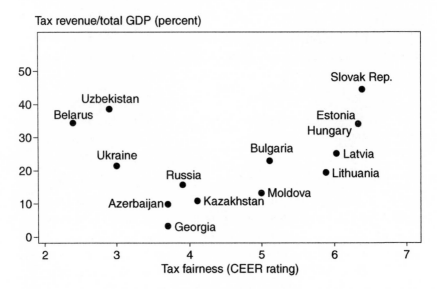

Figure 7.8 Tax fairness and tax revenue, selected transition economies, 1995. *Sources: Central European Economic Review* and European Bank for Reconstruction and Development (EBRD), 1996.

but not high enough for a large amount of tax revenue. Belarus and Uzbekistan are anomalous because the high level of political repression enables the state to keep firms in the official sector (and therefore to maintain its revenue), even though tax fairness and the level of public goods provision are both low.

Our model assumes that tax revenue and government spending are equivalent. Figure 7.9 shows that tax revenues are highly correlated with government spending. This figure suggests that internal and external borrowing generally are not critical determinants of the government budget in these countries, and justifies our assumption that tax revenue equals spending.

Figure 7.10 shows a positive relationship between tax revenue and quality of legal safeguards. It supports the importance of the public finance mechanism suggested by our model; namely, that countries with fair tax systems raise more revenue and hence supply more public goods. In turn, the better supply of public goods may enhance the tax base and tax revenues.

Tax revenue/total GDP (percent)

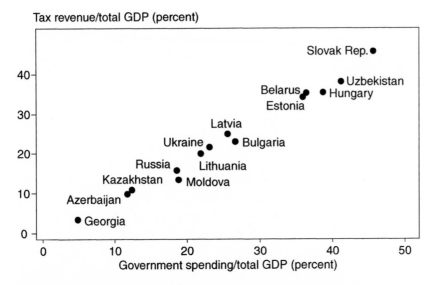

Figure 7.9 Tax revenue and government spending, selected transition economies, 1995. *Source:* European Bank for Reconstruction and Development (EBRD), 1996.

Tax revenue/total GDP (percent)

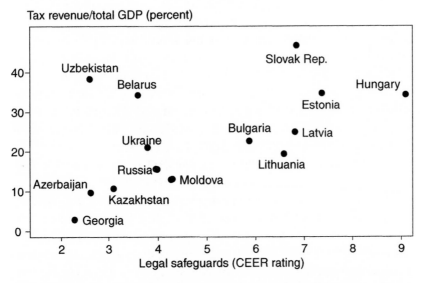

Figure 7.10 Legal safeguards and tax revenue, selected transition economies, 1995. *Sources: Central European Economic Review* and European Bank for Reconstruction and Development (EBRD), 1996.

7.3.5 Summary

The results of regressions using the share of the unofficial economy (U) on the left-hand side confirm our theoretical predictions for both the tax rate (t) and public goods (Q) in the state sector. Liberalization, privatization, fairer taxation, and fewer regulations are all associated with a smaller unofficial economy. Better provision of public goods to the official economy is associated with a relatively larger official economy. Finally, public finance mechanisms do appear to be at work: countries with less distortionary tax and regulatory systems collect more tax revenue and provide more public goods to their official economies.

An ex ante plausible criticism of the model is that our electricity-based calculations of the unofficial economy are founded on too many implausible assumptions and are therefore too noisy to be useful. But if our estimates of the size of the unofficial economy are pure noise, why do they line up so well with the measures of t and Q? The objection loses much of its power in light of the extremely strong raw correlations between our constructed measures of the unofficial economy and a variety of other variables. At this cross-sectional level, then, the predictions of the theoretical model are strongly confirmed.

7.4 Conclusion

This chapter develops a simple framework for understanding the relationship between taxation and the provision of public goods in an economy, and puts forward several propositions about how tax and regulatory policies affect the relative size of the unofficial economy. The economic transition of formerly communist countries since 1989 offers an opportunity to test this theory. The available evidence broadly supports it.

There are three types of transition economies in Eastern Europe and the FSU. First, there are politically repressed economies with highly distortionary taxes, low provision of public goods, but still, a small unofficial sector; Belarus and Uzbekistan are striking examples in our sample. Second, there are economies with relatively fair taxes, relatively light regulation, high tax revenues, and relatively good provision of public goods in the official sector; these are concentrated in Eastern Europe. Third, there are economies with relatively unfair taxes, relatively onerous regulation, low tax collection, and relatively poor public goods; these are concentrated in the FSU. Comparing the second and third groups, the former has a lower share of unofficial activity than the latter.

These findings pinpoint the crucial difference between Eastern Europe and the FSU in the progress of institution building. It widely agreed that over the next couple of decades, the East European economies will converge to West European living standards. The fate of the economies of the FSU poses a tougher question. In a pessimistic scenario, they would be stuck in a bad equilibrium for a long time to come, with poor institutions, a large unofficial economy, and an ineffective state. In a more optimistic scenario, appropriate policies would get these countries out of a bad equilibrium and set them on the growth path achieved by the East European countries. The central policy question is how to make the second scenario come true. How can institutions be built in the FSU?

One strategy is to draw on massive foreign assistance. Indeed, the IMF has played a crucial role in helping Russia achieve macroeconomic stabilization. Nonetheless, foreign assistance has not brought Russia to East European institutional standards. Foreign economic assistance does not, by itself, ensure the transition to growth through improvements in the budget situation. This is not a criticism, but rather a recognition that the political environment can lead to a very poor rate of conversion of money into public goods.

Our analysis suggests that reforms must focus primarily on the elimination of the distortions associated with existing government activities, including tax collection, and on the effectiveness of the conversion of available public revenues into market-supporting public goods. This approach would correspond to an upward shift in the $Q(T)$ function in our model, which, if large enough, can eliminate the bad equilibrium. In the context of Russia, several reforms that correspond to these strategies have been proposed. These include a tax reform aimed at increasing government revenues while reducing marginal tax rates and simplifying tax rules; revision of the federal system, designed to improve the incentives of local governments to collect tax revenues and supply public goods; and improvements in the provision of law and order. Typically, the design of these institutional reforms is not very complicated. The question is whether they are politically feasible.

We believe that there is cause for optimism, at least in some countries of the FSU—most notably, Russia. One reason is that with privatization and macroeconomic reforms completed, there is relatively widespread agreement about the necessity of institutional reforms. By contrast, in Belarus, Ukraine, Uzbekistan, Tajikistan, and Turkmenistan, there is much less support within the elite for essential public finance reforms and deregulation.

In addition, Russia and some other countries in the FSU, such as Georgia and Azerbaijan, have now achieved a modicum of political stability that could ease the passage of institutional reforms. Boris Yeltsin was reelected President of Russia in 1996, and apparently remains committed to reform. To be sure, the government and the parliament still have major tactical disagreements about particular policies, and there is no guarantee that the institutions that emerge out of the political process will be nearly as market friendly as those in Eastern Europe.

Finally, it is worth noting that institutional reform is possible even in countries with little history of functioning market institutions. Certain East Asian countries have achieved such reforms in relatively short periods of time. In Russia, as well, there have been some considerable successes, such as the creation of a stock market and a legal infrastructure supporting financial markets and institutions. The lack of market history is an impediment to institutional reform, but it is not insurmountable.

To be sure, because so many market-supporting institutions have yet to be set up and because many missteps are likely along the way, we do not expect Russia to achieve spectacular growth in the near future. But it is important to remember that considerable growth is possible without institutional perfection: many East European countries have had their own institutional problems, as do many countries in the West. Reform of the tremendously distortionary tax system will take Russia far along the path of reducing the unofficial sector, increasing government revenues, and achieving growth. Russia is moving in the right direction quite rapidly, by both its own and comparative standards. This progress gives cause for cautious optimism about its economic, as well as its political, future.

Appendix: Measures of Reform

This appendix provides descriptions and sources of the various measures of reform that we use in this chapter. Although the EBRD indexes are on a scale of 1 to 4*, there is no apparent reason for using 4* rather than

5. As it says, "most advanced economies would qualify for the 4* rating for almost all transition indicators" (EBRD, 1996, p. 11n1). We convert 4* to 5 throughout.

Parameter *t*

INTERNAL LIBERALIZATION. Liberalization of "internal markets": price liberalization and elimination of state trading monopolies. Scale is 0–1, where a higher score means more liberalized. *Source:* For 1989–94, de Melo, Denizer, and Gelb (1996, sect. 3); updated for 1995 using unpublished data provided by Ratna Sahay of the IMF.

EXTERNAL LIBERALIZATION. Extent of liberalization in "trade and foreign exchange system." Scale is 1–5. Score is 1 if "widespread import and/or export controls or very limited legitimate access to foreign exchange"; 2 if "some liberalization of import and/or export controls; almost full current account convertibility in principle but with a foreign exchange regime that is not fully transparent (possibly with multiple exchange rates)"; 3 if "removal of most quantitative and administrative import and export restrictions; almost full current account convertibility at a unified exchange rate"; 4 if "removal of all quantitative and administrative import and export restrictions (apart from agriculture) and all significant export tariffs; insignificant direct involvement in exports and imports by ministries and state-owned trading companies; no major nonuniformity of customs duties for nonagricultural goods and services"; and 5 if "standards and performance norms of advanced industrial countries: removal of most tariff barriers; membership in GATT/WTO [General Agreement on Tariffs and Trade/World Trade Organization]." *Source:* European Bank for Reconstruction and Development (EBRD) (1995, Table 2.1, pp. 11, 12), updated in EBRD (1996, Table 2.1, p. 11).

LARGE-SCALE PRIVATIZATION. Extent to which large state-owned firms have been privatized. Scale is 1–5. Score is 1 if "little progress"; 2 if "comprehensive scheme almost ready for implementation; some sales completed"; 3 if "more than 25 percent of large-scale state-owned enterprise assets privatized or in the process of being sold, but possibly with major unresolved issues regarding corporate governance"; 4 if more than 50 percent of state-owned enterprise assets privatized in a scheme that has generated substantial outsider ownership"; and 5 if "standards and performance typical of advanced industrial economies: more than 75 percent of enterprise assets in private ownership with effective corporate governance." *Source:* EBRD (1995, Table 2.1, pp. 11, 12), updated in EBRD (1996, Table 2.1, p. 11).

TAX FAIRNESS. Scale is 0–10, where higher score means fairer taxes. One of 10 dimensions on which a panel of experts graded 26 transition countries "for their attractiveness as a place to do business over the coming year." A reasonable interpretation is that the experts took into account both tax rates and the quality of tax administration. *Source: Central European Economic Review* (CEER), "The Great Growth Race," December 1995–January 1996, pp. 8–9, 13 (published as a supplement to the *Wall Street Journal Europe*).

CRIME AND CORRUPTION. Scale is 0–10, where higher score means less crime and corruption. *Source:* CEER, "The Great Growth Race," December 1995–January 1996, pp. 8–9, 13.

REGULATION. Our scale, which reverses the Heritage Foundation's original scale, is 0–4, where a higher score means less regulation. Score is 4 ("very low") if free of corruption, existing regulations are straightforward and applied uniformly to all businesses, regulations are not much of a burden to business; 3 ("low") if licensing procedure is simple, no bribes, existing regulations are relatively straightforward and applied uniformly most of the time, regulations prove to be a burden to business in some instances; 2 ("moderate") if existing regulations may be applied haphazardly and in some instances are not even published by the government, complicated licensing procedure, regulations are a substantial burden to business, a significant state-owned sector exists, no bribes; 1 ("high") if government-set production quotas and state planning, major barriers to opening a business, complicated licensing process, very high fees, bribes sometimes necessary, regulations a great burden to business; and 0 ("very high") if government discourages new business creation, bribes mandatory, regulations are applied randomly. *Source:* Heritage Foundation, published in Johnson and Sheehy (1996).

Variable Q

LEGAL SAFEGUARDS. Scale is 0–10, where higher score means better legal safeguards. *Source:* CEER, "The Great Growth Race," December 1995–January 1996, pp. 8–9, 13.

RULE OF LAW. Scale is 0–10, where higher score means stronger rule of law. *Source:* CEER, "The Great Growth Race," December 1995–January 1996, pp. 8–9, 13.

LEGAL EFFECTIVENESS. "The effectiveness of legal rules on investment." Scale is 1–5. Score is 1 if "legal rules are usually very unclear and often contradictory and the availability of independent legal advice is very limited. The administration of the law is substantially deficient (for example, little confidence in the abilities and independence of the courts, no or poorly organized security and land registers)"; 2 if "legal rules are usually unclear and sometimes contradictory. Legal advice is often difficult to obtain. The administration and judicial support of the law is rudimentary"; 3 if "legal rules are reasonably clear and ascertainable through legal advice [but] administrative or judicial support is often inadequate (for example, substantial discretion in the administration of laws, few up-to-date registers); 4 if "law is usually clear and legal advice is readily available. Investment laws are reasonably well administered and supported judicially, although that support is sometimes patchy"; and 5 if "law is clear and readily ascertainable. Sophisticated legal advice is readily available. Investment law is well supported administratively and judicially, particularly regarding the efficient functioning of courts and the orderly and timely registration of proprietary or security interests." *Source:* EBRD (1995, Table 6.1, p. 103); updated in EBRD (1996, Box 2.1, p. 14).

LEGAL EXTENSIVENESS. "The extensiveness of legal rules on investment." Scale is 1–5. Score is 1 if "legal rules are very limited in scope, and impose substantial constraints on creating investment vehicles, security over assets or to the repatriation of profits. Indirect investment is not specifically regulated"; 2 if "legal rules are limited in scope and impose significant constraints on creating investment vehicles, adequate security over assets, or the repatriation of profits"; 3 if "legal rules do not impose major obstacles to creating investment vehicles and security or to repatriating profits [but] they are in need of considerable improvements"; 4 if "legal rules do not discriminate between foreign and domestic investors and impose few constraints on creating a range of investment vehicles and security instruments. Indirect investment is specifically regulated"; and 5 if "legal rules closely approximate generally accepted standards internationally and impose few restrictions, including on the creation of sophisticated investment vehicles or security. Indirect investment law is well developed." *Source:* EBRD (1995, Table 7.1, p. 103); updated in EBRD (1996, Box 2.1, p. 14).

FISCAL BALANCE. Budget deficit as a percentage of official GDP, calculated using IMF definitions. *Source:* Unpublished data provided by Ratna Sahay of the IMF. Fischer, Sahay, and Végh (1996a, 1996b) use an earlier version of these data.

— 8 —

Toward a Theory of Legal Reform

Virtually all observers of East European reforms have recognized the importance of the rule of law for the economic transformation. The rule of law means, in part, that people use the legal system to structure their economic activities and resolve disputes. This includes learning what the legal rules say, structuring their economic transactions using these rules, seeking to punish or obtain compensation from those who break the rules, and turning to the public officials, such as the courts and the police, to enforce these rules.

To be accepted, the legal system has to outcompete other, typically private, mechanisms of enforcing agreements and resolving disputes. One type of mechanism is legal but private contract enforcement through reputation or arbitration. Such mechanisms are extremely important, but they are not a perfect substitute for the public legal system: they either work in specialized markets with relatively few participants and repeat interactions (Bernstein, 1992), or ultimately rely on the legal system to enforce private arbitrators' decisions (Shavell, 1995). A second type of private enforcement is organized crime. As a method of dispute resolution, organized crime has the problem that criminals exert heavy, often distortionary and arbitrary, taxes on the parties they protect. The question asked in this chapter—using both theory and the example of Russia—is how to reform the legal system to make it more effective than organized crime in supporting private transactions.

By Jonathan Hay, Andrei Shleifer, and Robert Vishny; originally published in *European Economic Review*, 40 (1996): 559–567. © 1996—Elsevier Science B. V.

8.1 Aspects of a Dysfunctional Legal System

Why would people not use the legal system to resolve disputes? Presumably, they would use alternative methods of dispute resolution, such as private arbitration or crime, when these methods are less expensive. What, then, makes a legal system expensive for private parties to use?

Bad courts raise the cost of using the legal system. Court fees may be prohibitively high. Judges may be corrupt, and so disputants may be concerned about both having to bribe the judge and having the other party pay a higher bribe. Courts may be politicized in the sense of catering to the wishes of the politicians, especially when the government is a party to the conflict, or in the sense of favoring particular litigants for reasons unrelated to the dispute (for example, nationals over foreigners, state firms over private firms, and so forth). Courts may be so inefficient that it takes years to get a dispute resolved, by which time the value of damages that might be collected falls to zero in real terms. Courts may be unpredictable because they refuse to take cases, because their decisions are difficult to forecast from the law, or because judges are uninformed and incompetent. Likewise, the police often suffer from the same problems as the courts, making the legal system expensive to use.

A second reason that people do not use the legal system is the prevalence of bad laws on the books, laws that guarantee that virtually all business is operating extralegally. When private parties may already be breaking some laws (for example, tax, or registration), they may come to a court only to expose themselves to authorities without resolving their dispute. Indeed, Article 168 of the Russian Civil Code takes the extreme position that a transaction that violates any provision of the Russian law is void. With such laws, businesses may eschew courts altogether. A further problem with bad laws is that they contradict standard business practice and common sense, making it difficult for courts to reach decisions. How could a court enforce the payment of debts of a bankrupt company by its shareholders who have no limited liability (see Articles 56 and 105 of the Russian Civil Code)? If laws are so bad that courts can't reach decisions from them, people will not use the courts.

But even if two parties come to a court, they are both "legal," and the law does not invalidate their contract, there remains a critical problem of a dysfunctional legal system, namely that the courts cannot use the available laws to resolve disputes. For example, in a dysfunctional legal system, courts cannot effectively resolve contract disputes, even if they try, for two reasons. First, courts cannot easily verify whether a violation had taken place. For example, in the absence of standard accounting methods, courts cannot verify that one partner stole money from the other in their joint venture. Second, there is no body of law that specifies what a court should do even if there is a violation. For example, the Russian law does not specify who is liable when a buyer of securities discovers that these securities have been previously stolen (bona fide purchaser rules do not exist). In well-functioning legal systems, in contrast, a great deal more information is verifiable in court and the body of law and precedent is much more extensive, so that courts have a great deal more guidance as to what to do.

These problems can seriously handicap contracting. In particular, contracts may have to be very incomplete, in the Grossman and Hart (1986) sense, not because future contingencies are hard to describe, but because of severe limitations on what courts can verify and rule on. Nonverifiability of future states, which lies at the heart of incomplete contracts, may be a property of poor institutions such as accounting methods or access to information by the courts, rather than of the physical world. Moreover, this incompleteness of contracts can prevent many efficiency-improving contracts from being signed, or, even if they are signed, they will be enforced through extralegal means.

Finally, for the legal system to be used by private parties, the decisions of courts must be enforced by the coercive force of the state. If private parties need to enforce court decisions on their own, they often choose to use mafia in the first place. To be sure, there may be a lot of value in legal rules even if the government does not enforce court decisions, since private parties can use these rules to structure their transactions even when enforcement remains private. Indeed, Hart (1961, p. 91) argues that the importance of enforcement, relative to that of good legal rules and courts, has been greatly exaggerated by legal scholars, and gives examples of functioning legal systems with public courts and private enforcement of their decisions. Still, most modem legal systems rely on (ultimate) public enforcement of rules as well as on public laws and public courts.

Russia's legal system today has all the characteristics of a dysfunctional legal system. The courts do not function effectively. There are many bad laws on the books, a legacy of the communist system that aimed to ban private economic activity. The new laws are highly incomplete, and usually lag far behind business practice. The laws are often not written in ways that enable courts to verify violations (without a significant effort that judges refuse to incur). The police often fail to enforce the decisions of the courts. As a consequence, business people stay away from using the legal system, and use the services of organized crime instead.

The question addressed in the following sections is how to get more people to use the legal system. We believe that court and police reforms should not be the starting point, since those reforms are likely to take a long time. The legal system must begin to be used with the existing courts and police. To do so, legal reform should begin with the adoption of legal rules that the courts find usable, and that private parties find less expensive to rely on than other methods of resolving disputes. Such rules should have several obvious but important characteristics. First, bad rules—that keep people from using the legal system because they prohibit, or fail to support, legitimate market activity—need to be abolished. Second, the new rules should, to the extent possible, follow business practice, thereby enabling private parties to continue their business activities, but to rely on courts rather than crime to resolve disputes. Third, the new rules should help the courts resolve disputes by telling them what to do in the cases where existing laws are most conspicuously incomplete. In particular, courts, with their extremely limited resources, should be able to verify whether violations of these rules have occurred.

In the next section, we present a simple model that illustrates the need for legal rules, and shows how simple legal rules can facilitate contracting even in an undeveloped legal system. In the following section, we discuss our view of legal reform with a few more illustrations and examples.

8.2 A Model of a Dysfunctional Legal System

This section illustrates some of the ideas of the chapter using the example of a capitalist who wants to hire a manager. Suppose that a capitalist has an asset ($1 of capital) that can be put to productive use. If the capitalist works with this asset himself, he can produce output $1 + a$ next period. However, the capitalist has an alternative use of his time, valued at v, so his net payoff from working with the asset himself is $1 + a - v$.

Alternatively, the capitalist can hire a specialized manager to work with his asset, whose alternative wage is W. If the manager works with the asset, then the payoffs take the following form: with probability p, the payoff is $1 + G$ (the asset remains and there is extra output), and with probability $1 - p$, the payoff is 1 (only the asset remains). There is also a risk, however, that the manager sells the asset to his relatives at essentially zero price, in which case the capitalist receives zero. Every outcome is observable to the capitalist and the manager but outcomes need not be verifiable in court. Throughout, we assume that the manager does not have any resources of his own, and hence cannot either buy the asset from the capitalist and manage it himself, or even post a bond with the capitalist. We examine three contracting regimes of this model.

In the first regime, that of a well-functioning legal system, suppose that the income of the firm, as well as the fact of asset sale, are verifiable in court. The capitalist can then write a contract with the manager that gives the capitalist residual income and that also requires the capitalist's approval for any asset sale. If it pays to do so, the capitalist simply hires the manager at the wage W and retains the right to stop any disposition of assets. The condition for this contract being preferable to the self-management of the assets is that

$$(8.1) \qquad 1 - W + pG > 1 + a - v$$

that is, the surplus from delegated management exceeds the surplus from self-management. This is also the efficiency condition for delegated management, which we assume holds.

In the second regime, that of no legal contract enforcement, we assume that courts are not equipped to verify either the income of the firm, or even whether its assets have been sold. In this case, no matter what the contract with the manager is, he steals both the income and the asset, and the payoff to the capitalist is zero. Accordingly, as long as $1 + a - v > 0$, the capitalist would rather manage his asset himself than use the legal system to hire the manager.

Suppose that the capitalist has access to a (reputable) mafia, which for an up-front, non-negotiable fee of M ensures that the capitalist receives all the residual income. Then, as long as

$$(8.2) \qquad 1 - W + pG - M > 1 + a - v$$

the capitalist turns to the mafia to enforce the contract with the manager (for example, kill him if he steals). If equation (8.2) does not hold, the capitalist manages the asset himself. With no legal contract enforcement, the gains from trade either remain unrealized, or they are realized through the extralegal, and presumably expensive, system of contract enforcement.

In the third regime, that of simple rules, we suppose that the courts are not equipped to verify income, but can actually verify whether assets are sold, and in fact can stop an asset sale unapproved by the capitalist. In this case, the capitalist can contract the manager to run the firm except that any decision to dispose of assets must be approved by the capitalist. (We do not address the question of whether one needs just contract law, or more elaborate corporate law, to enforce this contract.) Suppose the manager gets a wage w (which we determine shortly). If the manager runs the firm, he cannot sell the asset, but he has no reason to report any income above 1, since income is not verifiable. The capitalist's payoff is then $1 - w$. The capitalist prefers legal delegation to running the firm himself if

$$(8.3) \qquad\qquad 1 - w > 1 + a - v.$$

To determine the manager's wage, note that he does not need to be paid W, since both he and the capitalist understand that he will steal G. In fact as long as $pG > W$, the manager is prepared to work for a zero wage (he would actually pay $pG - W$ for this job, but we are assuming that he has no cash to put up a bond). If $w = 0$, then the condition for employing the manager under these legal rules is $a < v$. As long as the capitalist's opportunity wage exceeds the amount he adds to the business, he would hire the manager rather than run the business himself.

Similarly, the capitalist prefers delegation under these legal rules to mafia enforcement if

$$(8.4) \qquad\qquad 1 - W + pG - M < 1.$$

In this case, if the capitalist chooses to hire a manager, he would choose to do so legally rather than through mafia enforcement. When condition (8.4) holds, legal rules outcompete the mafia.

One problem with the law that requires the capitalist's consent for the asset sale is that the manager may be ingenious enough to invent an alternative transaction, such as renting the capital to his relative at essentially a zero price. One potential way to prevent this from happening is by stipulating that the manager has a "duty of loyalty" to the capitalist.

In this case, a manager who undertakes any transaction that might be interpreted by the courts as a form of self-dealing is liable to the capitalist for damages. Unfortunately, such contract clauses require a developed body of precedent to be useful, or else the courts would either refuse to interpret them or do so arbitrarily. In the long term, such a body of precedent might develop, but in the short term, capitalists have to take the risk that managers outsmart them, and courts cannot identify a violation of existing laws. Laundry lists of bright line rules, which specify all the actions that managers are prohibited from taking without an explicit permission of the capitalists (or a super majority approval by shareholders), may make the legal system more effective even though they do not cover all the contingencies.

This simple model illustrates how legal rules can make the legal system more attractive to private parties than contract enforcement by the mafia. First, contracts suggested by economic theory may rely on information that courts cannot verify until other institutions—such as accounting standards—develop. Simpler rules and contracts may be more effective in transition economies in getting people to use the legal system. Second, these rules have to enable private parties to solve contracting problems they face (such as hiring a manager). Third, even simple rules, as long as they allow courts to verify violations easily, can be successful in getting private parties to structure their contracts using these rules, and thus can both facilitate trade and crowd out mafia as the means of contract enforcement.

8.3 Implications for Legal Reform

Our model may help the discussion of legal reform strategies. Note first that legal reforms often are not introduced by benevolent dictators or parliaments, but are rather an outcome of political pressure from the property owners. For example, Hunt (1936) presents the history of the repeal of the 1720s Bubbles Act in Britain. This Act, which prevented the incorporation of limited liability companies without consent of Parliament, was repealed only after a century of pressure from British business, covering most of the Industrial Revolution. Raeff (1983) similarly discusses how the legal system developed in Germany in the seventeenth and eighteenth centuries was shaped by pressures from the participants in an emerging market economy. In Russia today, the pressures on the

Duma for legal reform are also coming from the new business, as well as from the privatized business. This is not surprising, since these businesses (who are the capitalists in our model) stand to benefit most immediately from the legal reform, and therefore are prepared to lobby for it.

Several writers on transition (for example, Intriligator, 1994; Laffont, 1994) have argued for the introduction of legal and regulatory institutions before privatization, so that privatized firms can from the start operate in a market environment. Unfortunately, before privatization, when all property is state owned, no private parties are interested in institutional reform, and hence such reforms are unlikely to take place. The effective political pressure for legal reform appears only after privatization (Boycko, Shleifer, and Vishny, 1995). Surely, some of the laws that the property owners lobby for serve their private, rather than social, interest (protection from imports and from entry are good examples). Still, property owners would typically oppose the bad laws that prevent them from using the legal system, and support laws that conform to the standard business practice. Both of these positions are part of a good reform. Besides, some of the worst recent laws in Russia have been supported by the remaining state institutions (for example, the draft Land Code—supported by the managers of collective farms—makes private ownership of and transactions in land all but impossible). The politically feasible order of institutional reform, then, is privatization first, introduction of legal rules second, and bureaucratic reform only in the very long term.

This chapter has three observations to contribute to what the new laws should do in order to start off the use of the legal system. First, they should undo the effects of the bad laws, which keep private parties away from using the legal system more effectively than even the bad courts. Even the repeal of a few bad rules (such as that of unlimited liability in the Russian Civil Code that was recently repealed by a Presidential Decree) on the margin brings more activity into the legal system.

Second, to compete effectively with organized crime, bad rules should be replaced with those that facilitate and support the existing contractual arrangements and market transactions. In Russia, as elsewhere in Eastern Europe, business is developing at a fantastic rate, and a good goal for commercial laws is to keep up with good business practice. For example, some of Russia's recent draft laws, such as the Securities Law and the Law on Fund Transfers, essentially legalize already existing market transactions, thus enabling private parties to rely on the legal system to resolve disputes in their already ongoing activities. If, in contrast, laws make the existing market practice more difficult, as in the case of Russia's draft Land Code, they are only encouraging criminal enforcement of the existing practice.

Third, laws should enable very imperfect courts to verify violations and correct wrongs. In the language of the law school classrooms, bright-line rules are preferred to the vague rules. The bright-line rules have the disadvantage that they are necessarily incomplete. On the other hand, vague rules would leave courts too much discretion, and would therefore either not be used at all, or be abused by courts. Thus, as our model suggests, managerial duty of loyalty to shareholders is not a workable legal rule in Russia. In contrast, laundry lists of prohibitions against managerial misconduct, mandatory disclosure rules, and requirements of super majority approvals by shareholders of major corporate changes, may form the basis of a workable Corporate Law, even though, in the short run, they fail to cover all the cases of managerial misconduct (Black, Kraakman, and Hay, 1996).

Enforceable laws, even with poorly run courts, also serve the critical function of providing the threat points in private negotiations (Hay, 1994). Most of contract enforcement will remain private in the sense that parties will try to resolve their difficulties through bargaining. However, the ultimate threat to the nonperforming party may now be a lawsuit rather than death. If a manager is stealing from a capitalist, the capitalist will put a lot of resources into reducing this theft. But if he cannot keep his manager from stealing, it is better to have clear-cut laws that the manager has violated, so the capitalist may take the manager to court as the last resort. The private action of the capitalist in preventing his manager from stealing is here directed toward enforcing the public law, rather than undermining it. In this respect, introducing a simple legal system, but one that addresses the most egregious yet still verifiable cases of contract violation, can do a great deal to get private contract enforcement to reinforce, rather than supplant, public contract enforcement.

The strategy of legal reform described in this chapter may produce fairly crude and still incomplete laws. Why not instead simply borrow a legal system from another country? Although it is possible to borrow significant parts of, say, a Civil Code, as Russia has borrowed from Germany, this is not sufficient. As Merryman (1969) shows in general and

Buxbaum and Hopt (1988) for the case of corporate law, even in Civil Code countries most legal rules come either from subsidiary laws that are quite country specific, or even more important, from judicial decisions. Napoleon's hopes for a self-sufficient Civil Code notwithstanding, without a history of precedents, a Civil Code does not tell judges what to do in specific cases. In the short term, then, a reforming country needs a system of laws that is specific to its business practice, and that enables judges to make decisions and thus begin developing precedents.

In this situation, simple bright-line rules have the major advantage that they can immediately begin to be used by courts and hence by the private parties. Unlike the more elaborate rules, they fit the existing legal institutions and business practice. For example, if corporate law mandates that companies pay a fraction of profits (or sales) as dividends, or prohibits all asset sales, even the Russian courts might succeed in detecting the violations of these rules. As laws are used more, courts will begin to gain credibility and places to resolve disputes. They will also become more predictable as a body of precedents develop, and private parties begin to anticipate more clearly how courts make decisions. In this way, laws will converge to those of developed market economies even if the initial system is more primitive.

The basic point, then, is that to get to the rule of law in the intermediate term, it is best to begin with rules that are suitable for both private agents and the courts, and then to allow this system to develop as the needs of private agents and the capabilities of the courts develop over time.

— 9 —

Federalism with and without Political Centralization: China versus Russia

Over the past decade, China's gross domestic product (GDP) has grown at one of the highest rates in the world, Russia's at one of the lowest. The difference has come mostly from the growth of the new private sector. In China, the new private sector has thrived. In Russia, it has stagnated.

Why this sharp divergence between private sector evolutions? In both countries, the evidence points to the importance of the behavior of local governments. In China, local governments have actively contributed to the growth of new firms (Oi, 1992; Qian and Weingast, 1997). In Russia, local governments have typically stood in the way, be it through taxation, regulation, or corruption (Chapters 6 and 7; see also McKinsey Global Institute, 1999; EBRD, 1999).[1]

There are two main hypotheses for the attitudes of local governments in Russia. The first—call it "capture"—is that local governments have been captured by the initial rent holders, primarily by the old firms that dominated the Russian economy before the transition. In this view, local governments have worked both to generate transfers to these firms and to protect them from competition by new firms. In this first view, their hostile attitude vis-à-vis the new private sector has been deliberate. The second view—call it "competition for rents"—is that the behavior of local governments has been instead the unintended result of administrative disorganization. Too many agencies have tried to extract rents from new private firms, making it unprofitable to create or run a private business, at least legally.[2]

By Olivier Blanchard and Andrei Shleifer; originally published in International Monetary Fund, *IMF Staff Papers*, 48 (2001, Special Issue): 171–179. © 2001.

These two lines of explanation are plausible and not mutually exclusive, but they raise the obvious question of why things have been different in China. Here again, there are two main hypotheses.

The first is that the initial rent holders were weaker in China than in Russia. China started its transition from a very low level of economic development. Its agriculture did not rely on large collective farms, and its industry had relatively few large enterprises. Russia, in contrast, started its transition as a fully industrialized economy, dominated by large state firms and collective farms. According to this view, the potential for capture was simply more limited in China than in Russia.

The second view points to the strength of the central government in China. Transition in China has taken place under the tight control of the Communist Party. As a result, the central government has been in a strong position to either reward or punish local administrations, reducing both the risk of local capture and the scope of competition for rents (Huang, 2002). By contrast, transition in Russia has come with the emergence of a fledgling democracy. The central government has been neither strong enough to impose its views, nor strong enough to set clear rules about the sharing of the proceeds of growth (Shleifer and Treisman, 1999; Treisman, 1999b). As a result, local governments have had few incentives either to resist capture or to rein in competition for rents.

The aim of this chapter is to explore this last argument, and more generally to explore the role of federalism in transition. The question is an important one. Based on the experience of China, a number of researchers have argued that federalism could play a central role in development (Qian and Weingast, 1997; Roland, 2000). Indeed, a new term, "market preserving federalism," has been coined to emphasize the benefits of decentralization for Chinese growth. We agree, but with an important caveat. We believe the experience of Russia indicates that another ingredient is crucial, namely political centralization. In doing so, we echo a theme first developed by Riker (1964): for federalism to function and to endure, it must come with political centralization.

9.1 A Model of Federalism and Incentives

We start by writing down a model of federalism and local government incentives. The model is very simple, but it provides a convenient way to look at the facts and discuss the issues. This is what we do in the next two sections.

Think of the government as having two levels: central and local (in other words, ignore for the moment the fact that there are at least three relevant levels of government in both Russia and China: central, regional, and local).

Suppose each *local government* faces a simple choice. It can either foster growth, by limiting transfers of resources to state and former state firms and allowing new private firms to enter and to grow. Or it can kill growth, by transferring resources to old firms and/or preventing new firms from being created.

Why might a local government choose the second option? Under the "capture" view, it may want to protect state or ex-state firms from competition. Under the "competition for rents" view, it may be simply unable to prevent bribes and corruption by local officials. Sorting out the relative importance of the two should be high on the research agenda but is not essential here. For our purposes, both have the same implication: no growth.

Let y be the additional output under growth. With appropriate normalization, let y also stand for the additional amount of revenues available to the central and local governments under growth. Let b be the private benefits to the local government of killing growth. Under the capture interpretation, b may reflect the transfers back from existing firms to the local government, in the form of bribes, cash, or in-kind payments. Under the competition for rents interpretation, b may reflect the cost to a local government of reducing or coordinating bribe taking by local officials.

Now turn to the *central government*. Assume (an assumption to which we return later) that the central government wants to foster growth, and think of the central government as having two main tools, a carrot and a stick:

- Revenue sharing (the carrot): The central government can choose the extent of revenue sharing with local governments. Let a be the share of revenues from additional growth going to local governments: if a local government chooses to foster growth, it gets ay in revenues.
- Political centralization (the stick): The central government can affect the probability that the local government stays in power to

enjoy either the revenues from growth or the private benefits from killing growth. Denote by p_x the probability that the local government stays in power if it kills growth, and by p_y the corresponding probability if it fosters growth. Define $p = p_y / p_x$. The value of p clearly depends first on whether local officials are appointed or elected. If they are appointed, then presumably the central government can choose p freely and make it as high as it wants. If they are elected, the outcome depends on the ability of the central government to affect the outcome of the election, through endorsement and support of specific candidates. If the center has little control over the outcome, and capture is important, p may be less than one: the local government may be more likely to stay in power if it kills growth than if it fosters it. All it may take is for incumbent firms to be better organized politically than new entrepreneurs. Under these assumptions, the local government chooses growth if $p_y \, a \, y > p_x \, b$, or equivalently if

$$(9.1) \qquad\qquad p \, a \, y > b.$$

The local government is more likely to choose growth, the stronger the stick (the higher p), the bigger the carrot (the higher a), the larger the growth potential (the higher y), and the smaller the benefits of capture or the lower the costs of reining in competition for rents (the lower b). This formula provides a convenient way of organizing the discussion of Russia versus China.

9.2 Growth, Tax Sharing, Political Centralization, and Other Issues

Before proceeding to look at the empirical evidence on the various parameters of the model, one may well want to challenge the assumption that the central government is pro-growth, or at least more pro-growth than local governments. Surely, both China and Russia provide numerous examples where the policies of the central government destroyed the economy. In the context of transition and change, however, the assumption that the central government is less likely to be captured by initial rent holders than local governments seems reasonable. Local governments are smaller relative to state and ex-state firms, more directly affected by the unemployment implications of closing a particular firm, and more likely to respond favorably to requests for transfers or protection. Central governments may be captured, as well, but not necessarily by groups opposed to growth. Capture by the "oligarchs," for example, may well lead to a massive redistribution of wealth in their favor but not necessarily to lower growth.[3]

Much previous research has focused on y. If growth prospects are very good, then letting new firms enter and fostering growth is attractive. The example of Moscow, and of its mayor, Luzhkov, comes to mind here. But if growth prospects are dim anyway, the returns to allowing new business to enter and grow as opposed to protecting the old firms may be low, and y may be small.[4] This is particularly likely if the improvements from pro-growth policies take a long time to materialize, and the incumbent politicians are unlikely to benefit from them.

If y is small, there may be little the center can do to convince local governments to choose growth. Even large values of a and p may not change the inequality.

A number of recent studies have provided some evidence on a, both for Russia and for China. In an econometric study of the fiscal relationships between China's regional and central governments, Jin, Qian, and Weingast (1999) find a high value of marginal a, about 0.8. (In describing the evidence, we need to distinguish between the three levels of government: central, regional, and local.) No corresponding study exists for the relations between China's local and regional governments. Wong (1997) suggests that the nature of the contracts between local and regional governments, and therefore the outcomes, may be similar to those for the relationships between central and regional governments.

In an econometric study of the fiscal relationships between Russia's local and regional governments, Zhuravskaya (2000) finds that marginal a is only about 0.1, giving local governments only weak incentives to increase the tax base. No corresponding study exists for the relationships between Russia's regional and central government. In personal correspondence, however, Treisman reports that estimates of a obtained from regressions with a specification similar to that of Jin, Qian, and Weingast (1999) are not lower for Russia than they are for China.

In sum, the evidence is somewhat murky. At the local level, a might be somewhat higher in China than in Russia. It seems difficult to conclude, however, based on the available evidence, that differences in a are enough to explain the differences in the behavior of local governments in Russia and China.

Turn finally to p, the relative probability of staying in power if pursuing pro-growth policies. In China, the Communist Party has the power to appoint and dismiss governors, and it has exercised this power both to support the governors whose regions have performed well economically and to discipline governors who have followed anti-growth policies (Huang, 2002). Perhaps as an ultimate prize, the governors whose regions perform well have been brought into the national government in Beijing. It is clear that, in China, p is a large number—if the power of the Communist Party is viewed as absolute, then p is close to infinity.

In Russia, governors are now elected, not appointed. The ability of the national government to reward or penalize governors through administrative and electoral support has been limited. For this reason, p in Russia is much lower than in China; it is arguably less than one.

This difference in political control, rather than the difference in revenue sharing arrangements, may therefore be the reason why inequality (9.1) holds for China and not for Russia. For a high enough p, even a low a may sustain pro-growth policies. The Chinese central government has allowed a substantial share of tax revenues, as well as spending responsibilities, to stay with the regions, but, given its power of appointment, it might have gotten away with a lower value of a. For the Russian government, on the other hand, there may have been no value of a that would lead local governments to foster growth. As a result, there may have been little incentive for the central government to maintain a high value of a anyway.

It is interesting to look at the evolution of the relationship between central and regional governments in Russia in the 1990s in the light of this model. In the early 1990s, Russia's central government relied on the use of $a > 1$ for most of the regions. It did this by taxing a few oil-producing regions and by using deficit finance to compensate for the resulting lack of net revenues at the center (Treisman, 1999a). During that period, particularly in 1992–93, Yeltsin also had administrative control over the governors, so p was higher than afterward. As Treisman (1999a) shows, this policy worked tolerably well for a while and bought the center peace with the regions.

In the mid- to late 1990s, that equilibrium fell apart. First, stabilization policies forced the central government to reduce a for most regions, as the central deficit had to be reduced and hence large transfers to the oblasts became unaffordable. Second, political decentralization and party-free gubernatorial elections reduced p significantly. Third, the continued recession reduced at least the expectation of y. In Russia's federal structure today, equation (9.1) fails, in part because a might be low but also, and more importantly, because p is low. To return to Riker (1964), the peripheralized federalism that characterizes Russia today may simply not be sustainable.

Our focus on the role of political parties in Russia achieving—or not achieving—political centralization may be too narrow. In Russia, two forces have become at least partial substitutes. The first is the national media. Media companies in Russia are private and controlled by interests closely tied to political movements, particularly the government and the center–left opposition. The media groups used television and newspapers aggressively to get their preferred candidates elected in the 1996 presidential election (when both supported Yeltsin) and especially in the 1999 Duma elections. The second centralizing force has been the energy monopolies, especially Gazprom and United Energy Systems. The first holds monopoly over the supply of gas in Russia; the second controls the electricity grid. Both companies, while nominally private, have been close to the government. Both have been used by the government to provide cheap energy, as well as energy without payment, to cooperative regions. In this way, both have been used to make the conduct of regional governments more responsive to the needs of the center. How efficient or desirable these substitutes have been, however, is an open question.

9.3 Discussion and Implications

Our analysis has a number of implications for China, for Russia, and for the economic theory of federalism. With respect to China, our analysis implies that, to the extent that federalism has played a helpful role in promoting China's economic growth, such federalism relied crucially on the centralizing role of the Communist Party.[5] If the Communist Party, as it yields power in the future, is not replaced or supplemented by other national parties that influence the appointment or the election prospects of governors, p will fall, leading to greater rent seeking and lower efficiency in its federal arrangements. The message of our analysis for China is clear: the competitive benefits of "market preserving federalism" emphasized by China scholars depend very much on political centralization.

With respect to Russia, our analysis suggests that federalism has failed precisely because of political decentralization. There is no question that carefully designed tax and other fiscal policies can raise a in Russia. These policies would require a clearer division of tax bases between the central and the regional governments, as well as a division of tax collection and spending responsibilities that does not exist today.[6] Nevertheless, given the low level of political centralization, such fiscal measures may not be enough to induce local governments to foster growth.

Will centralization come, and if so what form will it take? In principle, centralization in Russia could come through the creation of national parties that exercise influence over the governors needing their support in elections. Centralization may alternatively take the form of greater administrative control over governors through more aggressive bargaining over issues that bear on their regions and remain under the control of the center, such as the allocation of electricity and gas. Centralization may also involve the suspension of the democratic process. Presumably, a turn to a competitive national party system is more compatible with political freedom than are the alternatives. Yet some form of centralization is probably necessary for the federal equilibrium in Russia to change—for a switch in the sign of inequality (9.1).[7]

From this perspective, Mexico provides a very instructive, though not in every way appealing, example. In the 1920s and 1930s, the Mexican economy presented a far more extreme version of peripheralized federalism than Russia presents today (Diaz-Cayeros, 1997). Following the revolution, the Mexican states were each run by their own dictator, or *cacique*, who controlled the regional sources of military power, collected the regional taxes without remitting them to the center, and erected trade and other barriers against other Mexican states. The result was fiscal disorder and economic stagnation. In 1938, President Calles, with the support of the military, transformed the Partido Revolucionario Institucional (PRI) into a national hegemonic party. He convinced the regional leaders to join the party and to adhere to its national policies with an offer of a carrot and a stick. The carrot was a promise of long, secure, and profitable careers under the protective wing of the PRI, which would gain control over the nomination (and effectively the election) of governors. The stick was a threat of personal violence against the *caciques* who declined to join. Nearly all joined; a few who did not were killed. As part of this deal, the central government obtained full centralized control over tax collection in Mexico, leaving the states to rely on transfers from the center, as well as control over trade and regulatory policies that turned Mexico into a common market. The economic benefits of the 1938 arrangement were large, but they did come with tremendous political centralization. It may have been "market preserving federalism," but the political market was not the one that was preserved.

The last example leads us to the implication of our analysis for federalism in general. This implication is not new, and draws on Riker (1964), yet it has been neglected in the recent discussions of China praising the decentralization benefits of federalism. As best we can tell, the economic benefits of decentralization obtained from federalism rely crucially on some form of political centralization. Without such centralization, the incentives to pursue regionalist policies are too high, and cannot be eliminated solely through clever economic and fiscal arrangements. It is possible that a federal country can "muddle through" without political centralization, as Russia has done in the 1990s and Brazil and India have done for longer, but some political system of aligning the interests of national and regional politicians is needed to get beyond "muddling through."

— 10 —

A Normal Country

10.1 Introduction

During the 1990s, Russia underwent extraordinary transformations. It changed from a communist dictatorship into a multiparty democracy in which officials are chosen in regular elections. Its centrally planned economy was reshaped into a capitalist order based on markets and private property. Its army withdrew peacefully from Eastern Europe and the former Soviet republics, allowing the latter to become independent countries. Twenty years ago, only the most naïve idealist could have imagined such a metamorphosis.

Yet the mood among Western observers has been anything but celebratory. By the turn of the century, Russia had come to be viewed as a disastrous failure and the 1990s as a decade of catastrophe for its people. Journalists, politicians, and academic experts typically describe Russia not as a middle-income country struggling to overcome its communist past and find its place in the world, but as a collapsed and criminal state.

In Washington, both left and right have converged on this view. To Dick Armey, then Republican House majority leader, Russia had by 1999 become "a looted and bankrupt zone of nuclearized anarchy" (Schmitt, 1999, p. A12). To his colleague, Banking Committee Chairman James Leach (1999a, 1999b), Russia was "the world's most virulent kleptocracy," more corrupt than even Mobutu's Zaire. Bernard Sanders (1998), the socialist congressman from Vermont, described Russia's economic per-

By Andrei Shleifer and Daniel Treisman; forthcoming in *Journal of Economic Perspectives*, 19 (2005).

formance in the 1990s as a "tragedy of historic proportions"; liberal reforms had produced only "economic collapse," "mass unemployment," and "grinding poverty."

More recently, a glimmer of optimism returned. President Bush, in late 2003, praised President Putin's efforts to make Russia into a "country in which democracy and freedom and the rule of law thrive" (U.S. Department of State, 2003). But the happy talk did not last long. When Russian prosecutors arrested the oil tycoon Mikhail Khodorkovsky in October 2003, the *New York Times* columnist William Safire (2003b) reported that Russia was now ruled by a "power-hungry mafia" of former KGB and military officers, who had grabbed "the nation by the throat." When the pro-Putin United Russia Party was announced to have won more than 37 percent of the vote in the December 2003 parliamentary election, Safire (2003a) lamented the return of "one-party rule to Russia," and declared the country's experiment with democracy "all but dead."

Are conditions in contemporary Russia as bad as the critics contend? In this chapter, we examine the country's recent economic and political performance, using a variety of data on growth, macroeconomic stability, income inequality, and company finances, as well as reports of election monitors and surveys of business people and crime victims. We find a large gap between the common perception and the facts. After reviewing the evidence, the widespread image of Russia as a uniquely menacing disaster zone comes to seem like the reflection in a distorting mirror—the features are recognizable, but stretched and twisted out of proportion.

In fact, although Russia's transition has been painful in many ways and its economic and political systems remain far from perfect, the country has made remarkable economic and social progress. Russia's remaining defects are typical of countries at its level of economic development. Both in 1990 and 2003, Russia was a middle-income country, with gross domestic product (GDP) per capita around $8,000 at purchasing power parity, according to the UN International Comparison Project—a level comparable to that of Argentina in 1991 and Mexico in 1999. Countries in this income range have democracies that are rough around the edges, if they are democratic at all. Their governments suffer from corruption, and their press is almost never entirely free. Most also have high income inequality, concentrated corporate ownership, and turbulent macroeconomic performance. In all these regards, Russia is quite normal. Nor are the common flaws of middle-income, capitalist democracies incompatible with further economic and political progress.

To say that Russia has become a "normal" middle-income country is not to overlook the messiness of its politics and economics or to excuse the failures of its leaders. Most middle-income countries are not secure or socially just places to live. Nor are all middle-income countries alike. None of the others has Russia's nuclear arms or its pivotal role in international affairs. Yet other countries around Russia's level of income—from Mexico and Brazil to Malaysia and Croatia—face a common set of economic problems and political challenges, from similarly precarious vantage points. Russia's struggles to meet such challenges closely resemble those of its peers.

10.2 Economic Cataclysm?

10.2.1 The Output "Collapse"

Russia started its transition in the early 1990s as a middle-income country. The United Nations International Comparison Project, which calculates cross-nationally comparable income figures, estimates that Russia's per capita GDP as of 1989 was $8,210—around the level of Ukraine, Argentina, Latvia, and South Africa. (By 1991, when Gorbachev left office, it had fallen to $7,780.) This level was higher than Mexico and Brazil, but only about 65–75 percent of that in poorer west European countries such as Portugal, Greece, and Spain; less than half the level of France or Italy; and just over one-third that of the United States.

That Russia's output contracted catastrophically in the 1990s has become a cliché. According to Russia's official statistical agency, Goskomstat, Russian GDP per capita fell about 39 percent in real terms between 1991, when Gorbachev left office, and 1998, when the economic recovery started.[1]

Yet there are three reasons to think that Russia's economic performance in the 1990s was actually far better. First, official statistics greatly exaggerate the true value of Russia's output at the beginning of the decade. Much of recorded GDP under the Soviet Union consisted of military goods, unfinished construction projects, and shoddy consumer products for which there was no demand. In the early 1990s, military procurement dropped sharply. With the introduction of markets, firms also stopped making consumer goods they could not sell. Cutting such production reduces reported economic output, but does not leave consumers any worse off. Moreover, much of reported output under the Soviet system was simply fictitious. To obtain bonuses, managers routinely inflated their production figures. With the end of central planning, managers now wished to under-report output so as to reduce their tax bill. Consequently, Russia's economic decline was probably smaller than officially reported (Aslund, 2001).[2]

Second, Russia's unofficial economy grew rapidly in the 1990s. Estimating unofficial activity is difficult. But one common technique for measuring the growth of the whole economy—both official and unofficial—is to use electricity consumption, on the theory that even underground firms must use electricity (see Chapter 7). Figure 10.1 shows the trend in reported GDP, deflated for price rises, between 1990 and 2002, alongside figures for electricity consumption. While official GDP fell 26 percent in this period, electricity consumption fell only 18 percent. This suggests that Russia's output decline in the 1990s was not as sharp as the official statistics indicate. Since under market conditions firms are likely to use electricity more rationally, even the observed decline in electricity consumption may overstate the output drop.[3]

Third, other statistics suggest that average living standards fell little during the decade, and, in some important respects, improved. Retail trade (in constant prices) rose 16 percent between 1990 and 2002, as shown in Figure 10.1. Goskomstat's figures for final consumption of households (in constant prices) rose by about 3 percent during 1990–2002. Average living space increased from 16 square meters per person in 1990 to 19 in 2000, and the share of this living space owned by citizens doubled during the decade, from 26 to 58 percent (Goskomstat Rossii, 2001, p. 200). The number of Russians traveling abroad as tourists rose from 1.6 million in 1993 to 4.3 million in 2000. The shares of households with radios, televisions, tape recorders, refrigerators, washing machines, and electric vacuum cleaners all increased between 1991 and 2000. Private ownership of cars doubled, rising from 14 cars per 100 households in 1991 to 27 in 2000, with large increases occuring in almost all regions (Goskomstat Rossii, 2001, pp. 193–194). At the same time, however, con-

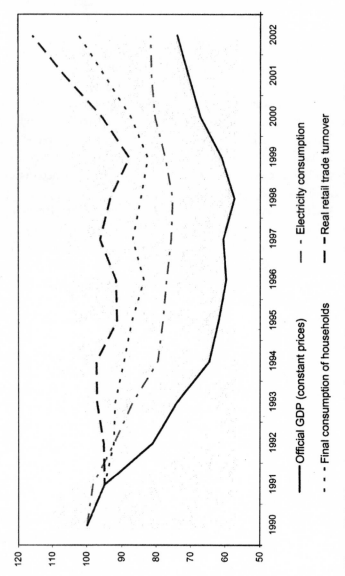

Figure 10.1 Measuring economic change in Russia, 1990–2002. *Sources:* Goskomstat Rossii (Moscow, Russia), *Rossiiskiy Statisticheskiy Yezhegodnik 2001, 2003; Rossia v Tsifrakh 2002;* Goskomstat updates.

sumption of some previously state-provided or state-subsidized services—trips to the movies, theaters, museums, and state-subsidized summer camps for children—fell.

Russia has, without doubt, experienced an increase in inequality (as we discuss below). But some indicators also suggest improvement toward the bottom of the social pyramid. Since 1993 (when comprehensive figures begin), the proportion of Russia's housing with running water has increased from 66 to 73 percent; the share with hot water grew from 51 to 59 percent; and the percentage with central heating rose from 64 to 73 percent. Since 1990, the proportion of apartments with telephones has increased from 30 to 49 percent (Goskomstat Rossii, 2001, pp. 201, 468).

One indicator often taken as evidence of a catastrophic decline in living standards is the sharp drop in Russian life expectancy in the 1990s. Between 1990 and 2000, average life expectancy fell by about four years, from 69.2 to 65.3. However, this does not seem to be related to increased poverty, malnutrition, or poorer access to healthcare. If poverty were to blame, one might expect the death rate to rise most among the most economically vulnerable groups. In the early 1990s, the poverty rate was highest among children aged 7 to 15; among adults it was higher among women than men. But there was practically no increase in mortality among children of any age, and the death rate jumped much more for men than for women (Goskomstat Rossii, 2001, p. 126). Higher mortality is also hard to link to malnutrition. In 1992–93, as the death rate jumped sharply, the Russian Longitudinal Monitoring Survey found no evidence of serious malnutrition in Russia. In fact, the proportion of people whose body weight increased during these years exceeded the share that lost weight (Shkolnikov et al., 1998). As for access to health care, the percentage of adults getting required checkups fell slightly, from 89 percent in 1990 to 86 percent in 1992, before rising to 91 percent in 2000 (Goskomstat Rossii, 2001, p. 246). The state's fiscal crisis did reduce resources of the health system in some ways. But in other ways, resources increased. The number of doctors per capita, already one of the highest in the world, rose still higher in the 1990s (Goskomstat Rossii, 2001, p. 242). Infant mortality—one indicator of the effectiveness of basic health care—although rising a little initially, fell during the decade, from 17.4 per 1,000 live births in 1990 to 15.3 in 2000 (Goskomstat Rossii, 2001, p. 127).

Most specialists agree that the rise in mortality in the early 1990s, concentrated as it was among middle-aged men, had much to do with increasing alcohol abuse (DaVanzo and Grammich, 2001; Shkolnikov et al., 1998). This may have been stimulated by a sharp drop in the relative price of vodka in these years. For the average monthly income, Russians could buy 10 liters of vodka in 1990 but 47 in 1994.[4] Several causes of death that increased dramatically have been associated with binge drinking (Shkolnikov et al., 1998). Stress induced by the economic transition may also have contributed (Brainerd and Cutler, 2005). Either way, there is little sign the increased death rate was caused by falling income. As per capita GDP rose by about 30 percent between 1998 and 2002, life expectancy again dropped by 2.2 years.

A close look at Figure 10.1 also casts doubt on the popular theory that Russia's economic decline was caused by misguided government policies pursued in the 1990s, especially Yeltsin's privatization program and his "loans-for-shares" scheme (Goldman, 2003). As Figure 10.1 makes clear, most of the fall in both Russia's official GDP and electricity consumption occurred prior to 1994, before the significant part of the mass privatization program was completed, and before the "loans-for-shares" program was even contemplated.

Comparing Russia's economic performance in the 1990s to that of other postcommunist countries suggests two additional points, illustrated in Figure 10.2. First, officially measured output fell in all the postcommunist economies of Eastern Europe and the former Soviet Union (FSU), with no exceptions. It declined in new democracies, such as Russia and Poland; in continuing dictatorships, such as Belarus and Tajikistan; in rapid reformers, such as the Czech Republic and Hungary; and in very slow reformers, such as Ukraine and Uzbekistan. The universality of the contraction suggests common causes. One possibility is a universal decrease in military and economically useless activities that were previously counted as output. A second is the temporary dislocation that all countries experienced as their planning systems disintegrated (Blanchard and Kremer, 1997; see also Chapter 2). Consistent with both these explanations, officially measured output began to recover after a few years almost everywhere. Second, the depth of the measured contraction was greater in some countries than in others. Generally, it was smaller in Eastern Europe and the Baltic states than in the rest of the FSU. Russia's official output fell slightly less than average for the 14 former Soviet republics for which figures are available.[5]

The patterns of decline in the postcommunist countries challenge another common theory about the output contraction. Some argue that excessive speed of reform exacerbated the decline, and compare the "gradualism" of China's economic policies favorably to the "shock therapy" of Russia's. In fact, among the East European and former Soviet countries, there is no obvious relationship between speed of reform and change in official output. Comparisons across these countries must be tentative since the quality of statistics varies, and the uneven impact of civil disorder and war complicates drawing connections between economic policy and performance. However, among the countries that contracted least according to the official figures are both rapid reformers (Estonia, Poland, Czech Republic) and slow or nonreformers (Belarus, Uzbekistan). Those with the largest declines also include both nonreformers (Tajikistan, Turkmenistan) and some that tried to reform (Moldova). A comparison of Russia with Ukraine is particularly instructive (see Figure 10.2). Ukraine had a large population (about 52 million), an industrial economy, significant natural resources, and a "culture" similar to Russia's prior to transition. Unlike Russia, it retained the old communist leadership, albeit renamed, and pursued more cautious reforms, keeping a much larger share of the economy in state hands. Yet Ukraine's official drop in per capita GDP of 45 percent between 1991 and 2001 was almost twice as large as Russia's.

In comparison with other nations of Eastern Europe and the FSU, Russia's economy performed roughly as one might have expected. Our best estimate is that its genuine output drop between 1990 and 2001 was small, and probably completely reversed by 2003 (Aslund, 2003). Considering the distorted demand, inflated accounting, and uselessness of much of the pre-reform output, Russians today are probably on average better off than they were in 1990.

10.2.2 Financial Crises

The 1990s was a decade of extreme macroeconomic turbulence for Russia. Between December 1991 and December 2001, the ruble's value dropped by more than 99 percent against the dollar. Three years after the authorities managed to stabilize inflation in 1995, a financial crisis led to a devaluation of the ruble and a government moratorium on foreign debt payments.

But such financial crises are common among emerging market economies. As bad as the 99 percent drop in the ruble's value sounds, an

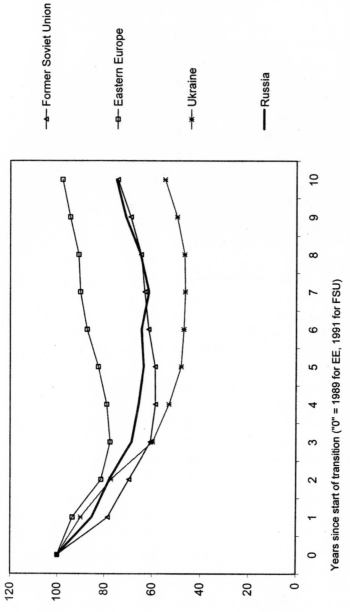

Former Soviet Union

Eastern Europe

Ukraine

Russia

120

100

80

60

40

20

0

0　1　2　3　4　5　6　7　8　9　10

Years since start of transition ("0" = 1989 for EE, 1991 for FSU)

Figure 10.2 Official GDP per capita (at constant prices) in postcommunist countries, first 10 years of transition. Eastern Europe: unweighted average of Albania, Bulgaria, Hungary, Poland, Romania, Slovakia, and Slovenia. Former Soviet Union: unweighted average of Armenia, Belarus, Estonia, Georgia, Kazakhstan, Kyrgyzstan, Latvia, Lithuania, Moldova, Russia, Tajikistan, Turkmenistan, Ukraine, and Uzbekistan. Data unavailable for Azerbaijan. *Sources:* calculated from EBRD, 1997 and World Bank, *World Development Indicators* (Washington, DC: World Bank, 2003).

examination of the IMF's International Financial Statistics (April 2002) shows that 11 other countries—including Brazil, Turkey, Ukraine, and Belarus—suffered even larger currency declines during the 1990s. In the 1980s, depreciations this large were even more frequent, with larger ones recorded by Peru, Argentina, Bolivia, Brazil, Uruguay, Nicaragua, Vietnam, Lebanon, and even Poland, later seen as the greatest success story of transition from socialism.

During Russia's 1998 crisis, the ruble fell 61 percent in the months of August and September. But during the decade from January 1992 to December 2001, two-month currency collapses at least this large occurred 34 times, in a total of 20 countries. Russia's crash in 1998 was not an isolated phenomenon: it came in the middle of a wave of similar currency crises that stretched from Thailand and Indonesia to Brazil and Turkey. Moreover, the consequences of Russia's 1998 financial crisis were far less dire than claimed at the time. The devaluation was followed by a multiyear spurt of rapid growth and a reinvigorated drive toward liberal economic reform.

10.2.3 Economic Inequality

Russia's economic reforms are said to have exacerbated economic inequality, with privatization often fingered as the primary culprit. The European Bank for Reconstruction and Development (EBRD, 1999, p. 110) wrote: "[U]nder the 'shares-for-loans' scheme implemented in 1995, many of the key resource-based companies fell into the hands of a small group of financiers, the so-called 'oligarchs'. This has led to very sharp increases in wealth and income inequality—by 1997 the Gini coefficient for income in Russia was around 0.5."[6]

Inequality has increased sharply in Russia since the fall of communism. There is some question about the precise numbers, but no dispute about the trend. Goskomstat (2001, p. 187) shows the Gini coefficient for money incomes rising from .26 in 1991 to .41 in 1994, after which it stabilized at about .40 through the end of the decade.[7] The World Bank, in various issues of the annual *World Development Reports* and *World Development Indicators*, gives figures for Russia's Gini for expenditure of .496 in 1993, .480 in 1996, .487 in 1998, and .460 in 2000. For comparison, the Goskomstat figure of .41 is almost exactly the same as that for the United States (.408 in 1997). The higher World Bank estimate of .496 is about the same as that of Malaysia (.492) or the Philippines (.462), but below that of Hong Kong (.522), Mexico (.531), South Africa (.593), or Brazil (.607).

The trouble with the claim that privatization caused inequality is that inequality came first. Russia's Gini coefficient rose sharply between 1991 and 1993 and peaked in 1994, before any effects of privatization could possibly materialize. Nor is unemployment responsible. In 1992–93, unemployment remained below 6 percent. It was in 1994–98 that it grew to 13.2 percent, while inequality declined slightly (Goskomstat Rossii, 2001, p. 133). The growth of entrepreneurial income also played at most a limited role. Branko Milanovic (1998, p. 22) of the World Bank finds that 77 percent of the inequality increase can be attributed to growing dispersion of wage incomes. Although some Russians worked in successful firms that rapidly benefited from free prices and open trade, others remained in declining firms and in the state sector. Unfortunate as the growth of inequality has been, it is largely the result of the upheavals associated with rationalizing economic activity.

10.2.4 Oligarchical Capitalism

Russia's economic reforms are often said to have fueled the rise of a small class of "oligarchs" who stand accused of stripping assets from the companies they acquired. This, in turn, is said to have depressed investment and economic growth (Hoff and Stiglitz, 2002; Stiglitz, 2002).

Russia's big business is certainly dominated by a few tycoons. However, in this Russia is quite typical. In almost all developing capitalist economies and even in most developed countries, the largest firms are either state or family controlled, with a few dominant families often controlling a large share of national production through financial and industrial groups (Claessens, Djankov, and Lang, 1999; La Porta, Lopez-de-Silanes, and Shleifer, 1999). This is overwhelmingly true of middle-income countries, such as Mexico, Brazil, South Korea, Malaysia, or South Africa, but it also applies to developed countries such as Italy, Singapore, and Sweden. The big business families are inevitably politically connected, sometimes receiving loans and subsidies from the government (as in South Korea and Italy), often actively participating in privatization (as in Mexico and Brazil), and quite regularly holding high government offices while retaining a connection to their firms (as in Italy and Malaysia) (Faccio, 2003). Following the Asian financial crisis of 1998, this system of political ownership and control has been pejoratively rechristened "crony capitalism," even though it has been associated with some of the most rapid growth ever seen, as well as a remarkable recovery from crisis in Malaysia and South Korea. Such patterns of ownership have also emerged in transition economies from Latvia to the Central Asian states.

Have Russia's oligarchs depressed economic performance? Russia's tycoons, like those elsewhere in the developing world (not to mention America's robber barons of the nineteenth century), grew rich in part through deals with the government. But the claim that this accounts for poor growth in Russia makes little sense. Russia's sharp decline in official output came before—not after—the oligarchs emerged on the scene in 1995–96. A few years of stagnation followed, and then rapid growth. Oligarch-controlled companies have performed extremely well, and far better than many comparable companies that remained controlled by the state or by their Soviet-era managers. They are responsible for much of the dramatic increase in output in recent years, as well as the amazing stock market boom.

Consider three of the most notorious cases. In "loans-for-shares," Mikhail Khodorkovsky (now in jail) obtained a major stake in the oil company Yukos. Boris Berezovsky (now in exile) won control of the oil company Sibneft along with his then-partner Roman Abramovich. Vladimir Potanin acquired the nickel producer Norilsk Nickel. Between 1996 and 2001, the reported pretax profits of Yukos, Sibneft, and Norilsk Nickel rose in real terms by 36, 10, and 5 times, respectively.[8] Their stock market valuations also soared (those of Yukos and Sibneft rising by more than 30 times in real terms). This performance is markedly better than that of the gas monopoly Gazprom or the electricity utility UES, which stayed under state control, or of major private companies, such as Lukoil, that remained controlled by pre-privatization management (Boone and Rodionov, 2001).

Have the oligarchs stripped assets from the companies they acquired in privatization? The audited financial statements of these companies suggest they actually invested, especially since 1998. Yukos' assets rose from $5.3 billion in 1998 to $14.4 billion in 2002, although this might reflect in part higher world oil prices (see Table 10.1). Norilsk Nickel's assets rose from $6.6 billion in 1999 to $9.7 billion in 2002. Sibneft's assets did fall from 1996 to 1999, in part due to an accounting change (which might reflect asset stripping). But since 1999, they have increased from $4.3

Table 10.1 Total assets and investment of three leading Russian companies

	1996	1997	1998	1999	2000	2001	2002
Yukos							
total assets, bn US $	4.7	5.2	5.3	6.0	10.3	10.5[e]	14.4[e]
Investment,[a] mn US $				226	589[e]	954[e]	1263[e]
Sibneft							
total assets, bn US $	7.6	5.6[d]	5.0	4.3	4.6	5.7	7.5
Investment,[b] mn US $			154	129	231	619	959
Norilsk Nickel							
total assets, bn US $				6.6	7.2	10.9[c]	9.7
Investment,[b] mn US $				168	638	510[c]	351

a. Additions to property, plant, and equipment.
b. Capital expenditures.
c. Restated in 2002 Annual Report.
d. Book assets reduced by $1.3 bn because of accounting change.
e. As in 2002 Annual Report.
Sources: Audited financial statements and annual reports.

billion to $7.5 billion in 2002. Recently, the major oligarchs have been investing hundreds of millions of dollars annually in their companies. In 2002, Yukos invested $1.26 billion in property, plant, and equipment, and Sibneft made capital expenditures of $959 million. Guriev and Rachinsky (2004), in a systematic study of the performance of oligarch-controlled companies in 2001, found that such companies invested significantly more that year than firms controlled by other Russian owners.

In contrast, the greatest asset stripping scandals have concerned companies that remained under state control. Gazprom's former management has been accused of stealing assets via complicated networks of trading companies. The state-owned airline Aeroflot's reported assets dropped between 1998 and 2001. By and large, the companies privatized to the oligarchs performed far better than those left under state control. That the leading oligarch-controlled oil companies generally outperformed other oil firms such as Lukoil, which remained under Soviet-era management, suggests that their success was due to better management and not only to rising oil prices.

None of this is to say the oligarchs are public spirited, politically naïve, or protective of their minority shareholders. They benefited from sweetheart deals with the government and massively diluted the value of minority shares in order to consolidate their control. Investor protection and corporate governance in Russia remain weak. But here again, Russia is typical of middle-income developing countries, where expropriation of minority shareholders is nearly universal (Johnson et al., 2000).

In fact, the claim that the oligarchs privatized companies in order to strip their assets and are impeding economic growth has it precisely backward. The oligarchs stripped assets from state-controlled companies in order to buy others in privatization. Indeed, the concern with such theft from state firms was one of the reasons to accelerate privatization in 1992. The oligarchs also tried to buy assets in privatization at the lowest possible prices, often offering politicians various deals. Once in control, they attempted to increase their ownership stakes, both legally and illegally. But once oligarchs became full owners, they acted as economic theory predicts: they invested to improve their companies' performance. This is what oligarchs have done in every other country—from J. P. Morgan and John D. Rockefeller to Silvio Berlusconi and the owners of Korean chaebol.

In sum, Russia's economy is not a model of capitalism that one finds in introductory textbooks. Like other middle-income countries, Russia suffers from inequality, financial crises, and a large unofficial sector. Economic and political power are intimately intertwined. Nonetheless, Russia started the 1990s a disintegrating, centrally planned economy, and ended it a market system in a burst of rapid growth.

10.3 Autocratic Kleptocracy?

10.3.1 Democracy

Western evaluations of Russia's political institutions in the last 10 years have often been scathing. Even before Putin's recent consolidation of power, the *Economist* magazine declared the country's democracy to be "phony" (June 24, 2000, p. 20). The advocacy group Freedom House, which rates countries' institutions, has since 2000 given Russia a 5 for political freedom and a 5 for civil liberties on a seven-point scale that ranges from 1 (highest) to 7 (lowest). This puts Russia's political regime below Brazil's military junta of the late 1970s, and its civil liberties below those of Nigeria in 1991 under the dictatorship of Major General Ibrahim Babangida. (According to Freedom House's own report, in Nigeria at this time military tribunals were charged with trying cases of sedition and the regime had made a practice of incarcerating "innocent relatives of suspected political offenders to draw the suspects out of hiding" (Gastil, 1992, p. 353). Even Kuwait—a hereditary emirate where political parties are illegal, women cannot vote in legislative elections, and criticism of the emir is punishable by imprisonment—gets a better rating for political freedom than Russia.

Critics of Russia's democracy focus on several points. Those in power are accused of manipulating elections through control of the state media, harassment or censorship of the independent press, and use of judicial and administrative levers to intimidate or incapacitate rivals. Voters are portrayed as apathetic and gullible. At the same time, big business is seen as subverting the democratic process through financial support of favored candidates. The combination of voter apathy and official manipulation means, in the grim but quite representative view of one *New York Times* reporter, that in Russia during the last decade "there has been no truly democratic choice of new leaders" (Myers, 2003, pp. 1, 5).

Just how bad is Russia's democracy? Russia's political institutions and civic freedoms are certainly imperfect in many ways. Relative to that under Yeltsin, the situation under President Putin has deteriorated considerably. However, Western condemnations of Russia's institutions in the last 10 years have been grossly overblown. Russia's politics have been among the most democratic in the region. The defects of the country's democracy resemble those found in many other middle-income countries.

Eight national ballots—four parliamentary and four presidential—took place in Russia between 1991 and 2004. A variety of candidates ran in each, representing all parts of the political spectrum. With few exceptions, parties and electoral blocs were free to organize, and a large number managed to register. International observers, although critical of imbalance in media coverage and episodic improprieties, have generally given these elections high marks. The Organization for Security and Cooperation in Europe (OSCE), a regional security organization headquartered in Austria with 55 member nations, regularly monitors elections in Russia and other countries. Its report on the 1999 Russian Duma election, for instance, praised the country's electoral laws for providing "a sound basis for the conduct of orderly, pluralistic and accountable elections" and the vote-counting procedures for "transparency, accountability and accuracy that fully met accepted international standards." The OSCE's predecessor organization, the Conference for Security and Cooperation in Europe, reported after the 1993 election that voters had been able to "express their political will freely and fairly" and called the 1995 election "free and fair."[9]

Does such language merely reflect a reluctance to criticize? Such fears are belied by the OSCE's blunt condemnations of elections in other nearby countries, such as Azerbaijan in 2000 ("primitive falsification"), Georgia in 2000 ("ballot stuffing and protocol tampering" that "has discredited Georgia's democratization"), and Ukraine in 1999 ("flagrant violations of voting procedures" and a "widespread, systematic, and coordinated campaign by state institutions at all levels to unduly influence voters"). The OSCE expressed stronger reservations about Russia's 2003 parliamentary and its 2004 presidential elections, complaining of bias in the state-controlled media and abuses by some local officials, although it still praised the Central Election Commission for its "professional" organization of the elections.

As for voter apathy, turnout in Russian elections since 1991 never dipped below about 54 percent and rose as high as 75 percent in 1991, compared to about 50–51 percent of the voting-age population in recent U.S. national elections. In all Russian national elections since 1993, voters had the option to vote "against all" candidates. The number doing so has never exceeded 5 percent.

In a phony democracy, one expects reported election results to match the desires of incumbents, but in Russia, at least before Putin's presidency, the results often shocked political elites. In 1991, an outsider candidate, Boris Yeltsin, beat the favorites of Gorbachev and the Soviet Communist leadership to win the Russian presidency with 57 percent of the vote. In 1993, elites were horrified by the high showing of Vladimir Zhirinovsky and his clownish ultranationalists. In 1995, the Communist Party surprised observers by coming first in the party list vote, with 22 percent, a feat it repeated in 1999, when it won 24 percent. The main party associated with the incumbent regime won only about 15 percent in 1993 and 10 percent in 1995.

Some falsification and improprieties have definitely occurred. In regional elections, Russian officials have used technicalities to disqualify candidates, and incumbents at all levels have misused state resources to campaign for reelection. Limits on campaign spending have been breached. However, such problems do not appear to go beyond the violations common in middle-income democracies like Mexico or Brazil, where stories of coercion, intimidation, and vote-buying also abound.[10]

Many have attacked Russia's "super-presidentialist" constitution, which was drafted by presidential appointees and endorsed by a 1993 referendum in which the turnout figures have been questioned. While this constitution clearly tilts the balance of power in favor of the executive, it hardly renders Russia's system undemocratic. For example, the Russian constitution allows the president to issue decrees on matters on which the laws are silent. But these decrees can be overruled by the Duma (albeit with a two-thirds majority) or ruled unconstitutional by the Constitutional Court. In this regard, Russia is not very different from the presidential democracies of Argentina and Brazil.

In the last few years, President Putin has stepped up efforts to scare off potential political rivals. The arrest of Mikhail Khodorkovsky was widely believed to be designed to punish the oil tycoon for funding liberal political parties. The October 2003 and August 2004 presidential elections in Chechnya, both of which brought to power the Kremlin's current favorite, had all the credibility of ballots held in the shadow of a tank. The December 2003 parliamentary election clearly saw official pressures on the media, biased coverage, and harassment of rival campaigns, though at rates comparable to those in previous Russian elections and in other middle-income democracies. That these practices swayed the voters more than in previous elections seems unlikely. Some viewed the high reported vote share for the pro-Putin United Russia Party as prima facie evidence of falsification. In fact, the vote share for this party, 37 percent, was almost exactly the total won in 1999 by the two blocs—Unity and Fatherland–All Russia—that had later joined together to form United Russia. Although ballot-stuffing in some regions may have shaded the vote by a few percentage points, the official results were mostly close to those found by independent exit polls. Given that real incomes of the population had grown by an average of 10 percent a year after Putin took over, it would be surprising if pro-Putin parties were not popular.

From Malaysia to Venezuela to Argentina, political rivals of incumbent politicians in middle-income countries have ended up in jail in recent years, victims of dubious or at least selective prosecutions. In Mexico, such rivals have been assassinated. In disputed territories from Chiapas to Eastern Turkey and Mindanao, elections have been held under the alert watch of the military. Russia's record on democratic practices is unenviable, and has shifted recently toward the illiberal end of the spectrum, but it is not unusual.

10.3.2 Freedom of the Press

Russia's press has come in for particularly harsh scrutiny. Freedom House rates the level of "political pressures, controls, and violence" against the media in countries around the world. In its 2002 ratings, Russia scored a 30 on a scale that runs from 0 (best) to 40 (worst), putting it below Iran (Sussman and Karlekar, 2002, pp. 43, 32). Iran, as the report itself pointed out, had imprisoned more journalists than any other country. It had banned 40 newspapers since April 2000 and had sentenced journalists to long prison terms, along with floggings of 30–50 lashes and prohibitions from practicing journalism for years.

Critics of Russia's press environment make two points. In the 1990s, some complained that major television stations and newspapers were controlled by oligarchs, who used them to further favored political or business goals. More recently, critics have focused on the state's efforts to harass and intimidate independent journalists and to close down oligarch-owned media, often on financial pretexts. Although the criticisms are not altogether consistent, they both have some validity. However, in these regards, Russia again fits the norm for developing—and some developed—states. Djankov et al. (2003) surveyed media ownership in 97 countries. They found that 92 percent of the largest television stations, radio stations, and newspapers in these countries were owned by either families or the state. This pattern was common to just about every country studied—from Brazil, Mexico, Argentina, and South Korea to Italy, Singapore, and Australia. On average, families controlled 57 percent of newspapers and 34 percent of television stations. By this standard, Russia—along with its postcommunist peers—stands out among middle-income democracies for the relatively large share of television stations and major newspapers owned by the government.

Press barons throughout the developing world slant the political coverage on their networks to help favored candidates. In many middle-income countries like Argentina and Colombia (Waisbord, 2000) or South Korea (Park, Kim, and Sohn, 2000), journalists and their bosses are accused of biasing their reports in return for bribes of cash, "entertainment," and favors in the privatization of media outlets. In Mexico payoffs to political reporters, often equal to about three months salary, go by the name of *chayotes* "after a small and tasty squash that fits in the palm of the hand" (Weiner, 2000, p. 12). Even in rich countries like Italy and the United States, journalists shape their broadcasts to further the political agendas of media tycoons such as Silvio Berlusconi and Rupert Murdoch.[11]

What about state harassment of the press? A single case of repression is already one too many. But state interference with news organizations is, sadly, almost universal among middle-income countries, and occurs even in some highly developed ones. The International Press Institute in Vienna collects figures on various kinds of state interference with journalism in the countries of the OSCE, and has published these for the 1999–2000 period. Of the 48 countries monitored, 26 had at least one incident in which media were censored or journalists were imprisoned or sentenced to "excessive" fines. In comparing the severity of such repression across countries, one possibility is to compare the total number of incidents in different countries. Within the OSCE, the total ranged from zero (for many countries) to 121 (for Turkey). On this measure, Russia looks relatively bad, coming in second place with 30 incidents during the two years.

However, to compare the absolute number of newspaper closures in a country with hundreds of daily newspapers (like Russia) to the number in a country with just three newspapers (like Macedonia) seems questionable. An alternative approach is to deflate the number of incidents of state interference by the number of media outlets. We could not find cross-national data on the number of television and radio stations, but UNESCO publishes estimates of the number of daily newspapers in countries around the world. Russia, as of the mid-1990s, had 285 (plus about 4,600 non-daily newspapers). Table 10.2 shows the number of cases of state censorship, imprisonment of journalists, and suppression of journalists "by law" per daily newspaper in the OSCE countries.[12] Of course, these measures are imperfect. If journalists are effectively intimidated, then a repressive state may not need to intervene to silence criticism, and its interventions may go unreported if it does. Dividing by the number of newspapers is a rough-and-ready adjustment—although likely to be less misleading than the raw numbers. By the deflated number, Russia's record of state interference with press freedom is only a little worse than

Table 10.2 Cases of state censorship, "suppression by law," and imprisonment of journalists in OSCE countries, 1999–2000

Absolute number		Per daily newspaper	
Turkey	121	Uzbekistan	3.33
Russian Federation	**30**	Azerbaijan	2.33
Azerbaijan	14	Turkey	2.12
Kazakhstan	10	Bosnia	2.00
Uzbekistan	10	Kyrgyzstan	1.67
Belarus	9	Belarus	1.13
Ukraine	8	Cyprus	0.67
Hungary	7	Macedonia TFYR	0.33
Bosnia	6	Armenia	0.27
Cyprus	6	Croatia	0.20
Kyrgyzstan	5	Ukraine	0.18
United Kingdom	5	Austria	0.18
Armenia	3	Hungary	0.18
Austria	3	Estonia	0.13
Greece	3	Lithuania	0.11
Croatia	2	**Russian Federation**	**0.11**
Czech Republic	2	Czech Republic	0.10
Estonia	2	Slovakia	0.05
Italy	2	United Kingdom	0.05
Lithuania	2	Netherlands	0.03
Germany	1	Italy	0.03
Macedonia TFYR	1	Greece	0.02
Netherlands	1	24 countries with zero:	
Slovakia	1	Albania, Belgium, Bulgaria, Canada,	
Turkmenistan	1	Denmark, Finland, France,	
United States	1	Germany, Iceland, Ireland, Latvia,	

23 countries with zero:
Albania, Belgium, Bulgaria,
Canada, Denmark, Finland,
France, Georgia, Iceland, Ireland,
Latvia, Luxembourg, Malta,
Moldova, Norway, Poland,
Portugal, Romania, Slovenia,
Spain, Sweden, Switzerland, and
Tajikistan.

Luxembourg, Malta, Moldova,
Norway, Poland, Portugal,
Romania, Slovenia, Spain, Sweden,
Switzerland, Tajikistan, and United
States.

Source: Data from International Press Institute and UNESCO.

average. Fifteen OSCE countries had poorer records in these years, including Ukraine, Belarus, Turkey, Cyprus, and even Austria.

Russia's problems with press freedom, although more widely reported in the West, are not very different from those in various other middle-income countries. In 2000–2001, Putin's government hounded the tycoons Berezovsky and Gusinsky out of the media business. At the same time, a strikingly similar campaign was unfolding in South Korea. In what was widely perceived as a politicized effort by President Kim Dae-jung to punish newspapers critical of his government, the Korean National Tax Service and Fair Trade Commission investigated 23 media companies and assessed them with multimillion-dollar fines. Prosecutors arrested executives from the three conservative newspapers most critical of President Kim and held them in solitary confinement. Kim's aide, Roh Moo-hyun, who later replaced him as president, reportedly said that the newspapers were "no different from organized crime" and told reporters he planned to nationalize them.

Since Putin's rise to power, criticism of the president on Russian national television has been effectively suppressed. This contrasts with major daily newspapers such as *Izvestia, Kommersant,* and *Nezavisimaya Gazeta,* in which criticism of Putin remains frequent and bitter. (Skeptics often note that these newspapers have relatively small readerships, but this is like saying the U.S. press is not free because only a fraction of citizens choose to subscribe to the *Washington Post* or the *New York Times.*) Despite national television's timid approach to political commentary, to compare such stations to their Soviet era counterparts—as some now do—is to distort reality. In fact, they provide far more information to viewers and fewer ideologically motivated lies. The difference is vividly apparent in the coverage of national tragedies. In 2002, the NTV channel provoked the Kremlin's fury for running live footage as Russian troops stormed a Moscow theater that had been siezed by Chechen terrorists. This did not stop NTV from broadcasting almost round-the-clock when, in 2004, terrorists captured a school in Beslan, North Ossetia. All three national channels showed harrowing pictures of children emerging, shell-shocked and wounded, from the school and being ferried to hospitals in civilian cars because of the shortage of ambulances standing by. It is inconceivable that such scenes would have been televised 20 years ago.

10.3.3 Corruption

In the late 1990s, the then Chairman of the U.S. House Banking Committee, James Leach (1999a, 1999b), wrote that he had made a study of the world's most corrupt regimes, including the Philippines under Marcos, Zaire under Mobutu, and Indonesia under Suharto. As bad as these were, each was outdone by the "pervasiveness of politically tolerated corruption" in postcommunist Russia. Other perceptions of corruption in Russia are equally grim. The anticorruption advocacy group Transparency International (TI) compiles annual ratings of countries' "perceived corruption," based on a range of business surveys. The World Bank has compiled a similar composite rating. Both of these make use, predominantly though not entirely, of surveys of business people or ratings by business consultancies based outside the relevant countries. In both ratings, Russia scores toward the bottom. For instance, in the 2001 version of the World Bank's "graft" index, Russia was 142 out of 160 countries. In TI's 2002 corruption perceptions index, Russia ranked 71 out of 102 countries.

But what about sources less dependent on the perception of outsiders? In summer 1999, the World Bank and the EBRD conducted a survey of business managers in 22 postcommunist countries. They asked respondents to estimate the share of annual revenues that "firms like yours" typically devoted to unofficial payments to public officials "in order to get things done." Such payments might be made, the questionnaire added, to facilitate connection to public utilities, to obtain licenses or permits, to improve relationships with tax collectors, or in relation to customs or imports. They also asked respondents to what extent the sale of parliamentary laws, presidential decrees, court decisions, and so forth had directly affected their business, in the hope of measuring the extent to which policymakers were coopted by business interests (Hellman et al., 2000).

Comparing Russian business managers to their peers in other postcommunist countries, Russia falls in the middle on both the "burden of bribery" and "state capture" dimensions. If one graphs per capita GDP on the horizontal axis and these measures of corruption on the vertical axis, Russia is almost exactly on the Ordinary Least Squares regression line in both cases. Administrative corruption is very high in the really poor countries, such as Uzbekistan, Armenia, and Azerbaijan; lower in

Russia, Bulgaria, and Lithuania; and lower still in the relatively rich Hungary and Slovenia (see Figure 10.3).[13]

How does corruption in Russia affect individuals? The United Nations conducts a cross-national survey of crime victims. In 1996–2000, it asked urban respondents in a number of countries the following question: "In some countries, there is a problem of corruption among government or public officials. During—last year—has any government official, for instance a customs officer, a police officer or inspector in your country asked you, or expected you, to pay a bribe for his service?" The proportion of respondents saying they had experienced demands for or expectations of bribes in the last year in Russia (16.6 percent) was lower than that in Argentina, Brazil, Romania, or Lithuania (see Table 10.3). Again, a simple regression shows that the rate for Russia is almost exactly what one would expect given its per capita GDP (Del Frate and van Kesteren, 2003; also United Nations, 2003, Table 21).

Looking at crime in general, the reported victimization rate in Russia is not particularly high. Only 26 percent of Moscow respondents said in 2000 that they had been victimized the previous year by property crimes, robbery, sexual assault, assault, or bribery, compared to 34 percent in Prague, 41 percent in Tallin (Estonia), 44 percent in Rio de Janeiro, and 61 percent in Buenos Aires. Moscow's rate was almost exactly that reported by urban respondents in Finland (26.6 percent) and lower than that for England and Wales (34.4 percent) (Del Frate and van Kesteren, 2003).

10.4 Conclusion

Russia's economy is no longer the shortage-ridden, militarized, collapsing bureaucracy of 1990. It has metamorphosed into a marketplace of mostly private firms, producing goods and services to please consumers instead of planners. The economy has been growing at an impressive pace. The country's political order, too, has changed beyond recognition. A few business magnates control much of the country's immense raw materials reserves and troubled banking system, and lobby hard behind the scenes for favored policies. Small businesses are burdened by corruption and regulation. Still, the dictatorship of the party has given way to electoral democracy. Russia's once all-powerful Communist Party no longer penetrates all aspects of social life nor sentences dissidents to arctic labor

Table 10.3 Percentage of respondents who had been victimized by administrative bribery, 1996–2000, major cities

Albania	59.1	Slovak Republic	13.5
Argentina	30.2	Paraguay	13.3
Indonesia	29.9	Hungary	9.8
Bolivia	24.4	Croatia	9.5
India (Mumbai)	22.9	Estonia	9.3
Lithuania	22.9	Costa Rica	9.2
Mongolia	21.3	Macedonia, FYR	7.4
India (New Delhi)	21.0	South Africa	6.9
Azerbaijan	20.8	Czech Republic	5.7
Belarus	20.6	Philippines	4.3
Colombia	19.5	Botswana	2.8
Uganda	19.5	Netherlands	0.9
Kyrgyz Republic	19.3	Northern Ireland	0.8
Romania	19.2	Denmark	0.5
Brazil	17.1	Scotland	0.5
Russian Federation	**16.6**	Finland	0.4
Georgia	16.6	England and Wales	0.3
Bulgaria	16.4	Sweden	0.2
Ukraine	16.2	Spain (Barcelona)	0
Latvia	14.3		

Sources: UN International Crime Victims Surveys; UN Human Development Report, 2002, Table 21; and A. Alvazzi del Frante and J. Van Kesteren, "Some Preliminary Tables from the International Crime Victims Surveys," *Criminal Victimisation in Urban Europe* (Turin: UNICRI, 2003).

camps. Instead, it campaigns for seats in parliament. The press, although struggling against heavy-handed political interventions, is still far more professional and independent than the stilted propaganda machine of the mid-1980s. In slightly over a decade, Russia has become a typical middle-income, capitalist democracy.

So why the dark—at times almost paranoid—view? Why the hyperbole about kleptocracy, economic cataclysm, and KGB takeovers? Why are Russian conditions often portrayed as comparable to those in Zaire or Iran, rather than to the far more similar realities of Argentina or Turkey?

Although many factors may have been involved, we believe that the exaggerated despair over Russia was fueled by a fundamental and widespread misconception.[14] Many Western observers thought that, as of the

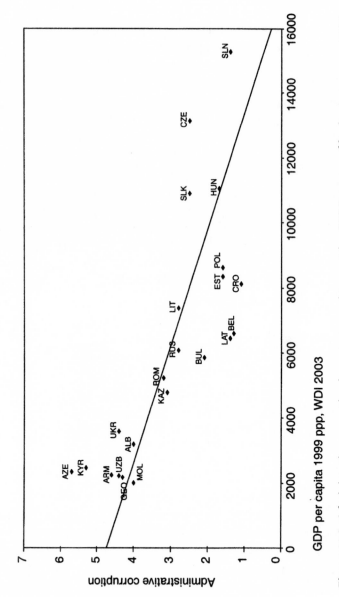

Figure 10.3 Administrative corruption in postcommunist countries, EBRD survey of business managers, 1999 (BEEPS). *Note:* "Administrative corruption" = percent of revenues paid in bribes by "firms like yours." *Source:* EBRD (1999).

early 1990s, Russia was a highly developed, if not wealthy, country. With its brilliant physicists and chess players, its space program, and its global military influence, Russia did not look like Argentina or South Korea. Thinking that Russia started off highly developed, these observers saw its convergence to the norm for middle-income countries as a disastrous aberration. The same misconception informed some academic analyses. One recent paper, for example, makes the remarkable observation that although institutions to support the rule of law are imperfect in all countries, "between Russia and most other developed, capitalist societies there was a qualitative difference" (Hoff and Stiglitz, 2002, p. 8). Indeed, there was a qualitative difference. Russia was never a "developed, capitalist society."

Such misconceptions have important consequences for Western policy toward Russia. They predispose decision makers to overreact to the inevitable volatility of Russian economic and political life. The result is extreme mood swings in the West's approach to Russia. When things go "well," markets and political leaders respond with enthusiastic rhetoric, ratcheting expectations up to ever more unrealistic levels. When things go "badly," Western Russia-watchers are prone to panic or denunciations, and are too ready to consider changing course completely. The discourse changes in a matter of days from one of partnership to one of isolation and containment. Such exaggerated swings are not helpful to either Russia or the West.

What does the future hold for Russia? Some see the sudden spurt of growth over the last five years as an indicator of more to come, and expect Russia soon to join Hungary and Poland in the community of poor developed countries, leaving behind the middle-income developing ones. They emphasize the country's advanced human capital, its reformed tax system, and its mostly open economy. Others see a serious barrier to growth in the bureaucratic regulations and politicized interventions. In politics, optimists anticipate continuing expansion of democratic competition and the emergence of a more vigorous civil society. Pessimists see an accelerating slide toward an authoritarian regime that will be managed by security service professionals under the fig leaf of formal democratic procedures.

None of these predictions can be ruled out. However, thinking about Russia as a normal, middle-income country suggests the implausibility of extreme forecasts. Middle-income countries rarely revert from democracy to full-fledged authoritarianism, although they often renegotiate the boundary between the two. Their democracies are incomplete, unpredictable, and subject to temporary reversals. When they grow at all, middle-income countries tend to grow in spurts that are often interrupted by financial crises. Russia has probably destroyed enough of the vestiges of central planning to stay a market economy, albeit one with flawed institutions and much counterproductive state intervention. Its bureaucracy will remain corrupt, although it will become less corrupt as the country grows richer.

That Russia is only a normal middle-income democracy is, of course, a disappointment to those who had hoped for or expected more. But that Russia today has largely broken free of its past, that it is no longer "the evil empire," threatening both its own people and the rest of the world, is an amazing and admirable achievement.

Notes

References

Index

Notes

1. Russia after Communism

1. The politics of economic reform in Russia has been the subject of two of my previous books, *Privatizing Russia* (with Maxim Boycko and Robert Vishny) and *Without a Map* (with Daniel Treisman). These books describe the political logic in the evolution of Russian reform.

2. The Transition to a Market Economy

1. World Bank (1991) and Shleifer and Vishny (1991) present evidence on Soviet economic performance through mid-1991.
2. There is a delicate issue here of whether the timber firms actually pay the marginal cost, or whether the government pays it, in which case they will produce as if the marginal cost were zero. The case we treat makes the comparison to the basic model most simple.
3. In a more elaborate model, the ministry creates a shortage by optimally choosing P to maximize the value of bribes (Shleifer and Vishny, 1993).

3. Privatizing Russia

1. Vining and Boardman (1992) survey the evidence on the relative efficiency of public and private firms.
2. For a discussion of distinction between cash flow rights and control rights in the characterization of ownership, see Grossman and Hart (1986).
3. Nellis (1988) presents evidence that incentive contracts of managers of public enterprises are often repealed when managers begin to restructure in earnest and thus violate the goals of the politicians. After their contracts are repealed, managers are told explicitly not to lay off workers, to continue building plants where politicians want them, and so on. Nellis's ex-

amples illustrate the fragility of corporatization as a depoliticization strategy.

4. Shleifer and Vishny (1986) stress the role of large shareholders in governing firms in the West. Frydman and Rapaczynski (1991), Lipton and Sachs (1990), and Blanchard et al. (1991) present privatization schemes that turn on the pivotal role of large shareholders in delivering governance to privatizing firms.

5. Boycko, Shleifer, and Vishy (1995) present a detailed description of the program. A legal description is found in Frydman, Earle, and Rapaczynski (1993).

6. Frydman, Earle, and Rapaczynski (1993), pp. 55–57.

7. Ibid., and Earle (1993), p. 67.

8. The case for the mutual fund scheme is presented by Lipton and Sachs (1990).

9. A more detailed discussion of voucher schemes versus mutual fund schemes is contained in Frydman and Rapaczynski (1991) and Boycko, Shleifer, and Vishny (1996).

10. See Bohlen (1993), p. A1.

11. Following Yeltsin's victory over the parliament in October 1993, the voucher price doubled to more than $20. Even with this increase, the total value of Russian assets remained very low. Nevertheless, the event demonstrates that the possible increase in the security of property that accompanied the demise of the parliament doubled the valuation of assets.

12. World Bank (1991) presents some evidence on industrial concentration in the Russian economy.

4. How Does Privatization Work?

1. A related survey was conducted around the same time in Eastern Europe by Earle et al. (1994).

2. We also asked whether a shop had a minor renovation *(kosmetichesky remont)*, which was a much more common restructuring measure than major renovation, but not one correlated with any of the determinants of restructuring investigated in this chapter.

3. Following Morck, Shleifer, and Vishny (1988), we checked for a systematic nonlinear relationship between management ownership and the probability of restructuring, but found none.

4. Even though we expressed a theoretical doubt concerning the validity of our instruments for the renovation equation, a χ^2 test fails to reject the null hypothesis that the instruments are exogenous.

5. We owe this term to Gary S. Becker.

7. The Unofficial Economy in Transition

1. See Frydman and Rapaczynski (1991), Shleifer and Vishny (1994a), Boycko, Shleifer, and Vishny (1995, 1996), Kaufmann and Siegelbaum (1997), and Shleifer (1997a, 1997b).

2. See *World Development Report 1996* (World Bank, 1996); *Transition Report* (EBRD, 1995, 1996); and for the IMF, Citrin (1995) and Fischer, Sahay, and Végh (1996a, 1996b). Leitzel (1995) analyzes changes in the character of unofficial activities in Russia as a result of reform. EBRD (1995, annex 2.1) contains estimates of the "hidden economy," based on surveys in Hungary, Estonia, Slovenia, Bulgaria, and Romania, although it is not clear whether the same methodology was used in all countries.

3. We use total—rather than just industrial—electricity consumption because new private sector activities probably use "nonindustrial" electricity; for example, when service sector firms operate out of apartments.

4. Gray (1995) reports that electricity prices for industry in 1994 were 5.2 cents per kilowatt-hour in Hungary and 5.6 cents in the Czech Republic, but only 2.7 cents in Russia and 1.4 cents in Ukraine. In addition, there is strong anecdotal evidence that payment arrears to electricity suppliers are much higher in the FSU than in Eastern Europe.

5. The elasticity is usually not the same when output is falling and when it is rising. Assuming an elasticity of 1.15 for the relationship between energy consumption and output when output is increasing (because energy use is becoming less efficient) is equivalent to assuming an elasticity of 0.87 (the inverse of 1.15) when output is falling. Similarly, the assumption of an elasticity of 0.9 for central and Eastern Europe when output is increasing (because of an improvement in energy efficiency) is equivalent to an elasticity of 1.11 when output is falling.

6. "Through a Glass Darkly," *Central European Economic Review*, February 1995, pp. 8–9; "The Great Growth Race," CEER, December 1995–January 1996, pp. 8–9, 13; "Continental Divide," CEER, December 1996–January 1997, pp. 10–11, 27.

7. EBRD (1995, 1996). There are no significant results in our regressions if we use the EBRD's measure of corporate tax rates (EBRD, 1996, annex 2.2). The posted rates are too similar across countries.

8. "We asked our panel to rank each of the 26 countries on the basis of their attractiveness as a place to do business over the coming year. Grades were given on a scale of 0 to 10 with 0 the lowest and 10 the highest score." ("The Great Growth Race," *Central European Economic Review*, December 1995–January 1996, p. 9) One of the categories is "tax burden." Although tax rates are relatively similar across countries, the scores for this variable

vary widely. Our interpretation is that the experts were taking into account both tax rates and the fairness of tax administration.

9. Johnson and Sheehy (1996), chap. 3. To facilitate comparison with measures of reform from other sources, we rescale their variables by multiplying by (-1) and adding 5, so that each index runs from 0 to 4, where a higher score is better.

10. See Aslund, Boone, and Johnson (1996, Table 3). Determining the first year of reform is uncontroversial for most countries. All members of the FSU (with the arguable exceptions of Lithuania and Estonia in the Baltics) clearly started reform in 1992, while Poland, Hungary, and Romania began in 1990, and Albania in 1992. The Czech Republic, Slovakia, and Bulgaria could be interpreted as having begun in 1990 or 1991. At least for the analysis in this chapter, these differences as to when reform "started" do not seem to affect the results.

11. These estimates of the unofficial economy are generally consistent with other estimates for particular countries, based on microsurveys and other independent estimations. For example, Kaufmann (1997), using firm-level surveys, finds that about half of value added is not reported in Ukraine. For Poland, Zienkowski (1996) estimates the unofficial economy at less than 20 percent by 1993.

We would emphasize, however, that our estimation procedure is subject to a margin of error. The pretransition estimates of the unofficial economy for Eastern Europe could be on the high side. Further, the energy efficiency gains from energy price adjustments in those countries may, in reality, have exceeded our assumed "efficiency elasticity" assumptions. But these effects would counteract each other, resulting in similar post-transition estimates of the unofficial economy. One could obtain significantly larger estimates than ours for the unofficial economics of Eastern Europe by the mid-1990s only if the initial baseline estimates were too low or the energy efficiency gains were substantially larger. For the FSU economies, it is plausible both that the initial estimate of 12 percent is somewhat low, and that there have been more gains in energy efficiency than we assume. Thus it may be that by the mid-1990s, the unofficial economy in the FSU was even larger than we estimate.

12. The CEER and Heritage Foundation estimates of tax fairness differ significantly. The Heritage Foundation's taxation index (in which a higher score means a greater effective tax rate) is not significantly correlated with the unofficial share of the economy. In the Heritage Foundation measure, tax fairness is relatively low (a score of 1 out of a potential 4) in economies with a relatively low unofficial economy share (such as the Czech Republic

and Hungary) and in those with a relatively high share (such as Russia and Azerbaijan). Since the Heritage Foundation does not provide data on Uzbekistan, we have only 14 data points when we use its measures of reform.

9. Federalism with and without Political Centralization

1. The McKinsey study of 10 sectors of the Russian economy, and of the specific obstacles faced by new firms in each sector, is particularly instructive in this regard.
2. Shleifer and Vishny (1993) show how such disorganization and competition for rents leads to a much worse outcome than monopoly corruption from an organized government. See also Chapter 6.
3. For more discussion, and a more agnostic view, of whether central or local governments are more likely to be captured, see Bardhan and Mookherjee (2000).
4. Our normalization that government revenues move with output may not be innocuous here: y, interpreted as government revenues, may be low not because additional output is low, but because the government—local or central—cannot successfully tax incremental output, which is hidden in the unofficial economy or through transfer pricing.
5. Even in China, control by the center is not absolute. Young (2000) argues, for example, that political centralization has not prevented regional governments from erecting trade barriers between provinces.
6. Shleifer and Treisman (1999) make one such proposal.
7. This chapter was written in December 1999, before President Putin came to power. His regional policies, including those toward governors, have been indeed very much focused on raising p.

10. A Normal Country

1. We use the change in real GDP figures from *Rossiiskiy Statisticheskiy Yezhegodnik 2001* for 1990–1995, and then newer updated figures for subsequent years from Goskomstat's Web site at *www.gks.ru*. We adjusted for change in population, using figures from *Rossiiskiy Statisticheskiy Yezhegodnik 2001* and *Rossia v Tsifrakh 2002*.
2. Some researchers argue that the Russian consumer price index (CPI) has been measured with significant bias during the transition period, leading to major overestimation of the transitional drop in living standards. The Russian official CPI is a fixed-weight (Laspeyres) index, which does not take into account consumer substitution away from higher-priced goods, and

therefore overstates the effect of rising prices on living standards when—as occurred in Russia—the prices of different goods rise at very different rates. See Gibson, Stillman, and Le (2004).

3. If electricity consumption by households and the government itself fell less than that by producers, the total drop in electricity consumption might understate the drop in economic output. However, rough calculations suggest the share of households was very low—maybe on the order of 4–6 percent of the total. Our guess is that use by the government was even lower.

4. Calculated from Russian Economic Trends database; Goskomstat Rossii (1994), p. 288; and Goskomstat Rossii (2001), p. 588.

5. One might have expected that the shift to world market prices in trade among the former communist countries would have disproportionately benefited Russia, which had been exporting subsidized energy to other Eastern Bloc countries.

6. The Gini coefficient ranges from 0 to 1, where 0 means perfect equality (everyone has the same income) and 1 means perfect inequality (one person has all the income). To calculate the Gini coefficient, plot a "Lorenz curve" where the horizontal axis is the percentage of households, ranging up to 100 percent, and the vertical axis is the percentage of income held by those households, also ranging up to 100 percent. A straight line, going up at a 45-degree angle, will show perfect equality of income. If the area between the line of perfect equality and actual Lorenz curve is A, and the area underneath the line that shows perfect equality of income is B, the Gini coefficient is A/B.

7. On the other hand, relative equality of incomes in the shortage economy of late socialism existed alongside highly unequal *access* to consumer goods.

8. Calculated from figures in *Ekspert* database, deflating by the CPI.

9. For the OSCE reports on Russian elections, see *www.osce.org/odihr/index .php?page=elections&div=reports&country=ru*. To compare with election reports on other countries, see *www.osce.org/odihr/index.php?page=elections &div=reports*. For the CSCE reports mentioned in the text, see *www.csce .gov*.

10. For instance, in Mexico international election observers from the human rights group Global Exchange reported after the 2000 presidential election that in "most of the communities [where its observers were stationed] voting day was marred by often flagrant violations of the electoral code. In the days immediately preceding the vote, episodes of vote-buying, coercion, and intimidation were commonplace. . . . The delegation heard numerous testimonies from opposition supporters of harassment and intimidation,

particularly in the marginalized and poor communities." See *www
.globalexchange.org*. In Brazil, according to one observer, "buying votes is
common practice . . . and spawns armies of voters ready to sell their votes
for a dish of beans" (Whitaker, 2000). Such observations are anecdotal, of
course, but so are the ones used to criticize Russia.

11. On Rupert Murdoch's Fox television network, see Neil Hickey, "Is Fox
News Fair?" *Columbia Journalism Review*, March–April 1998, which quotes
several former employees of the network complaining of " 'management
sticking their fingers' in the writing and editing of stories and of at-
tempting to cook the facts to make a story more palatable to right-of-
center tastes." On Italian television news under Silvio Berlusconi, see, for
instance Philip Willan, "Opposition 'Kept off Berlusconi-run TV,' "
Guardian, August 8, 2002, which cites a University of Pavia study that
found a sharp reduction in the amount of news time devoted to the opposition to Berlusconi after Berlusconi's appointees took over at the RAI network.

12. "Suppression by law" covers cases in which journalists were sentenced to
prison or excessive fines, including libel suits aimed at impeding the jour-
nalist's right to report freely, the introduction of restrictive legislation, and
official denial or suspension of credentials.

13. The World Bank and EBRD repeated the survey in 2002. In almost all
countries, the average percent of revenues paid in bribes dropped—it fell
in Russia during these three years from 2.8 to 1.4 percent. But the cross-
national pattern was almost the same. Again, Russia's level of administrative corruption was slightly lower than would be predicted from its income. And by 2003, it had become less corrupt on the administrative
corruption scale than Bulgaria and Belarus.

14. Contributing factors may have included: unreflective but sincere sympathy
on the part of Western publics for Russians dislocated by the transition;
sensationalism in the press; *schadenfreude* on the part of left-wing intellectuals, for whom turmoil in Russia proved the foolishness of liberal market
reforms; and presidential politics in the United States, where Republicans
sought to discredit Clinton and Gore, who had consistently supported
Yeltsin.

References

Aghion, Philippe, and Oliver Blanchard. 1993. *On the Speed of Transition in Central Europe.* NBER Macro Annual, Cambridge, MA.

Amaral, R., and C. Guimaraes. 1994. "Media Monopoly in Brazil." *Journal of Communication,* Autumn: 26–38.

Aron, Leon. 2002. "Structure and Context in the Study of Post-Soviet Russia: Several Empirical Generalizations in Search of a Theory." Working Paper, American Enterprise Institute.

Aslund, Anders. 2001. *Building Capitalism.* Cambridge: Cambridge University Press.

———. 2003. "Moscow Thrives." Memorandum.

Aslund, Anders, Peter Boone, and Simon Johnson. 1996. "How to Stabilize: Lessons from Post-Communist Countries." *Brookings Papers on Economic Activity,* 1: 217–314.

Atkinson, Anthony, and Joseph Stiglitz. 1980. *Lectures on Public Economics.* New York: McGraw-Hill.

Balcerowicz, Leszek. 1995. *Socialism, Capitalism, Transformation.* Budapest: Central European University Press.

Barberis, Nicholas, Maxim Boycko, Andrei Shleifer, and Natalia Tsukanova. 1996. "How Does Privatization Work? Evidence from the Russian Shops." *Journal of Political Economy,* 104: 764–790.

Bardhan, P. D., and D. Mookherjee. 2000. "Capture and Governance at Local and National Levels." *American Economic Review: Papers and Proceedings,* 90: 135–139.

Bates, Robert. 1981. *Markets and States in Tropical Africa: The Political Basis of Agricultural Policies.* Berkeley: University of California Press.

Bernstein, Lisa. 1992. "Opting Out of the Legal System: Extralegal Contractual Relations in the Diamond Industry." *Journal of Legal Studies,* 21: 115–157.

Black, Bernard, Reinier Kraakman, and Jonathan Hay. 1996. "Corporate Law from Scratch." In Roman Frydman, Cheryl Gray, and Andrzej Rapaczynski, eds., *Corporate Governance in Central Europe and Russia.* Vol. 2, pp. 245–302. Budapest: Central European University Press.

Blanchard, Olivier. 1997. The *Economics of Post-Communist Transition.* Oxford: Oxford University Press.

Blanchard, Olivier, Rudiger Dornbusch, Paul Krugman, Richard Layard, and Lawrence Summers. 1991. *Reform in Eastern Europe.* Cambridge, MA: MIT Press.

Blanchard, Olivier, and Michael Kremer. 1997. "Disorganization." *Quarterly Journal of Economics,* 112: 1091–1126.

Blanchard, Olivier, and Andrei Shleifer. 2001. "Federalism with and without Political Centralization: China versus Russia." *IMF Staff Papers,* 48 (Special Issue): 171–179.

Blanchard, Olivier, and Lawrence Summers. 1987. "Fiscal Increasing Returns, Hysteresis, Real Wages and Unemployment." *European Economic Review,* 31: 543–566.

Bohlen, Celeste. 1993. "Billions Bleed Out of Russia As Its Wealth Sent Abroad." *New York Times,* February 1, p. A1.

Boone, Peter, and Denis Rodionov. 2001. "Rent Seeking in Russia and the CIS." Paper presented at the tenth anniversary conference of the EBRD, London, December.

Boycko, Maxim, Andrei Shleifer, and Robert Vishny. 1993. "Privatizing Russia." *Brookings Papers on Economic Activity,* 2: 139–181.

———. 1995. *Privatizing Russia.* Cambridge, MA: MIT Press.

———. 1996. "A Theory of Privatization." *The Economic Journal,* 106: 309–319.

Brainerd, Elizabeth, and David Cutler. 2005. "Autopsy on an Empire: Understanding Mortality in Russia and the Former Soviet Union." *Journal of Economic Perspectives,* 19, forthcoming.

Buchanan, James, and Gordon Tullock. 1962. *The Calculus of Consent.* Ann Arbor: University of Michigan Press.

Buxbaum, Richard, and Klaus Hopt. 1988. *Legal Harmonization and the Business Enterprise.* Berlin: Walter de Gruyter.

Byrd, William. 1987. "The Impact of the Two-Tier Plan/Market System in Chinese Industry." *Journal of Comparative Economics,* 11: 295–308.

Central European Economic Review. 1995. "Through a Glass Darkly." 8–10. Published as a supplement to the *Wall Street Journal* Europe.

———. December 1995–January 1996. "The Great Growth Race." 8–9, 13. Published as a supplement to the *Wall Street Journal Europe.*

———. December 1996–January 1997. "Continental Divide." 10–11, 27. Published as a supplement to the *Wall Street Journal Europe.*

Citrin, Daniel. 1995. "Overview." In Daniel Citrin and Ashok Lahiri, "Policy

Experiences and Issues in the Baltics, Russia, and Other Countries of the Former Soviet Union, International Monetary Fund." Occasional Paper 133, Washington, DC.

Claessens, Stijn, Simeon Djankov, and Larry Lang. 1999. "The Separation of Ownership and Control in East Asian Corporations." *Journal of Financial Economics,* 58: 81–112.

DaVanzo, Julie, and Clifford Grammich. 2001. *Russia's Mortality Crisis: Drinking, Disease, and Deteriorating Health Care.* Santa Monica, CA: Rand Corporation.

Del Frate, Alvazzi, and J. van Kesteren. 2003. "Some Preliminary Tables from the International Crime Victim Surveys." In *Criminal Victimisation in Urban Europe.* Turin: United Nations Interregional Crime and Justice Research Institute.

De Long, Bradford, and Andrei Shleifer. 1993. "Princes and Merchants: European City Growth before the Industrial Revolution." *Journal of Law and Economics,* 36: 671–702.

De Melo, Martha, Cevdet Denizer, and Alan Gelb. 1996. "From Plan to Market: Patterns of Transition." Policy Research Working Paper 1564. Washington, DC: World Bank.

Demsetz, Harold, and Kenneth Lehn. 1985. "The Structure of Corporate Ownership: Causes and Consequences." *Journal of Political Economy,* 93: 1155–1177.

De Soto, Hernando. 1989. *The Other Path.* New York: Harper and Row.

Dewatripont, Mathias, and Eric Maskin. 1990. "Contract Renegotiation in Models of Asymmetric Information." *European Economic Review,* 34: 311–321.

Diaz-Cayeros, Alejandro. 1997. "Political Responses to Regional Inequality: Taxation and Distribution in Mexico." Ph.D. dissertation, Duke University.

Djankov, Simeon, Caralee McLiesh, Tatiana Nenova, and Andrei Shleifer. 2003. "Who Owns the Media?" *Journal of Law and Economics,* 46: 341–381.

Donahue, John. 1989. *Privatization Decision: Public Ends, Private Means.* New York: Basic Books.

Earle, John, Roman Frydman, Andrzej Rapaczynski, and Joel Turkewitz. 1994. *Small Privatization.* Budapest: Central European University Press.

EBRD. 1995. *Transition Report.* London: European Bank for Reconstruction and Development.

———. 1996. *Transition Report.* London: European Bank for Reconstruction and Development.

———. 1997. *Transition Report.* London: European Bank for Reconstruction and Development.

———. 1999. *Transition Report 1999: Ten Years of Transition.* London: European Bank for Reconstruction and Development.

Ekelund, Robert, and Robert Tollison. 1981. *Merchantilism as a Rent Seeking Society*. College Station: Texas A&M University Press.

European Corporate Governance Network. 1997. *The Separation of Ownership and Control: A Survey of 7 European Countries*. Preliminary Report to the European Commission. Vols. 1–4. Brussels: European Corporate Governance Network.

Faccio, Mara. 2003. "Politically-Connected Firms." Mimeo, Vanderbilt University.

Fischer, Stanley, Ratna Sahay, and Carlos Végh. 1996a. "Stabilization and Growth in Transition Economies: The Early Experience." *Journal of Economic Perspectives,* 10: 45–66.

———. 1996b. "From Transition to Market: Evidence and Growth Prospects." Mimeo, International Monetary Fund.

Freedom House. 1995. "The Comparative Survey of Freedom 1994–95." From *www.freedomhouse.org.*

———. 1997. "The Comparative Survey of Freedom 1995–96." From *www.freedomhouse.org.*

Freund, Caroline, and Christine Wallich. 1997. "Public-Sector Price Reforms in Transition Economies: Who Gains? Who Loses? The Case of Household Energy Prices in Poland." *Economic Development and Cultural Change,* 46: 35–59.

Frydman, Roman, John Earle, and Andrzej Rapaczynski. 1993. *Privatization in the Transition to a Market Economy: Studies of Preconditions and Policies in Eastern Europe*. New York: Pinter Publishers and St. Martin's Press.

Frydman, Roman, Cheryl Gray, Marek Hessel, and Andrzej Rapaczynski. 1999. "When Does Privatization Work? The Impact of Private Ownership on Corporate Performance in the Transition Economies." *Quarterly Journal of Economics,* 114: 1153–1192.

Frydman, Roman, and Andrzej Rapaczynski. 1991. "Evolution and Design in the East European Transition." *Rivista di Politica Economica,* 81: 69–118.

Frye, Timothy. 1997. "Contracting in the Shadow of the State: Private Arbitration Courts in Russia." In Jeffrey Sachs, ed., *The Rule of Law and Economic Reform in Russia*. Boulder, CO: Westview Press, pp. 123–138.

Frye, Timothy, and Andrei Shleifer. 1997. "The Invisible Hand and the Grabbing Hand." *American Economic Review: Papers and Proceedings,* 87: 354–358.

Gastil, Raymond. 1992. *Freedom in the World, 1991–1992*. Washington, DC: Freedom House.

Gibson, John, Steven Stillman, and Trinh Le. 2004. "CPI Bias and Real Living Standards in Russia during the Transition." Wellington, NZ, unpublished.

Goldman, Marshall. 2003. *The Piratization of Russia: Russian Reform Goes Awry*. New York: Routledge.

Goskomstat Rossii. 1994. *Rossiiskiy Statisticheskiy Yezhegodnik 1994.* Moscow, Russia.

———. 2001. *Rossiiskiy Statisticheskiy Yezhegodnik 2001.* Moscow, Russia.

———. 2002. *Rossiya v Tsifrakh 2002.* Moscow, Russia.

———. 2003. *Rossiiskiy Statisticheskiy Yezhegodnik 2003.* Moscow, Russia.

Gray, Cheryl. 1993. "Evolving Legal Frameworks for Private Sector Development in Central and Eastern Europe." World Bank Discussion Paper No. 209.

Gray, Dale. 1995. "Reforming the Energy Sector in Transition Economies: Selected Experience and Lessons." World Bank Discussion Paper no. 296.

Grossman, Sanford, and Oliver Hart. 1986. "The Costs and Benefits of Ownership: A Theory of Vertical and Lateral Integration." *Journal of Political Economy,* 94: 691–719.

Guriev, Sergei, and Andrei Rachinsky. 2004. "Ownership Concentration in Russian Industry." Washington, DC: World Bank.

———. 2005. "The Role of Oligarchs in Russian Capitalism." *Journal of Economic Perspectives,* 19, forthcoming.

Gwartney, James, and Robert Lawson. 1997. *Economic Freedom of the World 1997.* Vancouver: Fraser Institute.

Hart, H. L. A. 1961. *The Concept of Law.* Oxford: Clarendon Press.

Hay, Jonathan. 1994. "Law without Enforcement: The Case of Russia." Mimeo, Harvard University.

Hay, Jonathan, Andrei Shleifer, and Robert Vishny. 1996. "Toward a Theory of Legal Reform." *European Economic Review,* 40: 559–567.

Hellman, Joel, Geraint Jones, Daniel Kaufmann, and Mark Schankerman. 2003. "Measuring Governance Corruption and State Capture: How Firms and Bureaucrats Shape the Business Environment in Transition Economies." *Journal of Comparative Economics,* 31: 751–773.

Hickey, Neil. 1998. "Is Fox News Fair?" *Columbia Journalism Review,* 36: 30–36.

Hoff, Karla, and Joseph Stiglitz. 2002. "After the Big Bang? Obstacles to the Emergence of the Rule of Law in Post-Communist Societies." NBER Working Paper 9282.

Holmstrom, Bengt. 1979. "Moral Hazard and Observability." *Bell Journal of Economics,* 19: 74–91.

Huang, Yasheng, 2002. "The Industrial Organization of Chinese Government." *Political Studies,* 50: 61–79.

Hunt, Bishop Carleton. 1936. *The Development of the Business Corporation in England: 1800–1867.* Cambridge, MA: Harvard University Press.

IMD. 1997. *World Competitiveness Yearbook.* Lausanne, Switzerland.

International Monetary Fund. 2002. *International Financial Statistics.* Washington, DC: International Monetary Fund.

Intriligator, Michael. 1994. "Privatization in Russia Has Led to Criminaliza-
tion." *The Australian Economic Review,* 106: 4–14.

———. 1997. "A New Economic Policy for Russia." *The Economics of Transition,* 5: 225–227.

Jensen, Michael, and Kevin Murphy. 1990. "Performance Pay and Top Management Incentives." *Journal of Political Economy,* 98: 225–255.

Jin, Hehui, Yingyi Qian, and Barry Weingast. 1999. "Regional Decentralization
and Fiscal Incentives: Federalism, Chinese Style." Unpublished manuscript,
Nobel Symposium on Transition, University of Maryland.

Johnson, Bryan, and Thomas Sheehy. 1996. *The Index of Economic Freedom.*
Stanford, CA: The Heritage Foundation.

Johnson, Simon, Daniel Kaufmann, and Andrei Shleifer. 1997. "The Unofficial
Economy in Transition." *Brookings Papers on Economic Activity,* 2: 159–220.

Johnson, Simon, Rafael La Porta, Florencio Lopez-de-Silanes, and Andrei
Shleifer. 2000. "Tunneling." *American Economic Review: Papers and Proceedings,* 90: 22–27.

Johnson, Simon, and Gary Loveman. 1995. *Starting Over in Eastern Europe: Entrepreneurship and Economic Renewal.* Boston: Harvard Business School Press.

Kaufmann, Daniel. 1997. "The Missing Pillar of a Growth Strategy for Ukraine:
Institutional and Policy Reforms for Private Sector Development." In P.
Cornelius and P. Lenain, eds., *Ukraine: Accelerating the Transition to
Market.* Washington, DC: International Monetary Fund.

Kaufmann, Daniel, and Alexander Kaliberda. 1996. "Integrating the Unofficial
Economy into the Dynamics of Post-Socialist Economies." In B. Kaminski,
ed., *Economic Transition in the Newly Independent States.* Armonk, NY:
M. E. Sharpe.

Kaufmann, Daniel, and Paul Siegelbaum. 1997. "Privatization and Corruption
in Transition Economies." *Journal of International Affairs,* 50: 419–464.

Klitgaard, Robert. 1995. *National and International Strategies for Reducing Corruption.* Unpublished manuscript, University of Natal, Durban.

Laffont, Jean-Jacques. 1994. "Regulation, Privatization, and Incentives in Developing Countries." Mimeo, I.D.E.I., Toulouse.

Laffont, Jean-Jacques, and Jean Tirole. 1993. *A Theory of Incentives in Procurement and Regulation.* Cambridge, MA: MIT Press.

La Porta, Rafael, Florencio Lopez-de-Silanes, and Andrei Shleifer. 1999. "Corporate Ownership around the World." *Journal of Finance,* 54: 471–517.

Leach, James. 1999a. "The New Russian Menace." *New York Times,* September 10.

———. 1999b. "Opening Statement of Representative James A. Leach." In
"Hearing on Russian Money Laundering." U.S. House of Representatives,
Committee on Banking and Financial Services. September 21. *http://
financialservices.house.gov.*

Leitzel, James. 1995. *Russian Economic Reform*. London: Routledge.

Lipton, David, and Jeffrey Sachs. 1990. "Creating a Market Economy in Eastern Europe: The Case of Poland." *Brookings Papers on Economic Activity*, 1:75–133.

Loayza, Norman. 1996. "The Economics of the Informal Sector: A Simple Model and Some Empirical Evidence from Latin America." *Carnegie-Rochester Conference Series on Public Policy*, 45: 129–162.

Lopez-de-Silanes, Florencio. 1997. "Determinants of Privatization Prices." *Quarterly Journal of Economics*, 112: 965–1026.

McKinnon, Ronald. 1991. *The Order of Economic Liberalization: Financial Control in the Transition to a Market Economy*. Baltimore: Johns Hopkins University Press.

McKinsey Global Institute. 1999. *Russia's Economic Performance*. Moscow: McKinsey.

Megginson, William, Robert Nash, and Matthias van Randenborgh. 1994. "The Financial and Operating Performance of Newly Privatized Firms: An International Empirical Analysis." *Journal of Finance*, 49: 403–452.

Merryman, John Henry. 1969. *The Civil Law Tradition*. Stanford, CA: Stanford University Press.

Milanovic, Branko. 1998. "Explaining the Growth in Inequality during the Transition." Washington, DC: World Bank.

Morck, Randall, Andrei Shleifer, and Robert Vishny. 1988. "Management Ownership and Market Valuation: An Empirical Analysis." *Journal of Financial Economics*, 20: 293–315.

Murphy, Kevin, Andrei Shleifer, and Robert Vishny. 1992. "The Transition to a Market Economy: Pitfalls of Partial Reform." *Quarterly Journal of Economics*, 107: 889–906.

Myers, Steven Lee. 2003. "In Russia, Apathy Dims Democracy. . . ." *New York Times*, November 9, sect. 4, pp. 1, 5.

Nellis, John. 1988. "Contract Plans and Public Enterprise Performance." World Bank Staff Working Paper no. 118.

New York Times. October 29, 2000, p. 12.

Oi, Jean. 1992. "Fiscal Reform and the Economic Foundations of Local State Corporatism in China." *World Politics*, 45: 99–126.

Park, Myung-Jin, Chang-Nam Kim, and Byung-Woo Sohn. 2000. "Modernization, Globalization, and the Powerful State: The Korean Media." In James Curran and Myung-Jin Park, eds., *De-Westernizing Media Studies*. New York: Routledge, pp. 111–123.

Pinto, Brian, Marek Belka, and Stefan Krajewski. 1993. "Transforming State Enterprises in Poland: Evidence on Adjustment by Manufacturing Firms." *Brookings Papers on Economic Activity*, 1: 213–270.

Qian, Yingyi, and Barry Weingast. 1997. "Federalism as a Commitment to Pre-serving Market Incentives." *Journal of Economic Perspectives,* 11: 83–92.

Raeff, Marc. 1983. *The Well-Ordered Police State: Social and Institutional Change Through Law in Germany and Russia, 1600–1800.* New Haven, CT: Yale University Press.

Riker, William. 1964. *Federalism: Origins, Operation, and Significance.* Boston: Little, Brown.

Roland, Gerard. 2000. *Transition and Economics: Politics, Markets, and Firms.* Cambridge, MA: MIT Press.

Rosen, Sherwin. 1992. "Contracts and the Market for Executives." In Lars Werin and Hans Wijkander, eds., *Contract Economics.* Oxford: Basil Black-well, pp. 181–211.

Sachs, Jeffrey. 1994. *Poland's Jump to a Market Economy.* Cambridge, MA: MIT Press.

———. 1995. "Russia's Struggle with Stabilization: Conceptual Issues and Evi-dence." In *Proceedings of the World Bank Annual Conference on Development Economics.* Washington, DC: World Bank.

Sachs, Jeffrey, and Andrew Warner. 1996. "Achieving Rapid Growth in the Transition Economies of Central Europe." Stockholm: Institute of East Eu-ropean Economies, Working Paper Number 116.

Safire, William, 2003a. "The Russian Reversion." *New York Times,* December 10.

———. 2003b. "Siloviki versus Oligarchy." *New York Times,* November 5.

Sahay, Ratna. 1996. Private correspondence, November.

Sanders, Bernard. 1998. "Sanders: American Taxpayers Shouldn't Fund IMF's Russian Failure." September 10. *www.house.gov.*

Schmitt, Eric. 1999. "Republicans Step Up Attack on Clinton's Russia Policy." *New York Times,* September 15, p. A12.

Shavell, Steven. 1995. "Alternative Dispute Resolution: an Economic Analysis." *Journal of Legal Studies,* 24: 1–28.

Shkolnikov, Vladimir, Giovanni Cornia, David Leon, and France Meslé. 1998. "Causes of the Russian Mortality Crisis: Evidence and Interpretations." *World Development Report,* 26: 1995–2011.

Shleifer, Andrei. 1996. "Origins of Bad Policies: Control, Corruption, and Con-fusion." *Rivista di Politica Economica,* 86: 103–123.

———. 1997a. "Schumpeter Lecture: Government in Transition." *European Economic Review,* 41: 385–410.

———. 1997b. "Agenda for Russian Reforms." *Economics of Transition,* 5: 227–231.

Shleifer, Andrei, and Lawrence Summers. 1988. "Breach of Trust in Hostile

Takeovers." In Alan J. Auerbach, ed., *Corporate Takeovers: Causes and Consequences.* Chicago: University of Chicago Press, pp. 33–67.

Shleifer, Andrei, and Daniel Treisman. 1999. *Without a Map: Political Tactics and Economic Reform in Russia.* Cambridge, MA: MIT Press.

———. 2005. "A Normal Country: Russia after Communism." *Journal of Economic Perspectives,* 19: forthcoming.

Shleifer, Andrei, and Robert Vishny. 1986. "Large Shareholders and Corporate Control." *Journal of Political Economy,* 94: 461–488.

———. 1991. "Reversing the Soviet Economic Collapse." *Brookings Papers on Economic Activity,* 2: 341–367.

———. 1992. "Pervasive Shortages Under Socialism." *Rand Journal of Economics,* 23: 237–426.

———. 1993. "Corruption." *Quarterly Journal of Economics,* 108: 599–618.

———. 1994a. "Politicians and Firms." *Quarterly Journal of Economics,* 109: 995–1025.

———. 1994b. "Privatization in Russia: First Steps." In Olivier Blanchard, Kenneth Froot, and Jeffrey Sachs, eds., *The Transition in Eastern Europe,* Vol. 2, *Restructuring.* Chicago: University of Chicago Press, pp. 137–164.

Shor, Boris. 1997. "What's Behind the Freedom House Ratings and Deliberations?" *Transition,* 5.

Stigler, George. 1971. "The Economic Theory of Regulation." *Bell Journal of Economics,* 2: 3–21.

Stiglitz, Joseph. 2002. *Globalization and Its Discontents.* New York: W. W. Norton.

Sussman, Leonard, and Karin Karlekar, eds. 2002. *The Annual Survey of Press Freedom, 2002.* New York: Freedom House.

Talbott, Strobe. 2000. *The Russia Hand.* New York: Random House.

Tilly, Charles. 1990. *Coercion, Capital, and European States, AD 990–1990.* Berkeley: University of California Press.

Tirole, Jean. 1991. Privatization in Eastern Europe: Incentives and the Economics of Transition." *NBER Macroeconomic Annual,* 221–259.

Treisman, Daniel. 1999a. *After the Deluge: Regional Crises and Political Consolidation in Russia.* Ann Arbor: University of Michigan Press.

———. 1999b. "Decentralization, Tax Evasion, and the Underground Economy: A Model with Evidence from Russia." Mimeo, UCLA.

United Nations. 2003. *Human Development Report 2002.* New York: United Nations.

U.S. Department of State. 2003. "President Bush Meets with Russian President Putin at Camp David." September 27. *www.state.gov.*

Vining, Aiden, and Anthony Boardman. 1992. "Ownership vs. Competition: Efficiency in Public Enterprise." *Public Choice,* 73: 205–239.

Waisbord, Silvio. 2000. "Media in South America: Between the Rock of State and the Hard Place of the Market." In James Curran and Myung-Jin Park, eds., *De-Westernizing Media Studies*. New York: Routledge, pp. 50–62.

Walder, Andrew. 1995. "China's Transitional Economy: Interpreting Its Significance." *China Quarterly*, 144: 963–979.

Weiner, Tim. 2000. "Mexico Ending Coziness for Press and Powerful." *New York Times*, October 29, p. 12.

Whitaker, Chico. 2000. "Brazil's Free Elections." *Le Monde Diplomatique*, September.

Willan, Philip. 2002. "Opposition 'Kept off Berlusconi-Run TV.' " *Guardian*, August 8.

Wong, Christine, ed. 1997. *Financing Local Government in the People's Republic of China*. Hong Kong: Oxford University Press.

World Bank. 1991. *A Study of the Soviet Economy*. Washington, DC: The World Bank.

———. 1995. *Bureaucrats in Business*. London: Oxford University Press.

———. 1996. *World Development Report 1996: From Plan to Market*. London: Oxford University Press.

———. 2000. *World Development Report*. Washington, DC: The World Bank.

World Economic Forum. 1996. *World Competitiveness Report*. Davos: World Economic Forum.

Yavlinsky, Grigory, and Braguinsky, Serguey. 1994. "The Inefficiency of Laissez-Faire in Russia: Hysteresis Effects and the Need for Policy-Led Transformation." *Journal of Comparative Economics*, 19: 88–116.

Young, Alwyn. 1995. "The Tyranny of Numbers: Confronting the Statistical Realities of the East Asian Growth Experience." *Quarterly Journal of Economics*, 110: 641–680.

———. 2000. "The Razor's Edge: Distortions, Incremental Reform and the Theory of the Second Best in the People's Republic of China." *Quarterly Journal of Economics*, 115: 1091–1135.

Zhuravskaya, Ekaterina. 2000. "Incentives to Provide Local Public Goods: Fiscal Federalism, Russian Style." *Journal of Public Economics*, 76: 337–368.

Zienkowski, Leszek. 1996. "The Polish Experience in Estimates of the Hidden Economy." Research Bulletin of RECESS (Research Centre for Economic and Statistical Studies of GUS and PAN, abbreviated in Polish as ZBSE), No. 1.

Index